INFORMATION AND CONTROL IN ORGANIZATIONS

Goodyear Series in
Management and Organizations
Lyman W. Porter, Editor

Published:

Forthcoming:

INFORMATION AND CONTROL IN ORGANIZATIONS

Edward E. Lawler III

University of Michigan
and
Battelle Memorial Institute

John Grant Rhode

University of California, Berkeley

Goodyear Publishing Company, Inc.
Santa Monica, California 90401

Library of Congress Cataloging in Publication Data

Lawler, Edward E
  Information and control in organizations.

  (The Goodyear series in management and organizations)
  Bibliography: p. 199
  Includes index.
  1. Organization.   2. Communication in organizations.
I. Rhode, John Grant, joint author.   II. Title.
HD31.L3167   658.4'5   75-20582
ISBN 0-87620-424-8
ISBN 0-87620-425-6 pbk.

GOODYEAR SERIES IN MANAGEMENT AND ORGANIZATIONS

Y-4248-4 (Case)
Y-4256-7 (Paper)
Current printing (last digit):

10 9 8 7 6 5 4

Printed in the United States of America

To our parents, lovers, friends, and children . . .
who collectively maintain effective control.

CONTENTS

FOREWORD

The Goodyear Series in Management and Organizations embodies concise and lively treatments of specific topics within the broad area indicated by the Series title. These books are for supplemental reading in basic management, organizational behavior, or personnel courses in which the instructor highlights particular topics in the larger course. However, the books, either alone or in combination, can also form the nucleus for specialized courses that follow introductory courses.

Each book stresses the *key issues* relevant to the given topic. Thus, each author, or set of authors, has made a particular effort to "highlight figure from ground"—that is, to keep the major issues in the foreground and the small explanatory details in the background. These books are, by design, relatively brief treatments of their topic areas, so the authors have had to be carefully *selective* in what they have chosen to retain and to omit. Because the authors were chosen for their expertise and their judgment, the Series provides valuable summary treatments of the subject areas.

In focusing on the major issues, the Series' authors present a balanced content coverage. They have also aimed at breadth by the unified presentation of different types of material: major conceptual or theoretical approaches, interesting and critical empirical findings, and applications to "real life" management and organizational problems. Each author deals with this body of material, but the combination varies according to the subject matter. Thus, each book is distinctive in the particular way in which a topic is addressed.

A final word is in order about the audience for this Series: Although the primary audience is the student, each book in the series concerns a topic of importance to the practicing manager. Managers and supervisors can rely on these books as authoritative summaries of the basic knowledge in each area covered by the Series.

The topics included in the Series to date have been chosen on the basis of their importance and relevance for those interested in management and organizations. As new appropriate topics emerge on the scene, additional books will be added. This is a dynamic Series both in content and direction.

Lyman W. Porter
Series Editor

PREFACE

This book is about how information and control systems affect behavior in organizations. It covers the research that has been done in this area but it is not written for a scholarly or research-oriented audience. Rather, it is written with the beginning student in mind. No background in psychology, sociology or business is needed to read this book. The only requirement is a desire to understand how such organizational systems as budgets and computerized information and control systems affect behavior.

Most of the book is descriptive. Chapters 1 through 8 describe how people and organizations behave, how people react to information and control systems that measure their behavior, how people behave who develop and maintain the systems, and how decision makers use the results of the systems. The last part of the book is more prescriptive. Chapter 9 describes how the human organization should be measured and Chapter 10 discusses how systems should be designed in order to maximize organizational effectiveness.

The issue of how information and control systems affect behavior is a critical one for anyone interested in the determinants of organizational effectiveness. It is important to psychologists who are interested in understanding individual behavior in organizations. Information and control systems are such an important part of complex organizations it is impossible to explain much of the behavior that takes place in organizations without examining information and control systems. Further, since effective information systems are essential for organizations to function effectively, sociologists and others interested in organizational behavior need to seriously consider the impact of these systems on behavior.

Knowledge of how information and control systems affect behavior is also important for those who design and implement control systems. Their whole purpose is to develop systems that will influence behavior so as to make it more effective. Who is included in this large and somewhat diverse group? Most prominent are accountants who develop the financial information systems, budgets, and standard costs systems. Also in this group are the management scientists who specialize in developing computerized management information systems. In addition, industrial engineers who develop standards and measurement systems need to understand the effects of information and control systems on behavior.

Operating managers also should be aware of how information and control systems affect behavior. They need to know how to use the systems in order to influence the behavior of their subordinates. There is clear evidence that the impact of a particular information system is strongly influenced by the way line managers utilize the information the system produces. Good management practice must involve the utilization of information and control system data to influence behavior. It is unrealistic to expect managers to instinctively know how to best use the various information and control systems that exist in an organization to influence behavior. They need to be trained to respond properly to the information received.

There has been an increasing recognition during recent years that behavioral science knowledge and research should be used to understand how control systems should and do operate. Writers in the fields of accounting, industrial engineering, and systems design have called for the increased use of behavioral science knowledge in their fields. This call has been heard perhaps most clearly, loudly, and consistently in the field of accounting.

In 1966, Roy and MacNeill recommended that "the common body of knowledge for beginning CPA's include fundamental training in both psychology and sociology with emphasis upon those parts of both subjects focused upon the behavior of formal organizations (p. 234)." This view is in line with the definition of accounting developed in the same year by an American Accounting Association committee: "[Accounting is] the process of identifying, measuring, and communicating economic information to permit informed judgements and decisions by users of the information (1966, p. 1)." It is illuminating to contrast this definition with the following one, which might be described as a more traditional definition: "Accounting is the art of recording, classifying, and summarizing in a significant manner and in terms of money, transactions and events which are, in part at least, of a financial character, and interpreting the results thereof (AICPA 1941, p. 2)." This definition makes accounting much less of a behavioral issue than does the more recent American Accounting Association definition that emphasizes two important behavioral phenomena: communication and decision making. Once it is decided that a control system is created to influence behavior—in effect what the 1966

American Accounting Association definition says—then the study of human behavior must be part of the study of information and control systems.

Unfortunately, until recent years little information was available on how information and control systems affect behavior. Consequently, those people who designed control systems had to rely on untested and often invalid assumptions about the nature of human behavior. Three years ago we decided that this situation had changed sufficiently so that this research-based book on information and control systems could be written. Hopefully, this book is a first step in the direction of providing a better indication of the relationship between information systems and organizational behavior.

Any book of this nature is based on the contribution of many individuals. Ours is no exception and we would like to thank a few of our good friends and colleagues. Some of the individuals most essential to the completion of this text were William J. Bruns, Jr., Cortlandt Cammann, and James E. Sorensen who each made helpful comments on an earlier version of the manuscript. In addition, Chris Argyris was critical in stimulating our thoughts about the issues covered in the book. Finally, Ann Bishop Rhode provided the support and encouragement that not only kept the project alive, but also determined that it was completed with an agreeable balance between social and professional pleasures.

Edward E. Lawler III
John Grant Rhode

INFORMATION
AND CONTROL IN
ORGANIZATIONS

THE ROLE OF INFORMATION AND CONTROL SYSTEMS IN ORGANIZATIONS

During the spring of 1972, the Air Force recalled General John D. Lavelle from his command in Vietnam and demoted him for conducting 28 raids on North Vietnam that were in violation of White House rules (*Time,* 1972). How did General Lavelle manage to conduct 28 raids before he was caught? The General and his subordinates had developed a double accounting system. The Air Force required reports on all missions and checked them to be sure they violated no rules. According to Sergeant Lonnie Franks, however, he and 200 other men often made out two sets of reports—one true and one false. The false report was forwarded to the Pentagon, which became aware that it was receiving false information only some time later. Thus, the Pentagon lost control over the activities of General Lavelle at the same time that Henry Kissinger and the U.S. Government were trying to negotiate the Vietnam peace treaty. Consequently, when delicate coordination was most needed between the military and civilian segments of government, it was not present because a vital information system was not functioning effectively.

The literature concerned with accounting, auditing, and management information systems is full of many other anecdotes documenting the ineffectiveness and negative effects of information and control systems in organizations. For example, Dearden (1960, 1961) described managers who were reluctant to replace equipment, even when it was in the company's economic interest, because of the heavy book losses that would be reflected in their current performance reports. In a similar vein, Beyer (1963) has **1** noted a case of managers scheduling work on old equipment with low unit depreciation charges even though new equipment had lower variable costs. By trying to reduce the total costs reported on their performance reports, the managers increased the company's total processing costs. In a classic article, Jasinski (1956) has described how one company's production measures caused maintenance problems. As one foreman described the situation:

> We really can't stop to have our machines repaired. In fact, one of our machines is off right now, but we'll have to gimmick something immediately and keep the machine going because at the end of the month, as it is now, we simply can't have a machine down. We've got to get those pieces out. Many times we run a machine right to the ground at the end of the month trying to get pieces out, and we have to spend extra time at the beginning of the month trying to repair the machine (Jasinski, 1956, p. 107).

The many cases of information and control systems causing dysfunctional behavior raise some crucial issues about the general effectiveness of information and control systems. Probably the most important question is whether the kind of breakdowns described occur frequently. The answer seems to be yes. A large body of research suggests that information and control systems often fail to accomplish their purpose. The systems are often fed invalid data by the members of organizations and they often cause other dysfunctional behavior. Why does this happen? Can information systems be designed to be more effective? This book will explore these issues. But before we can deal with them, we need to understand why organizations create information and control systems, the different types of systems, and the characteristics that all systems share.

NEED FOR INFORMATION AND CONTROL SYSTEMS

One reason for information and control systems is the difficulty of coordinating and controlling the activities of members of organizations. A group of people constitute an organization only if there is some coordination among the activities they perform; some type of control is an inevitable result of the need to coordinate activities. The coordination and order created out of the diverse interests and potentially different behaviors of members of organizations is largely a function of control (Tannenbaum, 1968). Control of an organization and coordination of its activities are impossible without information about what is occurring in that organization, thus, information systems are developed.

Small organizations typically do not have extensive formalized information and control systems. Managers responsible for coordination and control often observe personally all the activities of their employees. As a result, these managers feel little need for a formal information system. For example, the neighborhood store may have a manager who represents the only information and control system in that store. However, large organizations, with substantial specialization of function, usually contain a number of formal information and control systems.

It is not accidental that control systems seem to be more prominent and better developed in large organizations where there is a division of labor and specialization of function. These are the organizations that most need control systems because they have the most severe coordination and information processing problems. They are usually so physically large that no one can personally observe and control all the activities. Consequently, they are in danger of having their operating "parts" fly off in different directions. General Creigton Abrams made this point clearly in his testimony on the Lavelle case.

> Rules have been our way of life out there. If I or any other commander picks and chooses among the rules, it will unravel in a way that you will never be able to control. A lot of these rules looked silly to many of the men. In a military, in a purely military sense, they appear silly, but they must be—if you are going to hold it together—they must be followed (*Time,* 1972, p. 14).

Abram's statement agrees with a study (Haire, 1959) that pointed out that large organizations frequently have proportionately more people involved in "holding the organization together" than do small organizations, because they have the greatest need to be held together.

The need to report to external groups is a second reason why organizations have information and control systems. Stockholders, government agencies, and even customers are among the many outsiders demanding reports on the activities of organizations.

To summarize, information and control systems are instituted in organizations because management and others feel they need information about what is going on in the organization so they can coordinate the activities of others. This need is felt most severely by managers of large organizations, since they are often far from what is going on and large organizations have the most severe coordination problems. Thus large organizations tend to have the best developed information and control systems.

TYPES OF INFORMATION AND CONTROL SYSTEMS

Organizations typically contain information and control systems, handling production data, personnel data, and financial data, among others. The development of computer technology has profoundly affected the kind of information systems now used in large organizations. Because machines have the ability to rapid- **3** ly process large amounts of information, they have made it possible for organizations to significantly expand their information systems. This development has made information systems an even more important part of most organizations.

In most organizations financial control systems are the most prominent and play a central role in influencing the behavior of individuals both inside and outside organizations. Financial-based systems permeate every complex organization because progress, or a lack of progress, is almost always measured in monetary terms. For example, when evaluating the performance of a hospital, city government, or automobile manufacturing plant, physical achievements such as number of patients treated, reduction in crimes of assault, or quantity of defect-free automobiles, are considered in the context of whether the budget was met or exceeded and how much profit or loss resulted during the reporting period.

Monetary quantification of organizational performance also exists for legal reasons. Regulatory and statutory agencies at all levels of government—municipal, state and federal—require that periodic reports be filed. Almost all adults must complete at least one financial report each year for the federal government to determine their income tax liability or refund. These reports are most conveniently made in a universal language—money.

Complex organizations usually have at least three financial control systems, for internal control, for budgetary control, and for external reporting. It is not sufficient for an organization to simply measure its gains or losses in financial terms. There must also be a safeguarding of the assets or resources of the enterprise. Thus, internal control procedures are established to insure that all cash received is properly credited to the organization, that cash disbursed represents payment for necessary and expected expenditures, and that inventory and other assets owned and controlled by the organization are safe from theft and properly used. The system that facilitates such safeguarding of cash and other assets is the internal control system—an extension of the financial reporting system and an integral component of the total information processing system. The need for a strong internal control system was well articulated by Carmichael (1970) in a series of hypotheses frequently held by accountants who design, operate, and audit internal control systems. These hypotheses maintain that individuals have inherent mental, moral, and physical weaknesses, that the threat of prompt exposure will deter an individual from committing fraud, and that an individual who is independent will recognize and report irregularities. In sum, these human weaknesses make an extensive internal control system necessary.

Together with the internal control system, the budget is one of the most critical financial statements available to managers in large organizations. Indeed, one of the most extensively researched areas in accounting is the budget and its effect on people and enterprises.

The traditional, or scientific management, view of employees as inefficient beings whose work activities must be closely controlled forms the basis for most of the logic defending the need for budgets. The primary concern of scientific management is to promote efficiency and thereby generate higher profits. Moreover, until Argyris' (1951) classic study, *The Impact of Budgets on People,* not much attention was paid to the negative behavioral side effects of budgets; much of the literature emphasized how the budget could help management make higher profits.

Although the behavioral impact of budgets and internal control systems exists primarily within organizations, published financial statements such as the balance sheet and profit and loss statement have a considerable effect on individuals outside the organization. Many more interested parties read and analyze an organization's published financial statements than ever see internally distributed reports on internal control or operating budgets. For example, the Securities and Exchange Commission (SEC), the Internal Revenue Service, the Interstate Commerce Commission, bankers, financial analysts, stockbrokers, United Auto Workers union officials, all of the bond holders, common and preferred stockholders, and any U.S. citizen who writes the SEC or the corporate headquarters can obtain without charge at least one copy of the annual report containing the current balance sheet and profit and loss statement for the General Motors Corporation (GM). On the other hand, none of these parties have direct access to the internal operating budget of GM. Several of GM's competitors would like to have access to the budget, but it is simply not available outside the company. In fact, only a few key executives within GM ever see the entire budget. Consequently, GM's budget potentially has a behavioral effect on fewer people than the annual report.

CHARACTERISTICS OF CONTROL SYSTEMS

In some ways many of the information and control systems that operate in organizations seem to have little in common. As we have noted, they differ widely in the kinds of information they deal with and in the audience they are intended for. Yet they do have three important characteristics in common.

First, they all have some similar structural characteristics.

1. They all collect, store, and transmit information in the form of abstract measures of reality. Usually, they deal with information about the condition of the organization in the form of measures that are quantitative (e.g., **5**

the cost and quantity of production) and that can be understood only by trained personnel.

2. The collected abstract information is stored and transmitted in a specific form and with a specific frequency. For example, a company makes quarterly profit reports based on a particular set of accounting practices regarding its method of treating inventory and depreciation.

3. The summarized information is distributed to a specific, usually predetermined, group of people. The group may or may not include all the members of the organization. Some information is given to only a few people in the organization while other information is more public (e.g., earnings reports for corporations).

Second, all information systems try to accomplish the same thing—influence behavior. The crucial aspect of any control system is its effect on behavior. As Anthony (1965) has noted, the central function of a management control system, therefore, must be motivation. The system needs to be designed in a way that assists, guides, and motivates management to make decisions and act in ways that are consistent with the overall objectives of the organization. Financial control systems provide clear examples of systems that are created to influence behavior. Different systems are intended to influence different groups of individuals but they all are intended to influence behavior.

Information and control systems typically try to influence behavior by specifying what kind of behavior is appropriate and by providing some means of gathering information about the adequacy of the behavior that takes place. Management uses this information for several purposes: to coordinate the activities of different parts of the organization; as a basis for taking corrective action when problems exist; and to reward and punish the behavior of members of the organization.

The third characteristic that all control systems share also has to do with human behavior. As Argyris (1957) clearly stated, implicit in the design of any control system is a set of assumptions about what causes human behavior. Traditional reward-based control systems assume that:

1. Man is rational and motivated to maximize his economic gain.
2. Man is not a social animal.
3. Man can be treated in a standardized manner.
4. Man needs to be stimulated by management if he is to work.

This set of assumptions about human behavior does not, of course, fit with what is known. It is precisely because people don't fit these assumptions that control systems often lead to dysfunctional behavior. Fortunately, a body of literature exists that can help us make valid assumptions about the causes of human behavior. From this knowledge it is often possible to predict how **6** individuals will react to information and control systems.

DESIGN OF THE BOOK

Human behavior is influenced by two general classes of factors. The first is composed of the personal characteristics that individuals have. These include such things as the person's needs, perceptions of the world, and learned expectations. The second is composed of those factors that make up the person's environment. Lewin (1935) stated the relationship of these factors as follows: Behavior = f (Person, Environment). This is a way of saying that someone's behavior is determined both by what the person brings to the situation (e.g., needs, abilities, and past experiences) and the characteristics of the situation (e.g., the rewards it offers). It follows that if we ever hope to understand the impact of information and control systems on behavior we must not only have a good knowledge of how information systems work in complex organizations, but also how people function.

The work that psychologists have been doing to understand human behavior in organizations has progressed well enough so that at this time we are in a position to make a number of statements about how humans function. Certainly, we are not yet able to predict behavior perfectly, but we can do a lot better than chance if we use the knowledge behavioral science has produced. This research knowledge also suggests what can be done to improve the effectiveness of information and control systems. Many practices that surround such things as budgeting systems have grown up as a result of myths and misconceptions. It is possible in many cases to recommend practices that are more congruent with the current state of our knowledge concerning human behavior. Further, as Massoud (1974) noted while describing the impact of different control systems on attitudes, organizations often change from one control system to another without any consideration of the human factor. The problems associated with such change are very real since managers will display a behavioral change in response to a new control system that measures their performance and assigns some value and reward to it. These problems can be solved. But before we can do this we must have a good grasp of the basic findings concerned with human behavior. Therefore, we will present a way of thinking about people that represents what is known about how people respond to their environments. This approach admittedly represents a partial simplification of human nature, but it is sufficiently complex and rich enough to use as a basis for predicting how people will responed to information and control systems.

Because all control systems share certain characteristics, common behavioral issues arise regardless of the specific control system being considered. In this book we will examine the theory 7 and research that are relevant to these issues. We will not look in detail at budgets, management information systems, or any other control systems; rather we will focus on the behavioral issues that arise when any control system is used. Behavior is more strongly influenced by certain generic differences in how information and control systems function than it is by the kind of information the systems collect. For example, in understanding behavior it is less important whether the system collects cost or production data than whether or not the information is used as a basis for giving pay increases or promotions. Similar behavioral reactions can be expected if information is used for reward purposes, almost regardless of the type of information that is gathered. Hence, when we talk of how people react to information and control systems, we will emphasize how differences in the way they function affect behavior. Later in the book, we will present a general model of information systems and discuss the crucial dimensions on which information systems vary. We will also point out the common characteristics of such things as budgets, computerized management information systems, standard cost systems, and production information systems. We will show that the research on any specific information and control system is relevant to most simply because they all utilize information to control behavior.

Individuals typically occupy one of three organizational positions with respect to each information and control system they interact with:

1. *The measured and controlled position.* This position involves being measured by the system. People in this position are usually at lower levels in the organization and are the ones whose behavior the system is supposed to measure and control.
2. *The system maintenance position.* This position involves the design and operation of the information and control system. Managers in staff positions in organizations usually have this relationship to information systems. Their primary task is seeing that the decision makers have the information they need.
3. *The decision maker position.* This position involves receiving the information from the control system in order to make decisions. High level managers in organizations usually have this relationship to information systems.

Information control systems have very different implications for the behavior of decision makers than they have for those whose behavior is being measured and controlled. A whole different set of behavioral issues are relevant for decision makers than are relevant for those whose behavior is measured by the system. This fact has been recognized by the research concerned with the impact of control systems on people occupying different roles with respect to the system and it has influenced the design of this book. First, we will look at issues concerned with the measured and controlled role, then we will consider the system maintenance role, and finally we will discuss the role of the decision maker.

In small organizations where jobs are not highly specialized the same person may occupy two of the roles. For example, someone may be both a system maintainer and a decision maker. Such individuals are subject to more complex influences on their behavior. In addition, in many organizations individuals may occupy different roles with respect to different systems. For example, they may be decision makers with respect to a production information system and be in a measured and controlled position with respect to a budget system. However, for the purposes of this book we will look at the research on these different roles separately and act as if different people always occupy the different roles. Also, we will not deal with problems associated with individuals having different roles with respect to different systems. This will allow for the clearest discussion of the most important ways control systems influence behavior.

A great deal of research has been done on the issue of how information and control systems affect the behavior of those people whose behavior is measured, and this is a major focus of our book. Basically, all of these studies have tried to determine how various features of the systems affect the attitudes and behavior of the organizations' members. Much of this research has been concerned with showing how certain kinds of control systems produce dysfunctional behavior. Still other studies have been concerned with how control systems affect employees' motivation to perform effectively. The results of these studies will be treated in detail later in the book because they suggest a number of things that can be done to make control systems more effective.

There is relatively little research on the attitudes and behavior of the individuals who maintain information and control systems. What research there is focuses on determining the types of people who occupy this role and the kind of satisfactions available to people who do this kind of work. This research is important because it looks at how the kind of system used is determined by the kind of people who occupy these roles and by the kinds of satisfactions these roles offer. Recently some research has also focused on how people in these roles try to influence decision making in organizations and how they can control the kind of results that control systems produce. In the discussion on decision making, the emphasis will be on how different kinds of information alter the decisions made. In this case, different kinds of information mean different data as well as the same data presented in different forms. Also relevant here are issues concerned with the information processing ability of people as well as the effects of information overload, information complexity, and frequency of feedback on

9

decision making. People differ in their information processing ability and styles. As a result, the same information may produce quite different reactions from two different managers.

The recent emphasis on the behavioral aspects of control systems is beginning to produce new developments in the design of control systems that have important implications for the use of control systems in organizations. It has led to the development of information and control systems that are designed to measure the human systems of organizations. Presently, most organizations don't measure this; they measure only the financial side of the organization. These new approaches, Human Resource Accounting and Human System measurement, will be considered after we have discussed the impact of information and control systems.

The final part of the book is concerned with summarizing and integrating what has been learned about information and control systems. It attempts the difficult task of specifying what characteristics information and control systems should have. It is by far the most speculative part of the book but it is also the most important in many ways since it suggests how to make organizations more effective. In a way each reader should be asked to design an effective control system based on what they have learned in this book. Certainly, there is no more rigorous test of the degree to which they have understood and integrated the results of the many research studies cited and discussed than to design such a system.

UNDERSTANDING HUMAN BEHAVIOR IN ORGANIZATIONS 2

There is an abundance of psychological theory that can be used to help explain human behavior in organizations. Not all theories are in complete agreement, but most agree on what the basic determinants of human behavior are. Knowledge of these determinants is crucial to understanding human behavior in organizations and effectively designing organizations. A now classic book on human behavior in organizations by McGregor (1960) illustrates just how important assumptions about human behavior can be in designing organizations. McGregor stated two opposing sets of assumptions about the nature of human beings, Theory X and Theory Y, which lead to quite different approaches to organization design and to different ways of treating the members of an organization.

Theory X emphasizes the control of people by the use of rewards and punishments. Theory Y emphasizes the ability of people to exercise self-control and their desire to perform effectively. Consequently, in the view of Theory X the employee who falsifies a report of how much was produced should be punished, and a better information system should be developed. According to the Theory Y view, the issue is why the system motivated the employee to report false data, and the possible cure might involve not letting the employee's superior see the production report and giving the employee more responsibility for controlling the production process.

Which view is correct, Theory X or Theory Y? The research evidence suggests that both are partially correct. The primary **11** reason they both have some validity is that people differ widely. Some individuals are more Theory X in orientation and some are more Theory Y in orientation. Thus, it is inappropriate to say that either view accurately describes human nature. Because of this we cannot use either position as an absolute guide to understanding behavior in organizations. The views are best regarded as contrasting, thought provoking statements about the nature of man that emphasize the relationship between the nature of man and the design of work organizations.

Are there any statements that can be made about the nature of man that will help us understand how information and control systems affect behavior? Yes. We have already stated a very important one: Individuals differ widely in a number of ways. Because of this, when looking at individual behavior, we must remember to expect that individuals will behave differently when faced with the same situation. Further, in considering any list of similarities or general principles about human behavior, it is vital to remember the important individual differences that exist and how much complexity they add to the problem of predicting how people will behave in a given situation.

What general principles can we state? A number of lists have been developed and they show a high degree of overlap. The following, which are based on those stated by Porter, Lawler, and Hackman (1975), seem to be a useful set for the purpose of understanding behavior in organizations.

PEOPLE TRY TO SATISFY MANY DIFFERENT NEEDS

Psychologists generally talk about human behavior as being stimulated or motivated by a set of needs. By a need they mean some internal state in a person that causes objects or outcomes to become attractive to the person. Thus, they speak of hunger or a need for food and relate it to objects (food) that satisfy the need. In the case of some needs, it is clear which internal states are related to the needs being experienced. For example, this is true for hunger and thirst (actual physiological states can be specified) but not for a number of other needs. Psychologists have pointed out that people seem to have a need for companionship, yet it is not known what internal state causes a person to experience this need. All that is known is that people do experience it and when it occurs the companionship of others becomes attractive.

For our purposes it is not crucial to determine how internal states are related to the attractiveness of outcomes. It is important, however, that we identify which needs people have and what

12

influences the strength of these needs. Only if we do this can we specify which outcomes or objects will be attractive to people.

How Many Needs Are There?

Originally, psychologists said needs existed only when a physiological basis could be established for the attractiveness of the objects sought by a person (e.g., food, water, sex). This proved to be too restricted since it failed to explain why people sought such things as social companionship, stimulating environments, achievement, and recognition. Now the term *need* is used to refer to clusters of goals or outcomes that a person seeks as ends in themselves regardless of whether a physiological basis for the attractiveness of the outcomes can be found. For example, various food objects seem to cluster together in the sense that when people desire one food object they usually desire others as well; and when they get enough of one, they often lose interest in the others. Thus, we say people have a need for food rather than saying that people have a need for roast beef or steak. By doing this we move to a more general level and begin to group outcomes more parsimoniously.

A number of theorists have tried to identify and document lists of basic human instincts, drives, and needs (Maslow, 1954; Murray, 1938). Often such lists are unnecessarily long. Unfortunately, as lists expand in length and diversity (some include thousands), they are less and less useful for understanding and predicting human behavior because they become mere catalogues of the outcomes people seek. The research on needs (Lawler, 1973) suggests that the following short list, based on Maslow's work, is the most useful one with which to work:

1. A number of "existence" needs, including sex, hunger, thirst, and oxygen.
2. A security need
3. A social need
4. A need for esteem and reputation
5. A need for self-control and independence
6. A need for competence, achievement and self-realization

These needs seem to be relatively independent in the sense that they relate to different outcomes. The list is conveniently short yet it covers most of the outcomes psychologists have found to be important to people.

One of the things that distinguishes the first five needs on the list from the others is that they can only be satisfied by outcomes external (extrinsic) to the person that have a concrete reality (e.g., food, money, praise from another). The need for self-realization and competence, on the other hand, seems to be satisfied only by outcomes given intrinsically by persons to them- **13** selves (e.g., a feeling of accomplishment and growth). It is true that certain environmental conditions need to be present before the internal outcomes can be obtained, but the outcomes themselves are not observable or controlled by others because they are intrinsic. Thus, it is important to remember that people seek *both* intrinsic and extrinsic outcomes. Chapter 4 will discuss how information and control systems affect extrinsic motivation while Chapter 5 deals with intrinsic motivation.

Scholars intent on generating the definitive list of human instincts, drives, or needs rarely state the obvious point that human beings are motivated toward a great diversity of ends. Furthermore, people's needs are constantly changing, what motivates people today may not be potent in determining their behavior tomorrow. Because of the large differences among people, it is impossible to state a universal list of factors that motivate all people. This, however, does not mean that the concept of need isn't a useful one in dealing with human behavior in organizations. It is necessary if we are to explain and predict the goal-oriented behavior that occurs in organizations. It also doesn't mean that a list of needs cannot be useful. A list can help us understand why outcomes are important to individuals and predict which outcomes will be important to specific individuals.

Is There a Hierarchy of Needs?

Maslow's (1954) need theory specifies that needs are arranged in a hierarchy. According to his theory, people move successively up a need hierarchy so that as their lower-order needs are satisfied their higher-order needs, like self-realization, become more important. In essence Maslow talks as if needs are arranged like a ladder that must be climbed one rung at a time. Thus, people will only be concerned with self-realization if their existence needs, their security needs, their social needs, and so on are satisfied. If, however, the satisfaction of a lower-order need is threatened, that need immediately becomes predominant and the person will forget about all higher-order needs. For example, when a person becomes hungry he or she will worry about obtaining food and forget about esteem, self-realization, and other higher-order needs.

Maslow also points out that a satisfied need is not motivating. As a result, once people have obtained enough food, the opportunity to obtain more food will not motivate them. It would be expected, therefore, that the kinds of things that motivate people may change as their career in an organization progresses and they move up the need hierarchy ladder.

There is a substantial amount of research relevant to Maslow's theory. It clearly supports part of the theory. As predicted, when

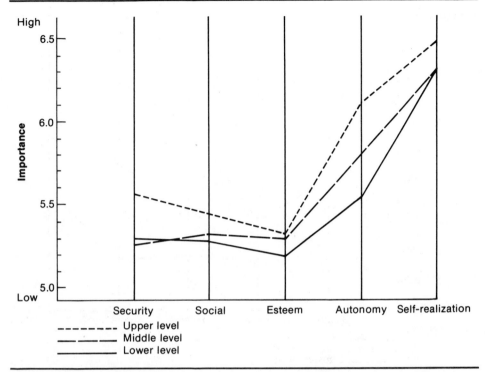

High

Importance

6.5

6.0

5.5

5.0

Low

| Security | Social | Esteem | Autonomy | Self-realization |

- - - - - - - - Upper level
— — — — Middle level
——————— Lower level

Adapted from L.W. Porter, *Organizational Patterns of Managerial Job Attitudes,* (New York: American Foundation for Management Research, 1964).

FIGURE 2–1
Importance
Attached to Five
Needs by Managers
at Three
Organizational
Levels

needs are satisfied they become less important. Figure 2–1 shows the stated importance of certain needs to a group of over 1,900 managers, and Figure 2–2 shows their satisfaction with these needs. Note that the least satisfied needs are also the most important. This has been a general finding in the research on need satisfaction. It appears that most needs can be satisfied and that once enough outcomes are obtained to satisfy a given need, people stop seeking outcomes relevant to that need. Thus, a satisfied need is not a motivator.

The one exception to this conclusion is the need for self-realization or growth. This need seems to be insatiable; the more individuals obtain the outcomes that satisfy it, the more important it becomes and the more of it they desire. Because of this, once self-realization appears, it usually continues to be a strong motivator. It is because of the need for self-realization that people are never satisfied and always want something.

Maslow's need hierarchy idea has not been supported by the research. There is evidence to support the view that unless the existence needs are satisfied the needs above them in the hierar- **15**

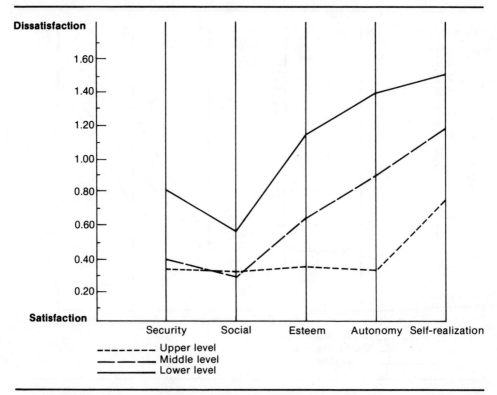

Dissatisfaction

Chart showing Dissatisfaction axis from Satisfaction to Dissatisfaction with values 0.20, 0.40, 0.60, 0.80, 1.00, 1.20, 1.40, 1.60 and horizontal categories: Security, Social, Esteem, Autonomy, Self-realization.

- - - - - - - Upper level
— - — - — Middle level
————— Lower level

FIGURE 2–2
Dissatisfaction
Attached to Five
Needs by Managers
at Three
Organizational
Levels

Adapted from L.W. Porter, *Organizational Patterns of Managerial Job Attitudes*, (New York: American Foundation for Management Research, 1964).

chy will not come into play. There is also some evidence that unless security needs are satisfied, people will not be concerned with the needs above them (Cofer and Appley, 1964). However, there is very little evidence to support the view that a hierarchy exists once one moves above the security level (see, e.g., Lawler and Suttle, 1972). For example, there is little evidence to indicate that social needs must be satisfied before people will be concerned with the need for self-realization. Thus, it probably is *not* safe to assume more than a two-step hierarchy with existence and security needs at the lowest level and all of the higher-order needs at the top level. This means that unless the lower-order needs are satisfied the others will not come into play and, if lower-order needs are threatened, they will become predominant. Thus, attempts to influence behavior that threaten lower-order needs will always have an impact because they dominate all others.

The existence of a two-step hierarchy means that any higher-order need may come into play after the lower ones are satisfied. This means that if the basic needs are satisfied no one need is likely to be the best or only motivator. In fact, the evidence suggests that two or more needs may be important simultaneously.

16

For example, it seems that a person can be motivated by both social and autonomy needs. However, people are rarely motivated simultaneously by existence needs and other needs. No one is likely to be motivated simultaneously by, say hunger and autonomy.

Can Outcomes Satisfy More than One Need?

A number of studies indicate that some outcomes (i.e., events, objects, behaviors) are useful in satisfying several different needs. That is, when certain outcomes are obtained by an individual, they affect a number of different kinds of satisfaction. A classic example is pay. Pay appears to be able to satisfy not only existence needs, but security and esteem needs as well (Lawler, 1971). Thus, to a person trying to satisfy any one of these three needs (i.e., existence, security, esteem), pay will be important. This helps explain why pay is a good motivator for most people. Pay can buy articles such as food that satisfy existence needs; it can provide a measure of personal security; and it confers on the person receiving high pay a certain amount of esteem and respect—in most societies.

Engaging in a behavior considered socially useful may also satisfy a variety of needs. Thus, while a person probably would not join a social action group out of a concern for existence-need satisfaction, joining such a group could reflect a desire to satisfy social, esteem, autonomy, and even self-realization needs.

How Important are Different Needs?

The data shown in Figure 2–1 indicate the importance of various needs (Porter, 1964). In particular, the data suggest that, for the 1,900 managers sampled, higher-order needs are more important than are needs lower in the hierarchy. It is, however, dangerous to place too much faith in data of this sort. People have difficulty reporting accurately how important different needs are to them. Different approaches to asking people which needs are most important to them produce quite different results. Thus, conclusions about the relative importance of different needs must be tentatively stated.

One statement can be made about need strength with great confidence: Large explainable individual differences exist in the strength of needs. These differences lead to individuals seeing different things in the same job and to different on-the-job behaviors. Because of these differences, a job that is satisfying and motivating to one person will often seem boring to another. Similarly, a reward system that will motivate one person may be irrelevant to others simply because the rewards provided by it are valued differently. **17**

Many differences in need strength are related to other characteristics of people. For example, urban workers tend to have different occupational values than rural workers (Hulin and Blood, 1968). In particular, urban workers seem to be more alienated from their work and less desirous of obtaining higher-order need satisfactions on the job. In addition, individuals with more education tend to be more concerned about self-realization and other higher-order needs.

By comparing the personal characteristics of people who have strong desires for various need satisfactions with those of individuals who have weak desires, it is possible to construct profiles to illustrate the personal characteristics that typify a person oriented toward certain needs. Here is an example of such a profile, provided from research data, for people who are strongly oriented toward money:

> The employee is a male, young (probably in his twenties); his personality is characterized by low self-assurance and high neuroticism; he comes from a small town or a farm background; he belongs to few clubs and social groups, and he owns his own home and probably is a Republican and a Protestant (Lawler, 1971, p. 51).

There is also evidence that shows that type of job is related to need strength. Some data suggest that pay and certain lower-level needs are more important to workers than managers (Porter and Lawler, 1965). Moreover, Dubin (1956) argues that the workplace is *not* a central part of the life of most industrial workers and that it is unwise to expect them to be concerned with fulfillment of higher-order needs on the job. Other data suggest that higher-order needs are important at all organizational levels, but that such needs may be more important at the higher, rather than the lower, levels.

The fact that differences in need strength are predictable if we know something about the backgrounds of individuals and their present jobs means that differences in need strength follow systematic patterns and can be understood. This is important because it means that knowing something about people makes it possible to predict how individuals will react to situations. For example, we can go beyond a simple prediction like, pay incentive plans will increase motivation, to predict which individuals will be motivated by pay incentive plans and which will not. It also means that we can tailor reward systems and control systems to fit the individuals who will be covered by them.

In Conclusion: The Nature of Human Needs

1. Needs are arranged in a two-level hierarchy. At the lower level are existence and security needs. At the higher level are social, esteem, autonomy, and self-realization needs.

2. The higher-level needs will appear only when the lower-level needs are satisfied.
3. Most needs can only be satisfied by extrinsic outcomes but the highest level needs can only be satisfied by intrinsic outcomes.
4. All needs except self-realization can be satisfied, and as they become satisfied, they become less important.
5. A person can be motivated by more than one need at a given point in time and will continue to be motivated by these needs until they are satisfied or until satisfaction of lower-order needs is threatened.

PEOPLE THINK ABOUT THE FUTURE AND MAKE CHOICES ABOUT HOW TO BEHAVE

The behavior of people at work is often discussed in terms of the way individuals react to organizational policies and practices. Individuals are seen as resisting the implementation of a new budgetary system, or as becoming more motivated because of the leadership strategies used by a supervisor, or as becoming more skilled in their work because of an organizational training program. This is a dangerously limited way of viewing human behavior in organizations.

It is true that people are often faced with situations where they must decide how to react and it is crucial that we understand how they decide what their reactions will be. The fact that individuals are usually reacting to situations others have placed them in should not obscure the great deal of initiative individuals demonstrate in seeking means to satisfy their personal needs and pursue their individual goals and aspirations. People take personal initiatives in virtually all settings. Like most behavior, work behavior is often goal oriented and proactive, rather than reactive, in nature.

Because people are purposive, proactive, cognitively-active beings, their behavior can be analyzed in terms of the plans they develop (or, alternatively, the choices they make) to deal with the world and achieve their personal goals.

How do individuals choose which plan to follow?

The general expectancy theory model of human motivation provides one answer. It shows how to analyze and predict what courses of action individuals will follow when they can make choices about their behavior. This theory has been usefully applied to behavior in organizations by a number of psychologists (see, e.g., Vroom, 1964; Porter and Lawler, 1968; Lawler, 1973). The model states that the motivation to engage in a given behavior is determined by (a) people's expectancies or beliefs about what outcomes are likely to result from behavior and (b) the valence or attractiveness people attach to the outcomes as a result of the outcomes' ability to satisfy their needs. Or, in symbols: **19**

$$M = (E \times V)$$
$$\text{where } M = \text{Motivation}$$
$$E = \text{Expectancy}$$
$$V = \text{Valence}$$

Figure 2–3 presents the expectancy model graphically. It shows that people, when deciding whether to try a certain behavior, consider both whether effort on their part will lead to the desired performance and what the outcome of that performance will be. The figure also shows that some outcomes are sought as ends in themselves (Outcomes 3 and 4) and some are sought because they lead to other desired outcomes (Outcomes 1 and 2). This figure emphasizes that two different types of expectancies must be considered: an expectancy concerned with the probability that effort will lead to the intended performance (an $E \rightarrow P$ expectancy) and a number of expectancies concerned with the outcomes that the performance will lead to ($P \rightarrow O$ expectancies). The figure does not show it, but expectancy theory is a choice model. Thus, it states that people compare the outcomes associated with different behaviors and then choose the most attractive one.

If the model is to be used to predict whether the individual will choose to produce at a high rate (e.g., fifty widgets per hour), one needs to do the following:

1. Determine whether the individual feels it is possible to produce at a high rate ($E \rightarrow P$ expectancy). There are a number of reasons why a person might doubt that he or she can produce at a high rate. The crucial physical

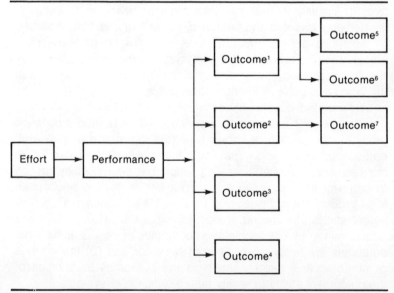

FIGURE 2–3
Diagram of an
Expectancy Model

supplies may be lacking or the person may lack the requisite skills and abilities. If the person feels the behavior is impossible then he or she will not try to engage in it regardless of how attractive it is.

2. Identify the outcomes the individual expects as a consequence of high productivity (P → O expectancy). These might be: "Being tired at the end of the day"; "Feeling that I'm really getting something done at work"; "Getting promoted on the job sooner"; or "Receiving negative reactions from my co-workers." Because most people consider only a few outcomes for any contemplated behavior such lists are usually short.

3. Determine the valence or attractiveness of each of the outcomes to the individual. Valence varies from highly negative to highly positive and is determined by the degree to which the outcome is need-satisfying.

4. Combine the performance outcome (P → O) expectancies of high productivity with the information on the valence of each outcome. If more positive than negative outcomes will result from high productivity, then the person will tend to engage in the behavior.

5. Determine how attractive various *alternative* behaviors are. People engage in behaviors they feel are highest in attractiveness, so it is necessary to compare high productivity with other possible behaviors. This means that E → P beliefs, P → O beliefs, and valences need to be determined for alternate behaviors.

Rationality and Work Performance in Organizations

The expectancy model of decision making suggests a high level of rational, effective decision making on the part of the individual. It is tempting to assume that individuals will always select behavioral alternatives that maximize their payoffs. However, people do not have, and do not attempt to obtain, complete knowledge of the outcomes of their behaviors nor do they proceed rationally and methodically toward their objectives, even when these objectives are ones they personally endorse. One reason for this is that people are not capable of processing all the information available to them.

If people truly attempted to optimize their behavior, they would be so heavily involved in search and evaluation activities aimed at meeting the test for optimal behavior that they would never do anything, or at least they would never be able to make all the decisions required to maintain a day to day existence. Fortunately, optimal decision making is not required for survival; many situations can be dealt with in a kind of automatic way that doesn't involve conscious decision making, and often several kinds of behavior will result in satisfying outcomes.

Simon (1957) has argued that, in general, people's behavior is directed more toward obtaining satisfactory outcomes than obtaining optimal outcomes. By this he means that a person will look for a course of behavior that is satisfactory or good enough, and finding it, take action. Or, for ongoing performance activities, individuals will persist until they feel their performance has reached some level of personal acceptability, even though that level of performance may be far from optimal. **21**

Because individuals often perceive the same situation differently, what looks rational to one person may not to another. As will be discussed later in this chapter, there are a number of reasons why individuals perceive the same situations differently. It is sufficient to note at this point that because they do, people often engage in behavior that appears irrational and nonoptimal.

Does this mean behavior in organizations is irrational and unpredictable? Not necessarily. Behavior generally is predictable if we know how the person perceives the situation and what is important to him or her. While people's behavior may not appear to be rational to an outside observer, there is reason to believe it usually is *intended* to be rational and it is seen as rational by them. An observer often sees behavior as nonrational because the observer does not have access to the same information or does not perceive the environment in the same way. We infer from this that if we are to understand and predict behavior in organizations, we must deal with how individuals see the world as well as with objective reality.

In Conclusion

A general model has been proposed for analyzing and predicting the decision-making behavior of individuals in organizations. Central to the model are three factors: (a) the expectancies individuals hold about whether they can perform certain behaviors ($E \rightarrow P$ expectancies); (b) the expectancies individuals hold about the outcomes of contemplated behaviors ($P \rightarrow O$ expectancies); and (c) the valence or attractiveness of these outcomes to the person. It was stressed that unless behaviors are seen as capable of being performed and as resulting in positive outcomes no motivation will be present to engage in them.

It should be emphasized that the expectancy model is just that—a model, and no more. People rarely sit down and list their expected outcomes for a contemplated behavior, estimate expectancies and valences, multiply and add up the total, unless, of course, they are asked to do so by a researcher. One reason for this is that people are limited in their ability to process information. Yet, people *do* consider some of the likely outcomes of their actions, weigh and evaluate the attractiveness of various alternatives, and use these estimates in coming to a decision about what they will do. The expectancy model provides an analytic tool for mirroring that process and for predicting its outcome, but it does not purport to perfectly reflect the actual decision-making steps taken by an individual in making behavioral choices.

PEOPLE HAVE LIMITED RESPONSE CAPABILITIES

An important factor limiting individuals' behavior is response capability. Stated in other terms, people cannot respond in all the ways that might seem possible and desirable. This has already been mentioned in two contexts—one having to do with high production and people's physical capability to produce at high rates, and the other having to do with people's abilities to process large amounts of information. These two points highlight that individuals are limited in both their physical and mental response capabilities. No baseball player can hit a home run every time at bat just as no author writes only great fiction. In fact, most people are not capable of hitting a home run or writing great fiction.

One reason information and control systems come into existence in organizations is because people are limited in their ability to store and process information. Because of their complexity and storage capacity, information and control systems can sometimes capture and summarize information that individuals cannot.

Traditionally, psychologists have divided behavior into those responses that are innate and therefore not subject to improvement by training, and those that can be altered and learned. This way of thinking about human characteristics seems to be outmoded. Now it appears that even measures like intelligence (IQ), which was once thought to be innately determined and fixed, can be influenced significantly by training and experience. It remains true, however, that IQ can only be influenced within a limited range because of physiological constraints. Consequently, it now seems reasonable to think of human response capacities in terms of a continuum. At one end of the continuum are those responses that are relatively uninfluenceable as a result of training and experience, and at the other end are those responses that are relatively open to change and not significantly constrained by genetic or physiological factors.

Figure 2–4 presents an illustration of the kind of continuum that can be constructed. It shows that some abilities (e.g., reaction time) are relatively fixed, while others are relatively malleable and can be improved by training. The significance of this point for understanding behavior in organizations is substantial. It directly raises the issue of what type of training and development programs organizations should run. If, for example, managerial style is relatively fixed, it hardly makes sense to spend money training managers. It would seem far better to attempt to *select* managers who have the desired response capabilities. Similarly, if people cannot be trained to deal with the kind of information that complex management information systems produce, then it makes no sense to **23**

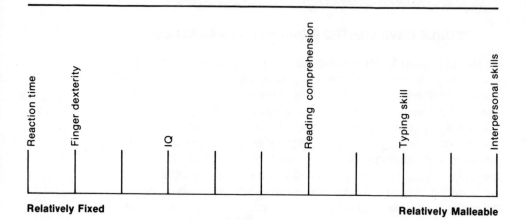

Relatively Fixed

Relatively Malleable

FIGURE 2–4
Human Response
Capabilities

Adapted from L.W. Porter, E.E. Lawler, and J.R. Hackman, *Behavior in Organizations*, (New York: McGraw-Hill, 1975).

do training in this area. It does, however, make sense to select people who can deal with these data and to change the data so that more individuals can deal with them.

Measuring Individual Differences

The major contribution of psychologists interested in individual differences has been the development of valid measures of people's response capabilities. A large number of psychological tests have been developed, and research has shown that they can predict future behavior in organizations. Tests have been developed to measure response capabilities that are relatively fixed and those that can be changed by experience and training. The latter tests are often called skill tests, while the former are called aptitude tests. Both kinds of tests often play an important role in a variety of personnel decisions, including hiring, firing, promotion, and training decisions. Psychologists have been much less successful in developing valid tests of people's personalities and needs. Thus, these are much less frequently used as a basis for personnel decisions.

Mental Capabilities

Most of the research that has attempted to relate mental ability to job performance suggests a relatively simple classification scheme (Ghiselli, 1966). One dimension of the system is quantitative or numerical ability, and the other is verbal ability. The distinction turns out to be important since quantitative and verbal abilities differentially predict success in various jobs. For some jobs (e.g., certain sales jobs) verbal ability seems to be the best predictor while for others (e.g., financial and engineering jobs) quantitative

24

ability predicts better. This is not surprising, given the different demands jobs put on people. Consequently, for understanding individual behavior in organizations it is probably important to maintain this distinction between verbal and quantitative skills.

Interpersonal Skills and Style

A number of studies have shown that how individuals deal with each other influences organizational effectiveness in general and the operation of information and control systems in particular (see, e.g., Argyris, 1964). A recent study (Cammann, 1974b), for example, shows that the impact of an information system is partially determined by the interpersonal skills and abilities of the manager who uses the system. This suggests that interpersonal competence should be thought of as an important skill for organization members to have (Argyris, 1962).

A person's interpersonal style (how they deal with others) frequently is thought of in terms of response predispositions, i.e., as reflecting largely how a person *wants* to respond or behave. But, interpersonal behavior is influenced not only by response disposition but also by response capability (Wallace, 1966). This view leads to an abilities conception of personality that considers the response capabilities of people to be an important determinant of people's interpersonal behavior. It is clear that people are limited in the interpersonal behaviors of which they are capable. Some people cannot, for example, express emotions in groups. Others don't trust co-workers and still others find it impossible to praise subordinates who perform well. These behaviors are difficult for some people not because of dispositional tendencies but simply because they *do not know how* to express themselves. They have never learned to express emotions openly. Instead, they have learned only how to cover them up, or at most, express them indirectly. Interpersonal competence, then, can be likened to calculus; many people can be taught it, but few people can discover it for themselves.

It is also clear that people's interpersonal behavior is strongly influenced by their dispositional tendencies. Sometimes people do not express emotions even though they can because they feel the group will punish them for it or their boss will not approve of it. In summary, then, the argument is that interpersonal behavior is strongly influenced by both "can do" and "want to" issues.

Unfortunately, there simply are no well-validated approaches to classifying interpersonal style and no well-developed measures of it. There are, however, a few approaches to studying leadership, and these will be considered in later chapters because of the important role leadership plays in determining how individuals react to information and control systems.   **25**

In Conclusion

People are limited in the behaviors they are capable of performing. Training and education can help overcome some but not all of these limitations. Particularly relevant to control systems in organizations are the limitations of people in mental ability and interpersonal style. To some extent it is possible to measure what people's response capabilities are, and this provides helpful data for understanding behavior in organizations. The most important point to remember is the basic one that behavior in organizations is a function of both what people are motivated to do and what they *can* do. Thus, in analyzing behavior and designing information and control systems it is important to determine what people are capable of doing.

PEOPLE ARE ACTIVE PERCEIVERS OF THE WORLD

Experiencing the environment is an *active* process in which people try to make sense out of their environment. In this active process individuals selectively notice different aspects of the environment, appraise what they see in terms of their own past experience, and evaluate what they experience in terms of their needs and values. Since people's needs and past experiences often differ markedly, so do their perceptions of the environment. For example, people in the same organization often develop very different expectancies of what kinds of behavior lead to rewards like pay increases and promotions. This has a very important implication for understanding behavior in organizations. It is not safe to assume that the same management policy, practice, or decision will be seen in the same way by members of an organization. Thus, the same control system is likely to be seen quite differently by the members of an organization.

Selective Noticing

Environments provide their members with many more stimuli than any individual is cognitively able to handle. Therefore, in perceiving a given situation, individuals do not notice many aspects of the environment and, as was noted earlier, they must decide not to deal with many aspects they do notice. It is precisely because of this characteristic of human perception that it is often useful to combine data into summary reports and indices. Which aspects of the environment *are* noticed and processed depends partly on the nature of the stimuli and partly on the previous experience of the individual.

Stimuli that are highly distinctive within the usual organizational context are more likely to be noticed than stimuli that do not stick out in some unusual way. The written memo from the central office may not be a very distinctive input to members of an organization that generates dozens of such memos every week. But a videotaped message from the company president that occurs rarely will be distinctive and will likely be attended to by almost all employees. Similarly, daily or weekly productivity reports may be ignored by most employees while published quarterly earnings statements are watched carefully.

In addition to stimulus distinctiveness, the previous learning of organization members plays an important part in determining what is noticed. Organization members quickly become able to recognize the stimuli they need to pay attention to in order to satisfy their needs and those they may safely overlook. For example, a manager may learn that it is generally unnecessary to read the accounting department's extensive budget reports, but that it is important to read carefully reports concerned with quality control because possible promotions and pay increases hinge on these reports.

In summary, then, people are not able to respond to all stimuli and must be selective. What *is* noticed is a joint function of the distinctiveness of the stimuli and a member's learning which messages have important personal consequences for him or her and which do not.

Appraisal

Even when a stimulus is noticed, there is no guarantee that it will be perceived accurately. The meaning any given objective stimulus has for an organization member is influenced by the needs and values of the member. Individuals tend to distort stimuli so that they are more congruent with their needs and values (Jones and Gerard, 1967). It is difficult to predict for any given person the specific nature of the distortion of a particular event; there are too many idiosyncratic factors involved in the nature of the event and in the psychological and emotional makeup of the individual. It is possible, however, to predict the amount of distortion likely to occur. Distortion of an event in an organization is likely when there is emotional involvement in the situation in which the event takes place. Emotional involvement usually occurs when the situation relates to the central needs of individuals. For example, when an organization announces a new policy about promotions, the possibility of distortion and misunderstanding of that message is high for those who aspire to make it big in the organization. The chances for distortion are also high when the organization performance measurement system produces information on the performance of individuals. **27**

In Conclusion

In several places in this chapter it has been pointed out that individuals often perceive the same environment differently. This is because perceiving the environment is an active process that leads to selective noticing and appraisal. There are a number of implications of this point for understanding behavior in organizations. Probably the most important is that to understand and predict the behavior of people we must see the world through *their* eyes. This point also has some interesting implications for understanding the reactions of individuals to information and control systems. For example, it suggests that systems will often be misperceived when they are part of a reward system that distributes important rewards.

INDIVIDUALS HAVE AFFECTIVE REACTIONS TO WHAT HAPPENS TO THEM

People are rarely neutral about things they perceive or experience. Instead, they tend to evaluate most things in terms of whether they like or dislike them. Moreover, this evaluative response (or "gut reaction") is one of the most important influences on future behavior, because it establishes the attractiveness of events and stimuli. For many years psychologists have been concerned with measuring and understanding the causes of the feelings people have about their work. Thousands of studies have been done on the satisfaction of organization members. Studies have focused on overall job satisfaction as well as satisfaction with such specific aspects of the work environment as pay, promotion opportunities, the task to be performed, fringe benefits, personal relationships, security, and the leadership style of the supervisor.

Part of the reason for the original interest in the causes of job satisfaction was the widely held belief that job satisfaction was a major determinant of job performance. Research, however, has not supported the view that job satisfaction can cause job performance. Quite to the contrary, recent research shows that when a relationship exists between satisfaction and performance it is usually because the performance causes the satisfaction (Lawler, 1973). This has by no means, however, signaled the end of interest in studying job satisfaction. Psychologists still are concerned with job satisfaction, but it now is seen more as a *reaction* to one's work and one's organizational membership than as a *determinant* of one's performance. Viewed in this way, satisfaction has become an important topic of study in its own right and an outcome that it is important to increase for humanistic reasons.

28

Moreover, satisfaction is a reasonably strong determinant of absenteeism, tardiness, and turnover. The more satisfied an employee, the less likely he or she is to be absent, late to work, or to resign from the organization (Porter and Steers, 1973). This seems to come about because satisfaction influences people's expectancies about the consequences of coming to work. Satisfied employees naturally see more positive outcomes associated with going to work and hence are more likely to show up for work and to remain members of their organization.

Unfortunately, no real theory of job satisfaction has been developed, although several contributions to such a theory are available (see Locke, 1976, for a review). In general, it appears that satisfaction is determined by the difference between the amount of rewards people receive and the amount that they feel they *should* receive. The larger the discrepancy, the greater the dissatisfaction. Moreover, the amount people feel they *should* receive has been found to be strongly influenced by what they perceive others to be receiving (Lawler, 1971). People seem to compare what they are putting into a work situation and what they feel they are getting out of it with what others receive for what they put into it. If this comparison reveals that their outcomes are not equal to those of others, then dissatisfaction results. As would be expected, since this is an important area, individuals often misperceive the inputs and outcomes of other people as well as their own.

An illustrative satisfaction model is presented in Figure 2–5. It shows that people compare their perception of what they receive (Box B) with what they feel they should receive (Box A) and that they are satisfied when there is a balance between the two. It also shows that sometimes people feel they receive more than they should. However, research has shown that this tends to be a relatively short-lived and infrequent phenomena.

The figure indicates that people's perceptions of what they should receive are influenced by their personal inputs as well as by the inputs and outcomes of others. The greater the inputs of a person the higher the perception of what they should receive. This means that high input individuals must receive more outcomes to be satisfied. The model can be used to understand either satisfaction with a particular job facet, such as pay or job design, or overall job satisfaction. The switch from satisfaction with a specific facet to overall satisfaction is accomplished by combining the degree of satisfaction that exists with each facet.

Much of the research on job satisfaction has focused on various determinants of satisfaction. Sufficient research has now been done that it is possible to specify, in general, how people react to various managerial and work practices they experience **29**

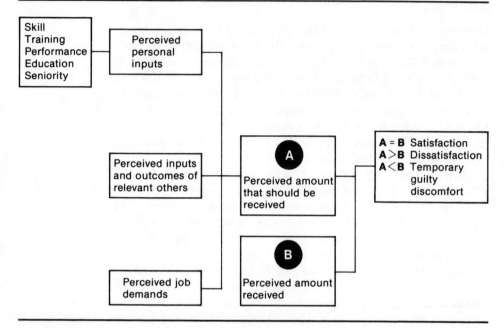

FIGURE 2–5
A satisfaction
model

in organizations. It is also possible to point out how individual differences influence the effects of organizational practices on satisfaction. In the chapters to follow, the effects of many organizational policies and practices with respect to information and control systems on member satisfaction will be considered. In addition, attention will be given to the kinds of satisfactions available in information and control system jobs.

In Conclusion

Job satisfaction is best thought of as a reaction people have to what happens to them at work. It is strongly influenced by what happens to others, since people evaluate their own situation by comparing it with that of others. For this reason people often are dissatisfied even though they appear to be well off by some standards. There also are differences in how people react to work situations, because people differ in their needs and in who they compare their work situation with. Finally, it is important to note that satisfaction is not a cause of performance, although it does influence the willingness of employees to come to work and their tendency to change jobs.

UNDERSTANDING ORGANIZATIONS AND CONTROL SYSTEMS 3

Information and control systems are only one element of a formal organization. If we are to understand why these systems exist, how they function, and finally how they affect behavior, we need to understand how organizations operate and how the other elements of organizations interact with information and control systems. This chapter will begin by focusing on the nature of complex organizations. It will then consider the nature of information and control systems, how they operate, and which of their generic attributes are the crucial determinants of behavior.

WHAT IS AN ORGANIZATION?

The basic nature and features of organizations have been the subject of study for several decades. Among the many theorists who have studied organizations, there is surprisingly little agreement about what defines an organization and what its key features are.

The difficulty in defining an organization is captured in one theorist's statement: A person "who has not tried his hand at framing a one-sentence (or even one-paragraph) definition of organization has denied himself an educational experience of high value (Waldo, 1961, p. 218)." Two other authors note, "It is easier and probably more useful to give examples of organizations than to define the term (March and Simon, 1958, p. 1)." Needless to say, they do not try to define the term.

At this point the reader may wonder if there is any agreement about what an organization is. In fact there is, and it centers around a few characteristics that most organizations have. A recent book (Porter, Lawler, and Hackman, 1975) captures the agreement in the following:

"Organizations" are:
Who: composed of individuals and groups
Why: created in order to achieve certain goals and objectives
How: operated by means of differentiated functions that are intended
   to be rationally coordinated and directed
When: in existence through time on a continuous basis

This approach to defining organizations suggests a number of statements about organizations that can help understand the role of control systems and their relation to the whole of which they are a part.

ORGANIZATIONS ARE SOCIAL ENTITIES THAT HAVE BOUNDARIES

Organizations are social institutions that contain certain interaction patterns. These patterns can be used to differentiate organizations. For example, the interaction patterns associated with particular organizations vary in the degree to which they occur between insiders and outsiders. This is another way of saying that organizations have boundaries and that some people are seen as inside the organization and others are not. This has an important impact on the nature of social interactions that take place and it emphasizes the fact that organizations exist in an environment. Open systems theory in fact emphasizes that organizations have frequent interactions or exchanges with their environment (Katz and Kahn, 1966). Organizations receive inputs from the environment and send outputs back. It is the existence of this kind of input-output process in most organizations that suggests our second point about the nature of organizations.

ORGANIZATIONS HAVE GOALS AND OBJECTIVES THAT INVOLVE THE EXTERNAL ENVIRONMENT

A number of organization theorists have emphasized that organizations have certain goals and objectives. The goals and objectives typically involve the input-output process of organizations. Often the goals are stated in terms of the nature and amount of output and its impact on the external environment. For example, selling X number of widgets at Y amount of dollars, or in the case of the American Cancer Society, eliminating cancer. Sometimes the goals of organizations focus more on the nature of the internal activities an organization engages in to generate its output. These may be concerned with the efficiency with which the organization processes its inputs (e.g., labor cost effectiveness) or with the size and internal health of the organization itself. Frequently, these internal or process goals are secondary or subgoals that must be met for the output or external goals to be achieved.

Recently, some organization theorists (e.g., Haas and Drabek, 1973) have argued that organizations don't really have goals that individuals do. They point out that organizations don't consistently pursue a single set of goals, and that within organizations there is often low agreement about what the goals are. There is no question that some organizations have many goals, and these goals are often changing. Further, it is quite clear that different groups in an organization often see different goals for it. Top management, for example, often sees quite different goals for an organization than the personnel manager. The stockholders of a corporation typically have goals for an organization that are quite different from those that are held by blue collar workers. For example, the stockholder wants the organization to maximize profits so that a large dividend may be declared whereas the blue collar worker wants large profits so that salary increases—especially to the labor force—can be given.

Even though different individuals and groups do not agree on what the goals of their organizations are, the concept of goal orientation is useful in understanding organizational behavior. Most people believe that organizations should have goals and many try to influence the goals of their organization. One way to view power in an organization is in terms of how much an individual or group can influence an organization so that it will pursue the goals they want it to pursue. In most organizations management has the most power in this sense. One reason they have power is because they develop reward systems and maintain information and control systems. As we shall see, the reward systems are used to motivate goal directed behavior, and the information and control systems are used to direct behavior and measure progress toward the goals.

ORGANIZATIONS REWARD AND PUNISH INDIVIDUAL MEMBERS

Chapter 2 pointed out that the behavior of individuals is governed by the kinds of outcomes they expect to receive. They join organizations because they expect to receive certain rewards that they cannot obtain without joining. Work organizations pay people in return for their membership, attendance, and effort. The rewards for joining voluntary organizations are often less obvious **33** but no less important. For example, the rewards for joining the United Fund are usually not monetary, but they are very real and important to some people. Membership is an important status symbol in some communities—particularly suburban areas near large cities.

Usually a psychological contract develops between an individual and an organization. The individual agrees to be part of the organization as long as he or she receives certain rewards. And the organization agrees to give the person these rewards as long as the person performs in agreed upon ways.

There is a second way organizations use rewards and punishments that is very important in any discussion of control systems. Just because a person is a member of an organization does not mean that the person is contributing towards the goals of the organization. Membership motivation and performance motivation are quite different. Pay may motivate people to come to work, but it doesn't automatically make them perform effectively. Realizing this, organizations often relate rewards and punishment to performance. Pay incentive plans are a clear example of this. They create conditions where people's reward levels vary as a function of how they perform. Organizations also often punish individuals (for example, reduce their pay or temporarily suspend them) when they fail to perform in a designated manner.

All organization systems that attempt to motivate a certain kind of behavior by tying rewards or punishments to it require one thing—a way to measure the behavior. This, of course, is why there is a potential relationship between information and control systems that measure behavior and systems that are designed to reward it. For rewards to cause motivation they must be given on the basis of the measurement information developed by the information and control system.

Not all information and control systems are used for reward allocation. For example, sometimes they are only used to aid in long range planning decisions. Not surprisingly, as we shall see later, there are enormous differences in how information and control systems operate when rewards are related to measures of performance and when they are not.

ORGANIZATIONS CONTAIN A
NUMBER OF DIFFERENT ROLES

One of the most obvious features of organizations is that they often contain a large number of roles or jobs. The overriding reason for this is their tendency to have effectiveness- and efficiency-related goals. To produce a service or product, most organizations need more types of complex behavior than one person

34

can perform adequately. Even if a person were capable of performing them all well, the need for many of them to be performed at the same time in different locations compels some specialization. For example, organizations that use chemical processes must have persons stationed in different parts of the plant to carry out the necessary functions at the right time. Even in those organizations where tasks are simple, the strengths and weaknesses of individuals argue for role or job differentiation. Some people do certain things better than others, and the goal-oriented nature of organizations compels them to capitalize on this.

There are many ways the work to be performed in an organization can be subdivided differentially. For our purposes it is most useful to think of two major ways—those differing along the *horizontal* dimension of the organization and those differing along the *vertical* dimension (Porter, Lawler, and Hackman, 1975).

Horizontal differentiation refers to the division of activities among individuals and groups that occupy the same, or roughly the same, authority and responsibility level. Frequently, this kind of differentiation is labeled the division of labor. Unfortunately, this phrase carries connotations of applying only to industrial or manufacturing types of organizations and only to their lowest level, the rank and file worker. In point of fact, division of labor occurs in *all types* of organizations—governmental and educational as well as industrial—and at *all levels* within the organization. Thus, it is a universal characteristic of organizations.

Frequently, the jobs in organizations are differentiated on the basis of function. In the case of most business organizations, this means division into manufacturing, sales, marketing, etc. It also leads to the often stated distinction between line and staff employees. Line employees typically carry out functions designed to meet the direct output goals of the organization. Staff employees usually have support jobs in the sense that they provide specialized technical help to the line employees. Personnel, information system maintenance, and accounting are examples of functions that are called staff in most organizations. Horizontal differentiation may also be based on product responsibility or on geographic area responsibility. Organizations differ substantially in how horizontally differentiated they are and some recent research suggests that the degree of differentiation may influence their effectiveness (Lawrence and Lorsch, 1967).

Vertical differentiation involves differences along such dimensions as the amount of authority or power individuals have to influence organizational actions, the degree of responsibility they have for these actions, and the number of individuals they supervise or manage. The primary reason for vertical differentiation **35** within organizations is to coordinate the specialized activities that result from the division of labor on the horizontal level.

There are two things to note about the vertical differentiation of functions. Those people who are in the top positions (the deciders) are primarily oriented to goal formation and the monitoring of performance while those at the very bottom (the doers) are primarily functioning to carry out goals. Individuals in the middle of the vertical hierarchy are oriented to both goal setting and monitoring goal achievement for their segment of the organization. Thus individuals in these positions, i.e., middle and lower management, more than any others in the organization, need to be alerted simultaneously to the ends and the means for accomplishing them. A number of writers have stressed that the effectiveness of an organization is strongly influenced by its degree of vertical differentiation. Some have argued that it should be minimized (e.g., Likert, 1967; Argyris, 1957), while others have pointed out a high degree of it is often functional (e.g., Taylor 1911).

This brings us to our second point about vertical differentiation: Different performance demands are made on individuals at different levels in organizations (Porter and Ghiselli, 1957; Katz and Kahn, 1966). This is particularly true with respect to information and control systems since, as was noted in Chapter 1, some jobs involve making decisions based on the information they provide while others involve designing systems. This means that an individual who is an effective, satisfied performer at one level may not necessarily be well adapted to the requirements at other levels.

One basic characteristic of organizations in comparison with other social groups is that functions are differentiated along both the horizontal and vertical dimensions. In all organizations of any size, there are at least several horizontal divisions, as well as several vertical levels (of authority, responsibility, etc.). This means that a matrix of differentiated functions exists. In general, the larger the organization the more complex the matrix becomes.

ORGANIZATIONS HAVE SYSTEMS THAT ARE DESIGNED TO MONITOR GOAL-ORIENTED BEHAVIOR

The inevitable twin of differentiated function is intended rational coordination (that is, the combining or orchestrating of individual activities in such a way that they will accomplish the goals of the organization). The former creates the need for the latter (Porter, Lawler, and Hackman, 1975). In any situation where individuals are working on only part of a whole, there is a need to assure that the parts will come together to make an effective whole. This is true whether the whole is a TV set and the parts are transistors or the whole is a university education and the parts are different classes.

Most large, complex organizations contain a number of information and control systems for coordination. Not all control systems produce the same behavioral reactions, so, in order to go beyond a superficial discussion of the general impact of control systems on behavior, we must specify how different kinds of control systems impact on behavior. To do this, we need a classification system for control systems that lends itself to a discussion of the behavioral aspect of control systems. In other words, one is needed that distinguishes between systems in ways that are important from a behavioral impact point of view.

Our requirements for a classification system are quite different from those of engineers or economists. We are not interested in a classification system that will distinguish among information systems on the basis of the kind of support hardware they need or on the basis of whether or not they make certain economic assumptions. We are interested in a classification system that will distinguish among control systems on the basis of the impact they have on behavior. However, before we state such a classification system we would like to briefly review some of the more commonly used systems to show why they are unsatisfactory for our purposes.

Type of Information Handled

Control systems can be classified in terms of the kind of data they collect. Most systems collect one of three kinds: financial, production, or administrative. Budgets and cost accounting systems are examples of financial control systems. The daily production and quality control reports issued by many organizations are examples of production information and control systems. Time clocks and other attendance measuring devices are examples of administrative systems. From a behavioral point of view this distinction is not very useful. The kind of data a system collects says little or nothing about how the system will impact on a person's behavior. It doesn't tell us how it will affect $P \rightarrow 0$ (Performance $\rightarrow$ Outcome) and $E \rightarrow P$ (Effort $\rightarrow$ Performance) beliefs or whether it will affect need satisfaction. To know about this, we need to know how the information will be used and who will see it, these are issues with a more direct influence on behavior.

It is undoubtedly true that, on the average, financial information systems have a slightly different impact on behavior than production information systems. However, they seem to have this impact not because of the kind of information they handle but because of the way they are designed to handle it and the importance they attach to it. As a result, in thinking about how a control system might impact on behavior, it is useful to know something about the kind of information it collects. Yet, this is just a small **37** part of the information needed to make accurate predictions of behavior.

Purpose of System

Control systems can be classified according to the purposes they serve in the organization (Anthony, 1965). Some measure performance to provide management with the information they need to control employees' present behavior. Others provide top management with the information they need for long-range planning. And a third group provides ongoing feedback to employees about their job performance.

Operating budgets and regular production reports are examples of systems used to control day to day behavior, although sometimes they are also used for long range planning. Capital expenditure budgets are a good example of a system used for long range planning. The dials and gauges on machinery are systems that operate primarily to give the employees feedback.

Behaviorally, the purpose for which a system collects data is important. As we shall see in Chapters 4, 5, and 6, the purpose determines the kind of P → O beliefs that develop concerning the behaviors measured by the system. Because of this, systems designed to provide management with the information they need to control the behavior of their subordinates have a quite different impact than those designed to give individuals the information they need to exercise self-control. Behavior surveillance systems, for example, often generate strong motivation because they are tied to reward systems. On the other hand, systems designed to assist self-control have to rely on the internal desire of the individual to do the job correctly.

The only problem with classifying control systems on the basis of the purpose of the system is that this distinction does not go far enough. To predict behavior in detail, we need to know more than just what the primary purpose of the system is. We need to know how the data are collected, who collects them, and how they are presented to the individual involved. In the case of a system designed to provide management with information it needs to control behavior, it is important whether or not the control will be achieved through financial incentives since this strongly affects the kinds of beliefs individuals develop. It also makes a difference who collects the information since this partially determines the validity of the data and the degree to which the system is seen as threatening by the employees.

In short, it is important to distinguish among control systems on the basis of the purpose of the system. Thus, in developing **38** a classification system for control systems this dimension needs to be considered. However, this distinction is not sufficiently detailed and precise to allow for good behavioral prediction; more information is needed.

More Complex Classification Systems

Recognizing that control systems cannot be adequately classified by using one dimension, several writers have proposed more complex classification systems. For example Reeves and Woodward (1970) have proposed that control systems be classified as either primarily personal or mechanical and as either primarily unitary or fragmented. The personal-mechanical dimension refers to the degree to which a control system functions through personal authority relationships. The ultimate personal control system is the owner-manager who gives his or her employees instructions and monitors their work. The ultimate mechanical systems are cost control systems, quality control systems, and the automatic control systems of continuous flow production plants. As Reeves and Woodward point out, impersonal mechanical controls operate more or less impartially and automatically.

The fragmentation dimension refers to the degree to which the various control systems in an organization are linked. It distinguishes between organizations where there is a single system and those where there is multi-system or fragmented control. Some organizations try to relate the different control systems so that they have an integrated system of managerial control while other firms do not. According to Reeves and Woodward, research shows that some firms have "made considerable and continuous efforts to relate the standards set for various departments by the different functional specialists, and the performance and adjustment mechanisms associated with them, into a single integrated system of managerial control" (p. 50).

By using the two dimensions suggested by Reeves and Woodward, a control system may be characterized as integrated or not and as personal or impersonal. Rackham and Woodward (1970) have done just this for a number of firms. They present data on the kinds of control systems different types of organizations tend to have. Their results show, for example, that unit and small batch production firms (e.g., job shops) tend to have unitary and mainly personal control systems while process production firms (e.g., oil refineries) tend to have unitary and impersonal control systems. Their work represents an interesting attempt to begin to relate the characteristics of organizations to the characteristics of their control systems. Research must be done in this area if we are to understand why organizations develop the kind of controls they have, if we are to have any idea of the frequency with which **39** the different kinds of control systems are present in organizations, and if we are to understand what kind of control systems are best for different kinds of organizations.

It is not clear, however, that the Rackham-Woodward kind of classification system is appropriate for looking at the impact of control systems on behavior within organizations. The distinctions made by it are helpful, but they don't go far enough. The unitary-fragmented distinction is useful, for example, since it leads to the prediction that in organizations with fragmented systems people will feel conflict. However, in order to predict behavior, we need to be able to predict what kinds of conflicting $P \rightarrow O$ beliefs will appear and the kind of behavior they will produce. This cannot be done with the simple integrated versus fragmented classification. The personal-impersonal classification also has relevance for behavior. Personal systems typically rely more on interpersonal rewards and influence, and they are more subject to bias; however, in order to know how this will affect behavior, we need to know more about how that system operates. In short, the Reeves and Woodward system does use behaviorally relevant variables, but it still is unsatisfactory from our point of view, because it doesn't go far enough to allow for the prediction of specific attitudes and behaviors.

The Thermostat Model

Eilon (1962) maintains that any control system, whether simple or complex, contains four elements: objective setting, planning, execution, and control. Objectives have to be set in relation to the behavior desired, plans have to be made about how these objectives can be reached, the plans have to be executed, and information gathered about the effectiveness of the action. These are not always discrete sets of activities, but they are the minimum elements of a control system. Planning, setting standards, and action are all prerequisites of control. Without some concept of what should be done, it is impossible to make any assessment of what has, in fact, been done.

McKelvey (1970) has drawn the analogy between a thermostat furnace system and the control systems that operate in many organizations. This analogy is useful because it elaborates on Eilon's idea about what functions are present in a control system. The thermostat system that controls the heating level in a room consists of (1) a *sensor* that measures the temperature of a room, (2) an adjustable device that sets a *standard* that is the desired temperature (often this is a temperature band), (3) a *discriminator* that compares the sensed information with the standard, (4) an *effector* that responds to the discriminator by turning the activity

40

(a furnace) on or off, (5) some wires for *communication,* (6) the *activity* itself, in this case a furnace, and (7) a source of *energy* that powers the activity.

Many organizational control systems contain these same seven functions. Probably the clearest analogy to the thermostat model is the budget system in most organizations. Like the thermostat it measures only one particular aspect of performance (financial expenditure), standards are set (budgetary goals), budgetary performance is compared with the standard (often by a controller or superior), action is taken when a deviance occurs from the standard, communication takes place in the form of financial reports, and an activity—spending money—takes place that derives its energy from the motivation of the people in the system.

The thermostat model suggests several possible classification systems. Control systems could, for example, be classified on the basis of whether or not they perform each of the seven functions of a thermostat. Not all control systems have each of the seven functions although all have most of them; otherwise, they would not be called control systems. Still not all control systems are as close to the thermostat model as the budget is. For example, many organizations have rules and regulations about how activities are to be performed, but they have poorly developed sensors or measures of how they are being performed. Also, production reports, unlike the thermostat, sometimes do not operate on the basis of standards and deviance from those standards. They simply sense and report how much of a given activity has taken place.

To predict the impact of a control system, like a budget, on behavior, it is not enough to know whether a control system has the same seven functions as a thermostat. We must also know how the functions are carried out. For example, it is important whether or not a standard exists, but in order to predict behavior we need to know how the standard was set and how it is perceived by the employees. In other words, we need to know not only what the parts of the system are but how they operate. Still, the thermostat model appears to provide an excellent basis for building a classification system. It raises the questions that are important from a behavioral point of view. The problem is it raises so many questions that it suggests a complex typology. However, this complexity is manageable since only certain questions are relevant when we consider each of the role relationships individuals can have with a control system. That is, only certain issues are important when the effects of control systems on decision makers, system maintenance people, and individuals whose behavior is measured are considered. But before this is specified we need to state in some detail the actual classification system we are proposing. **41**

A CLASSIFICATION SYSTEM

The classification system used throughout the remainder of this book is based on the thermostat model. It classifies control systems in terms of how the basic functions of thermostatic type information and control systems are handled.

Characteristics of the Measures

A crucial aspect of any control system is how *completely* or *inclusively* it measures the behaviors that need to be performed by a job holder. Control system measures vary in their completeness; some tap all the behaviors while others tap only part of them. Thus sensors or measures can be classified as either relatively complete or relatively incomplete. A system that measures only the number of products produced is a good example of an incomplete system while one that measures production, scrap, quality, and cost effectiveness is an example of a more complete one.

Systems also vary in terms of the *objectivity* and *impersonality* of the measures themselves. Some systems use objective measures while others use subjective ones. For example, production measurement systems that use electronic devices to count output or measure quality are relatively objective while systems that use ratings to measure customer good will or employee cooperation are subjective.

Finally, control systems differ in the degree to which what they measure can be *controlled* and *influenced* by the members of an organization. Some measures, like profits, are relatively difficult to influence, while others, like production rates, are easier for members to control.

Nature of Standards

The standards in control systems can be set by any number of people. From a behavioral point of view, it is crucial just who is involved in setting them. It is particularly crucial whether or not the person whose behavior is being measured is involved in setting the standards. Also, it often makes a difference whether people other than the individuals and their boss are involved. Obviously, there are a number of possibilities here. To mention just two, the individuals may set the standard in conjunction with their boss or their boss may set it in conjunction with a staff person.

Standards vary greatly in their *difficulty level*. Some are very easy for employees to reach; others are very difficult. Difficulty level has a strong impact on the behavior of those employees whose behavior is measured because of individual differences in people's ability to perform the same or dissimilar tasks and because of its effect on motivation.

Source of Discrimination

As with standard setting, it is crucial *who acts as the discriminator.* It can be the individuals whose performance is being measured, but it can also be their boss, a staff person, or even an automated system that makes the comparison between the standard and the performance. In the case of budgets, it is often a staff person or the boss, while in the case of some participative performance appraisal systems it is the person who is being measured.

Pattern of Communication

Control systems vary widely in terms of *who receives information* about deviations from the standard. This information may go to one or more of the following: the individuals whose activities are being measured, their superior, their peers, their subordinates, top management, staff members, or a variety of people outside of the organization. It is particularly important whether the information goes to the person whose behavior is being measured and whether it goes to someone who has reward power for that person. If it goes to the person, then self-control is possible; if it goes to someone who can give rewards, then it can be used as a basis for giving extrinsic rewards.

Speed and Frequency of Communication

Control systems differ in how *quickly* they report the results of their measurement process. Some on-line systems report almost instantly while others take months. For example, the annual financial performance of some companies isn't reported until months after the fiscal year has ended while in others it is known almost immediately. Systems also vary in how *often* they report. For example, some systems report continuously while others report yearly or even less often. The frequency and rapidness with which information is reported are important factors in determining the impact of the information. They influence both how the information will be used for decision making and the degree to which the information can facilitate self-control.

Form of Communication

There is some evidence to suggest that the form in which information produced by control systems is reported influences how decisions are made. At this point no one has developed a way of classifying the different forms. The research has been concerned with whether such things as footnotes on financial statements make a difference and whether summaries have a different impact than reports that include all the data. At this time the evidence **43** is not compelling on which formal characteristics are crucial and as a result our approach to classifying control systems will not include form of communication although it will be considered at various points in our discussion.

Type of Activity

The *activities* measured by control systems vary widely in terms of how *important* they are to the success of the organization. For example, financial control systems are typically seen as measuring an important area while systems designed to measure such things as job satisfaction are not. How people respond to control systems is strongly influenced by how important the measured activity is. Obviously, people weigh their reactions to important systems more carefully than they do their reactions to unimportant systems. As we shall see, sometimes this is functional and sometimes it isn't.

Motivation for Activity

Activities in organizations can be motivated by *intrinsic motivation, extrinsic motivation,* or some combination of the two. In the case of extrinsic motivation, rewards and punishment such as pay or dismissal are used to start and stop the activities. In the case of intrinsic motivation, the person is motivated by internal feelings and rewards. To predict the impact of a control system, we must know whether or not it relies on extrinsic rewards and punishment to start, stop, and motivate the activity being measured.

In Conclusion

Table 3–1 presents a summary of the classification taxonomy we propose. It argues for classifying information and control systems on eleven characteristics. The characteristics differ in the sense that some are continuous while others are not. A, B, C, E, H, I, and J can best be thought of as continuous variables. For example, the measure taken of B should be thought of as varying from highly subjective to highly objective and the activities being measured as varying from very important to very unimportant. Variables D, F, G, and K, however, involve classifying systems into discrete categories. For example, in the case of D, superiors either are or are not involved in setting the standards. The degree of involvement may vary, but the classification system is mainly concerned with whether or not they are involved.

In Chapters 4, 5, and 6 we will analyze the behavioral impact of the characteristics listed in Table 3–1 by looking at the relationships between these characteristics and the productivity, satis-

44

Characteristics of Sensor Measures	A. Complete—incomplete
	B. Objective—subjective
	C. Influenceable—noninfluenceable
Nature of Standards	D. Set by person being measured, superior, other higher level managers, staff people, or others (specify) _____
	E. Very difficult—very easy
Source of Discrimination	F. Person being measured, superior, other higher level managers, staff people, or others (specify) _____
Pattern of Communication	G. Person being measured, his superior, his peers, his subordinates, top management, staff personnel, or others (specify) _____
Speed of Communication	H. Immediate—delayed by_____ (hours, days, weeks, months, years)
Frequency of Communication	I. Continuous—every_____ (hour, day, week, month, year)
Type of Activity	J. Important—unimportant
Source of Motivation	K. Extrinsic, intrinsic rewards

TABLE 3–1
A Classification of
Control Systems

faction, defensiveness, rigidity, and information-reporting behavior of individuals whose behavior is measured. As we shall see, the importance of the different dimensions varies as a function of which behavioral reaction is being considered and which group of people is being discussed. However, the point remains that to predict the behavioral impact of a control system on the members in an organization, we need information on these characteristics.

4 EXTRINSIC MOTIVATION

Individuals are goal oriented and organizations have the power to administer rewards and punishments. Because of these two factors, which were stressed in Chapters 2 and 3, organizations can influence the extrinsic motivation of individuals. The principle involved is deceptively simple and very important: Individuals in organizations will be motivated to perform in the way they feel leads to rewards. This principle, which we will stress throughout this chapter, is supported by a large amount of research evidence. For example, Cammann (1974a) found that managers concentrated their efforts in areas where the results were measured and where the results influenced the rewards they received. The principle is deceptively simple in one sense: It sounds much easier than it actually is to create conditions where employees feel good job performance will lead to rewards they value. A number of conditions need to be right, and when they are not the result is often either no extrinsic motivation or dysfunctional behavior. What are the conditions? The best way to answer this question is to consider the characteristics on which control systems differ.

CHARACTERISTICS OF SENSOR MEASURE

Because individuals tend to try to perform better on measures that are tied to important rewards, the nature of the measure is a crucial determinant of behavior. Unless the measure meets certain criteria, the behavior motivated by the control system may end up being dysfunctional from the point of view of the organization.

In Chapter 3 we noted that the kinds of measures control systems use can be analyzed on three dimensions, completeness, objectivity, and influenceability. As a general rule, the less completely a control system measures the behavior individuals should demonstrate to perform their job adequately, the more likely it is to motivate dysfunctional behavior. If the measures are incomplete, a person will be motivated to perform only a portion of the behaviors needed for organizational effectiveness.

When incomplete measures are used, there is extrinsic motivation in the sense that individuals are motivated by the reward system to behave in certain ways. However, the extrinsic motivation is not functional for the organization. Examples of incomplete measures that end up motivating dysfunctional behavior are plentiful and will be discussed further in Chapter 6. At this point, it is worth noting a couple to clarify the point. When salesmen are measured only on number of sales calls made, they often end up making many calls and few sales. However, when salesmen are measured only on sales volume, they often end up doing things that damage customer relations. For example, they promise deliveries that cannot be made and they apply undue pressure in order to get a sale.

Research shows that the more objective measures are, the more likely they are to motivate behavior. For example, measures of sales value or units produced are much more likely to motivate behavior than are global performance ratings made by superiors. Extrinsic motivation is likely to be present only when individuals are sure what they have to do to perform well on a measure. It is only logical that if individuals don't understand how the measure operates because it is highly subjective, they will see little connection between their behavior and any reward based on the measure. It is usually clear what influences objective measures because they typically involve straightforward counting or other mechanical measurement procedures. Thus objective measures can be clearly tied to behavior.

Another reason objectivity of measures is important has to do with the climate of mistrust present in most organizations. When employees do not believe they will be evaluated fairly, they do not believe that good performance on their part will lead to rewards, and as a result motivation is low. Employees are especially doubtful that their behavior will be measured fairly when subjective measures are used. This seems to be particularly true when extrinsic rewards are involved. One reason for this is that in the past most individuals have been promised pay raises or other rewards and have not received them or have disagreed with their superiors' subjective assessment of their performance. Those who haven't experienced this seem to have heard of cases where it has hap- **47** pened (Viteles, 1953). Figure 4–1 shows the hypothesized relationship between trust, objectivity of the measure, and success of the measurement system. It clearly shows that unless trust is high, a subjective measurement produces little extrinsic motivation. It also indicates that some trust is necessary for successful measurement of any kind.

Many objective measures that at first glance seem ideal as measures of performance unfortunately are not very influenceable by individuals. For example, although corporate profits may be partially influenced by top management most individuals in large organizations have little control over them and what is most important, they realize this. Thus, to measure and reward individuals based on profits, as many profit-sharing plans do, is not likely to produce extrinsic motivation. Similarly, to measure and reward individuals based upon the market price of their company's stock is not likely to motivate them. There are numerous other examples of frequently used, relatively uninfluenceable measures. Although the use of such measures may be functional from some points of view, there is no reason to believe that their use contributes to extrinsic motivation because unless individuals feel that their behavior influences the measure, they won't see the connection between their behavior and rewards.

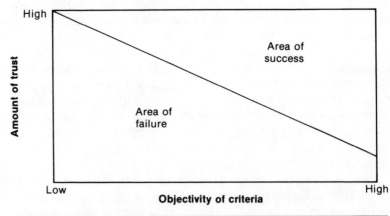

FIGURE 4–1
Relationship of Trust and the Objectivity of Performance Criteria to Success of the Program

NATURE OF STANDARDS

The research and theory on extrinsic motivation make one point quite clear: Employees are not motivated to reach goals that they don't feel they can achieve. Unachievable goals are not motivating because when a person's effort → performance (E → P) probability is zero, the net motivation for a person to behave is zero even if the behavior is attractive. This has direct implications for both the difficulty level of standards and for who should set standards. As far as difficulty is concerned, it suggests that standards should not be more than moderately difficult. But they should not be set at easy levels either. The research on goal setting (e.g., Locke, 1968) suggests that individuals tend to achieve easy goals but not exceed them. The result is mediocre performance. Thus it is not surprising that in a study of budget standards the highest performance occurred in situations with a tight budget (Cherrington and Cherrington, 1974).

To set goals at the proper level of difficulty, individuals who have information on where the standards should be set must be involved. Further, the individuals whose performance is being measured must be aware of the information that was used to set the standards so they will realize that the standards are reasonable. What does this mean in terms of most organizations?

One implication is that employees' superiors must be involved in setting the standard. This is hardly a revolutionary recommendation since most organizations already do this. A second implication, however, is that the person whose performance is being measured frequently should be involved. This recommendation is a bit revolutionary since it doesn't often occur. Typically, standards are set from above with the assumption that people will think they are reasonable. This top-down approach to standard setting can lead to unreasonable standards because it ignores information the employee can provide about reasonable levels. Often the subordinates have more information than anyone else about reasonable levels for standards concerning their jobs. It also ignores the importance of having individuals know about why their goals are set where they are. If employees don't participate in setting standards they may think that even reasonable standards are unreasonable because they don't know why they were set as they were. Participation in setting standards assures that not only will standards be reasonable, but that they will be perceived to be reasonable. It should be noted, however, that if reasonable standards can be set and perceived as reasonable without participation, it is not needed as far as extrinsic motivation is concerned. Participation is a means to an end in this case and to the extent that other means exist (e.g., a trusted, well-informed superior) it is not needed.

The main reason employees often aren't involved in setting standards can be captured in one word: trust. Superiors do not trust employees to provide valid data and behave responsibly when they are asked to set standards (Miles, 1965). There is a realistic basis for this concern. Subordinates do sometimes provide false data about what they can do and what they have done (see Chapter 6). This is particularly likely to happen when there **49** is poor communication and low trust between superiors and subordinates. This effect is so strong that when low trust exists it probably doesn't make sense to have employees involved in setting standards for their jobs. However, low trust is not always present and having employees participate in decisions such as these can help increase trust because it indicates to employees that the organization trusts them.

Another reason superiors often don't allow their subordinates to participate in standard setting is the pressures they are under to achieve high goals. Often they simply aren't in a position to allow participation because they can only accept very high goals (Hopwood, 1973). In organizations that operate this way participation is undesirable since it cannot be real. These organizations must change the way goals are set so that individuals lower down can have an influence if extrinsic motivation is to be present.

The peers and subordinates of employees also often have information that can contribute to reasonable standards being set. In addition, there is evidence that peers are often the best evaluators of a person's performance because they see more of it and they see it in unguarded moments (Lawler, 1967; Campbell et al., 1970). Usually, the peers and subordinates of employees are not involved in setting standards for the same reason the employees themselves are not: trust. Peers and subordinates are not seen as providing valid data about performance. When an organization is characterized by a poor climate, low trust levels, and high dissatisfaction, this probably is a safe assumption; but in many situations they can provide helpful data. For example, graduate students often set reasonable standards for their peers in terms of academic performance. Research also shows that employees set reasonable standards (often more stringent than those set by managers) when they are asked to establish personnel policy with respect to pay, absenteeism, tardiness, and disciplinary matters (see e.g., Lawler, 1973, 1975).

SOURCE OF DISCRIMINATION

Just as it is important who sets the standards, it is important who acts as the discriminator. The reason in both cases is very much the same. We have continually stressed that there will be extrinsic motivation only if individuals see a relationship between their performance and the extrinsic rewards they receive. For this to happen they must feel their performance is fairly measured and evaluated just as they must feel that standards are fair.

The objectivity of the measure and who makes the discrimination are two of the factors that determine whether employees feel that their performance is fairly measured and compared with the standard. For extrinsic motivation to be present the discriminator must be someone or something that the people feel they can rely on to accurately make the comparison. Otherwise, employees will not believe that their behavior will be fairly evaluated. When employees don't feel their behavior will be fairly evaluated, they in turn don't feel they can influence the rewards they receive and as a result they are not motivated. Particularly when extrinsic rewards are involved subordinates are likely to feel that the discriminator will always interpret the data so that they will not be able to make or exceed standards regardless of their performance (Whyte, 1955).

Who then should be the discriminator? Whoever it is must have two attributes: the knowledge to make the comparison and the trust of the person being measured. It is hard to generalize about who can meet these requirements. In some instances it may be the person's superior, in others it might be a well informed staff person, and in still others it might be the peers of the person. For example, in many research and development labs, the peers of a scientist do the evaluation because they are technologically up to date and have the greatest credibility. Of course, in most situations the superior is in a good position to act as a discriminator and must be involved. This can be a problem, however, if the superior lacks credibility. In fact, where the superior lacks credibility, it is often better not to try to tie the extrinsic rewards to performance.

It is also possible in many situations to automate the discriminator function. This in effect happens with budgets and many production measurement systems. These usually are trusted because of their objectivity, but when trust is very low employees sometimes suspect they are tampered with. This is a common occurrence among blue collar employees when piece rate systems are employed and it also occurs frequently when profit-sharing plans are employed (Lawler, 1971).

There is one person who always has high credibility to the person being measured and who is almost always seen as having the necessary technical knowledge: This, of course, is the person whose behavior is being evaluated. However, this person is seldom assigned the discriminator role because the organization does not trust that person to do the job fairly. This is not surprising since when important extrinsic rewards are involved, people sometimes do things to make their evaluations come out unreasonably high (Whyte, 1955). However, this does not necessarily mean that the individual should play no role in the discrimination function when extrinsic rewards are involved; it does mean that the individual typically should not be the only participant.

51

In line with this point it is interesting to note that most of the recent work on performance appraisal has emphasized that subordinates should actively participate in their evaluation (see e.g., Campbell et al., 1970; Barnes and White, 1971). In fact, some researchers have suggested that subordinates should participate as equals. The arguments for this include the fact that subordinates often have needed information and they are more likely to trust and understand the process if they are involved in it. Thus, it seems reasonable to conclude by pointing out that in most situations the person being measured should participate in the discrimination process. One exception to this would be when the measures and standards are very objective and clear cut (e.g., budgets) and thus the function can be done by an outsider (e.g., someone in the accounting department). Another exception would be the rare situation where the person simply lacks the technical knowledge or is so untrustworthy that he or she would not provide valid data.

RECIPIENTS OF COMMUNICATION

For extrinsic motivation to be present, the person who has the power to give rewards must receive the information about the results of the discrimination. This is a precondition to rewards being allocated on the basis of performance which in turn is a precondition to the perception that rewards are based upon performance. However, for this perception to exist, more people must receive information about the results of the discrimination than the person who has the power to give rewards. To be specific, it is desirable to have the person whose performance is being measured, and other employees who are doing similar work, receive the communication. The reason for this is that employees develop their perceptions about how extrinsic rewards are given in organizations by looking at how their performance and that of relevant others is measured and rewarded (Lawler, 1972). A very important social comparison process is involved here since extrinsic reward levels and performance results only have meaning in comparison to what happens to others. Raises and production levels, for example, only have meaning to individuals in the context of what others do and receive. A 5 percent raise can be either good or poor depending on what others receive. Similarly, if the only thing employees know is that they produced at X level and received Y for a pay raise, then they know nothing about the relationship of pay to performance. However, if they also know that others produced X + A and received Y + B, they know quite a bit more since they can see the actual relationship between pay and performance. If they are related, this in turn can establish extrinsic motivation.

Information can serve to increase employees' trust of the measurement system if the results compare with their perceptions of other employees' performance levels. When employees lack information about the pay and performance of others they cannot check their perceptions of what constitutes good performance and they are denied valuable feedback on their own performance. In addition, they often develop elaborate fantasies about how performance is measured and about how people have to perform to receive extrinsic rewards. Given the importance of extrinsic rewards, it is hardly surprising that employees often misperceive reality when an organization fails to communicate the results of its measurement process.

In most organizations information about management pay rates is kept secret and in some organizations the pay of all employees is kept secret. As the following note from the *Wall Street Journal* indicates, some organizations take their secrecy policies very seriously.

Money Talks: Jeannette Corporation illegally prohibited employees from discussing wage rates among themselves, an NLRB judge rules. He orders reinstatement of a secretary who was fired for talking about her pay, and tells the company to permit such conversations among employees. (*Wall Street Journal*, 1975, p. 1).

As would be predicted from the points made in Chapter 2 about perception, because pay is very important, secrecy often leads to misperceptions about how much individuals are paid. Employees overestimate how much other employees like themselves are paid and as a result are more dissatisfied with their pay. They also develop a confused perception of how rewards are tied to performance and as a result, are not motivated extrinsically.

Some organizations try to overcome the problem of pay misperceptions by releasing information on pay ranges and average pay for jobs, but stop short of releasing individual pay rates. This helps but still doesn't allow the employee to clearly see what the relationship is between pay and performance in the organization. Only if pay and the results of all performance measurement systems are made public will employees have a clear perception of the organization's reward system and, in turn, have a maximum level of extrinsic motivation. Some rewards are by their nature public (e.g., promotion). In the cases of these rewards, the issue is one of making the criteria for receiving them public. Often this is not done and as a result extrinsic motivation suffers. For example, despite their apparent advantages, few organizations have adopted open job posting and promotion systems. Of course, if extrinsic rewards are not related to performance it will do no good to make them and evaluation information public; in fact, it may lower extrinsic motivation and satisfaction.

53

SPEED AND FREQUENCY OF COMMUNICATION

As a general rule, communications about performance measures are most effective in producing extrinsic motivation when
they are fast and frequent. When communications about performance are delayed, it is impossible to closely tie rewards to the
actual performance of the person and this has the effect of reducing the perceived relationship between performance and rewards.
It also creates doubts among employees about the validity and
usefulness of the performance measurement data. There is something that doesn't ring true about performance results that are
months old and no longer reflect a person's performance. It is
also clear that the results of a performance measurement system
must be communicated regularly and frequently. If these communications are not frequent, then employees correctly perceive
that their behavior will not influence their rewards for a considerable or perhaps indefinite period of time. Extrinsic motivation is
reduced because performance isn't connected to rewards.

The optimal frequency of communication varies as a function
of the nature of the activity being measured. Despite the general
rule that communications should be frequent, they can be too
frequent. Jaques' (1961) concept of Time Span of Discretion
(TSD) explains why. TSD refers to the time between when an
activity is performed and when inadequate performance is detecta-
ble. Each job has a particular TSD. At the lower levels in organizations the TSD of jobs may be a few moments and it rarely exceeds
a few days. However, at the top levels of organizations the TSD
is often several years.

If performance is measured and reported on a frequency
shorter than the TSD it can threaten the validity and credibility
of the performance measure. Clearly, if the measurement system
tries to measure and report on the results of behavior before they
are apparent, employees will find it hard to believe that their performance is being fairly measured for a very straightforward reason: It won't be. In turn, they will not see a relationship between
their rewards and their performance.

Although it would seem obvious that organizations should
report on and reward performance in different parts of the organization with different frequencies, this often is not done. The policy
of many organizations is to collect and communicate results to
employees every quarter, year, and so on. For example, appraisals
of the performance of all individuals in organizations are typically
done yearly. This figure seems to be a compromise between how
frequently top and lower level people should be appraised. The
TSD concept suggests it is too frequent for top level jobs and
too infrequent for lower level jobs. It is too frequent for the top

levels because it does not allow enough time for the results of the person's performance to show up. It is too infrequent for lower level jobs because it separates performance and the visible results of it from communication and reward changes based upon it by too great a time period. What seems to be needed are appraisal systems that relate the frequency of the communication and reward change to the TSD of the job. Unfortunately, little research has been done to test the effectiveness of this approach.

Some research evidence suggests that it is important to take into account the nature of the person whose activities are being measured when decisions about the frequency and speed of communication are made. Specifically, people seem to differ both in terms of how far in the future they look in orienting their behavior and in how long a delay they can tolerate in receiving feedback about their performance and rewards based on it. Several psychologists have suggested that individuals who have grown up in a culturally deprived environment have a very short time perspective and need to see an almost immediate connection between their behavior and their rewards to be extrinsically motivated (see e.g., Porter, 1973). They explain that this comes about because they are trained to believe that they control little of what happens to them and that promises and delays are simply ways of avoiding giving rewards. In short, they believe that they will not be evaluated fairly by the system. Unlike middle class parents, their parents often do not stress that it is necessary to work for years in order to accomplish something worthwhile and that in the end the system will reward the good performer. In addition, their parents do not always tie rewards to their behavior during childhood (e.g., money for good grades in school). Thus they don't have a well-developed concept of performance-based rewards. This suggests that organizations should try to evaluate certain individuals almost daily and adjust their rewards accordingly so that they will see a connection between their rewards and their performance.

There are many practical problems in developing systems that regularly measure and reward performance so it is often difficult for organizations to do it with all employees. Even if an organization cannot do it for all employees it is particularly important that they do it for some groups. New employees are a case in point. They cannot be expected to develop high extrinsic motivation quickly in situations where delays occur because there will be no immediate visible connection between their rewards and their performance. It also seems that what happens to individuals early in their career has an important influence on their motivation because this is when they form a relatively permanent perception of how rewards are obtained (Berlew and Hall, 1966; Porter et al., 1975). This suggests that when employees from a culturally **55** disadvantaged background begin work, and, in fact, when any employee begins work, it is particularly important that there be an immediate and direct connection between their behavior and the extrinsic rewards they receive.

TYPE OF ACTIVITY

The importance of an activity to the success of an organization is not a direct determinant of how much extrinsic motivation is present to perform the activity. There can be tremendous extrinsic motivation to perform unimportant activities if performing them leads to extrinsic rewards. Typically, organizations are structured so that important activities do affect extrinsic rewards. Even if they don't directly and clearly affect such rewards as pay and promotion, they often do affect status and the amount of praise received from top management. Sometimes, however, this doesn't happen and great extrinsic motivation is generated to perform unimportant activities—what is often called bureaucratic behavior is an example of this. The term refers to behavior performed simply because it is called for by the rules rather than because it aids the effectiveness of the organization (see Chapter 6 for a discussion of bureaucratic behavior).

SOURCE OF MOTIVATION

Since extrinsic rewards vary considerably in their effectiveness, one of the most important decisions an organization has to make in designing an extrinsic reward system is which reward or rewards to use. In discussing the effectiveness of different outcomes as motivators, the basic issue we must consider is their importance. This is a necessary but not sufficient condition for extrinsic motivation. Which outcomes do employees value the most? Hundreds of studies have tried to answer this question without a great deal of success. As was stressed earlier, the importance of outcomes depends on the strength of different needs in the individual and the degree to which in a particular situation needs can be satisfied by specific outcomes. Because of this, there are large differences in how much individuals are concerned with different needs and, therefore, in how much they value different outcomes.

Chapter 2 pointed out that individuals have a number of needs and that outcomes gain their importance through their ability to influence need satisfaction. Outcomes that increase need satisfaction are rewarding and ones that decrease it are punishing. The importance of an outcome is determined by the strength of its effect on need satisfaction and by the strength of the need or needs it affects. The ability of an outcome to influence motivation is in turn a function of its importance. Unless it is important in either a positive or negative sense it cannot influence motivation. This means that for an outcome to influence motivation it must be related to the satisfaction of one or more important needs.

Many organizationally controlled outcomes can satisfy more than one need and for this reason are important to a wide range of employees. For example, pay has been shown to satisfy esteem, autonomy, security, and existence needs (Lawler, 1971). Because of this, it tends to be important any time one of these needs is important. Pay is not unique in this respect; many of the rewards and punishments that organizations control can potentially satisfy or threaten the satisfaction of a number of needs. Promotion, interesting work, dismissal, fringe benefits, and status symbols are all outcomes organizations control that satisfy a number of needs. Promotion, for example, can satisfy most of the needs mentioned in Chapter 2. Sometimes it can also threaten the satisfaction of security needs if the new job is one the employee is concerned about performing well. Thus, it is an outcome that satisfies some needs and threatens the satisfaction of others.

A mixed need satisfaction/dissatisfaction effect is true of many outcomes and for this reason individuals often have ambivalent feelings about receiving these outcomes. Praise from the boss is a good example; in many work situations this is an outcome that satisfies esteem needs but threatens social need satisfaction. This happens in situations where there is an antimanagement feeling in a work group and, as a result, employees who perform well are rejected by the work group. It also tends to happen in situations where the boss is not respected as a person.

The importance of needs is also influenced by a number of background and situation factors including how satisfied other needs are. Whether a particular outcome satisfies a specific need is very much determined by the culture in a particular work environment. For example, in many cultures money is a status factor, but in some it is not. Similarly in many situations promotion to management is a status factor, but in others it isn't (e.g., universities).

Despite the fact that the importance of outcomes varies among individuals, we can state some general conclusions about the importance of various outcomes. It is clear from a number of studies (Vroom, 1964; Lawler, 1971) that the extrinsic rewards of pay, promotion, job security, recognition from the supervisor, and more interesting work are important rewards to many people. One reason for this undoubtedly is that they are all rewards that satisfy more than one need and thus they are important to individuals who are different in terms of their needs.

Organizations have relatively little control over the value people place on extrinsic outcomes since it is largely determined by
aspects of the person over which the organizations have no control. There are, however, three ways an organization can influence
the importance of outcomes. They can affect the strength of people's needs either by increasing satisfaction with them or by threatening the level of satisfaction already obtained. For example, they
can give everyone tenure (a guarantee of permanent employment)
and high pay, thereby satisfying lower level needs and assuring
that the higher level needs will be important. They can also increase the degree to which an outcome satisfies a particular need.
For example, they can make all pay information public and emphasize the fact that it is performance based. This should increase
the degree to which pay is related to satisfying recognition needs.
They can also make certain objects and rights important by grant-
ing them only to certain people. Medals are used in this manner
by the military. Organizations can also vary the amount of some
of the rewards they give and thereby influence their importance.
A thousand dollar raise is usually valued more than a five hundred
dollar raise regardless of how much people value pay.

Organizations probably can do a reasonably good job of motivating employees by stressing those extrinsic rewards important
to most individuals. However, this approach is inevitably going
to miss some employees because even rewards that are important
to most people are not important to all. A better approach might
be for organizations to try to identify what outcomes are important
to individuals and then use those to motivate performance. This
approach calls for individualizing rewards (Lawler, 1975) so that
for each employee, there are valued rewards tied to performance.
This is not easy because of the differences in what people value,
the administrative problems of giving different rewards, and the
difficulty of accurately determining what individuals value. However, it is potentially more effective than using the same rewards
for all or trying to change the importance of outcomes.

There are a number of studies on what determines need importance that can be used as starting points to determine which
rewards individuals are likely to respond to (Lawler, 1973; Vroom,
1964). Age, education, and family background can provide helpful
information. Moreover, people are often quite clear in stating what
rewards they value. It is also often possible to make good estimates
of what people value simply by observing the choices they make.
In some situations it is possible to give people the choice of which
extrinsic rewards they will receive. For example, one company
allows workers who have finished their daily production quota the
chance to either go home or receive extra pay. Another organization allows individuals to choose the fringe benefits they wish to
receive.

In addition to varying in importance, extrinsic outcomes vary in other ways that we need to consider to evaluate their effectiveness as motivators. *Flexibility* is a desirable attribute because of the advantages of being able to give different amounts of an outcome. Without flexibility it is difficult to closely relate amount of reward to performance level. *Visibility* of outcomes is desirable because it influences the kind of needs they satisfy. In particular, it influences the ability of outcomes to satisfy esteem and recognition needs. Low visibility rewards cannot satisfy these needs and therefore are often less important. Rewards often must be given *frequently* in order to relate them closely to performance and sustain extrinsic motivation. Thus it is desirable to have outcomes that can be given frequently without losing their importance. Finally, *cost* is important because it is a constraint in organizations that must be considered.

Table 4–1 presents an evaluation of some outcomes in terms of their importance, flexibility, visibility, frequency, and cost. As can be seen from the table, none of the rewards rate highly on all of the criteria. Interestingly, pay seems to possess all the characteristics necessary to make it the perfect extrinsic reward except one, low cost. It is expensive to use as an extrinsic reward since individuals need to receive frequent pay increases or bonuses to sustain extrinsic motivation.

Outcome	Importance	Flexibility in Amount	Visibility	Frequency	Dollar Cost
PAY	High	High	Potentially High	High	High
PROMOTION	High	Low	High	Low	High
DISMISSAL	High	Low	High	Low	High
PRAISE FROM SUPERVISOR	Moderate	High	Indeterminate	High	Low
INTERESTING WORK	High	Moderate	High	Moderate	Low
TENURE	Moderate	Low	High	Low	High
STATUS SYMBOLS	Moderate	High	High	Low	Moderate

TABLE 4–1
An Evaluation of Outcomes as Motivators

It also should be noted that many organizations keep pay secret. This decreases its visibility and makes it a less important reward. It may also have the effect of blurring the relationship between performance and rewards in the situation. Low visibility, however, is not inherent to pay, it is a problem that organizations create.

Promotion, dismissal, and tenure are all low in flexibility. They simply cannot be easily varied in amount as the situation calls for. They also cannot be given very regularly. This makes it difficult to tie them closely to good performance over a long period of time. Tenure, for example, is a one shot motivator that once it is given loses all ability to motivate. These rewards also tend to be rather expensive. Their high cost is not as obvious as the cost of pay, but it is nonetheless real. Turnover, for example, can be expensive for an organization even when the dismissed employee is a poor performer. Recent research suggests that the replacement costs of employees is substantial, particularly in higher level jobs (Flamholtz, 1974; Macy and Mirvis, 1974).

Praise and interesting work are generally good motivators in terms of the criteria listed. Interesting work sometimes is low on frequency since in many situations it is difficult to give people more and more interesting work. For example, given the present technology, work on the auto assembly line can only be made moderately more interesting. Thus it is hard to make an assembly line worker's work more interesting as a reward for performing more effectively. Interesting work and praise from the boss are also particularly likely to vary in importance among people so they cannot be counted on to be important to all individuals.

In summary, there is no one outcome or class of outcomes that meets all the criteria for being a good extrinsic motivator. Furthermore, organizations have little control over how important different outcomes are to individuals. Organizations do control, however, which outcomes they will use and it is important that they carefully diagnose the situation and use the one or ones that are right for the situation. Organizations also determine the nature of their control systems and the way outcomes are tied to performance measures and control systems. These factors have tremendous impact on how effective any extrinsic outcome is in influencing motivation and on how effective control systems are in influencing behavior.

ORGANIZATIONAL FACTORS

In addition to the control system characteristics we have discussed there are a number of organizational factors that influence what the impact of relating extrinsic rewards to control system measures of performance will be. Organizational factors also influence the kind of measures that can be collected and thus they limit the kinds of reward system-control system relationships that can exist. Climate, technology, and structure are the most relevant organizational factors.

Organizational Climate

The reward system in an organization must fit the human relations climate of that organization (see e.g., Katz and Kahn, 1966; Leavitt, 1965; Lawler, 1975). Consider for a moment the suggestion that employees participate in measuring their performance. In the kind of organization that generally adopts a democratic or participative approach to management, participative performance appraisals develop naturally. On the other hand, in an autocratically run organization it is unlikely that meaningful participation can develop since it requires a climate of openness and trust. This is particularly likely to be a problem for autocratic organizations in which subjective measures of performance have to be used because they are the only ones that can be collected. Openness about pay and other rewards is another practice that should develop naturally where a participative approach to management is used.

What kind of reward system-control system relationship will work in an organization characterized by a low disclosure autocratic management style? Evidence suggests plans that tie rewards to hard criteria such as quantity of output, profits, or sales, and thus require a minimum level of trust, stand a much better chance of succeeding than approaches that depend on joint goal setting and soft criteria (Lawler, 1971; Whyte, 1955). The problem for traditional organizations occurs in jobs where no objective performance data are produced by the control systems and where trust and participation are needed if extrinsic rewards are to act as an incentive. As we will discuss further in Chapter 6, in this situation if the organization ties extrinsic rewards to control system measures then invalid data and rigid bureaucratic behavior are likely to be produced.

Technology

The kind of product being produced influences the kind of technology organizations use, and this in turn influences the appropriateness of different reward systems. Woodward (1958, 1965) distinguishes among industrial organizations that engage in mass production, unit production, and process production. Giving rewards on the basis of individual measures of performance makes sense in unit and mass production plants, but it rarely makes sense in a process production firm. On the other hand, giving rewards based on plant-wide control system performance measures seems well suited to many process production plants but not to most unit and mass production plants. This difference arises because of the difficulty of measuring individual performance in process production organizations and because of the importance **61** of rewarding cooperative or team behavior. In many nonindustrial, professionally-staffed service organizations, such as hospitals and schools, good control system measures of individual performance often cannot be developed and thus total organization measures of performance must be used.

In short, the type of product an organization produces influences the technology and production methods of the organization. Production methods in turn differ in the degree to which individual performance is identifiable and measurable by the control system and the degree to which team effort is important. Because of this, organizations that differ in the kinds of products they produce need different reward system-control system relationships if they are to avoid the dysfunctional outcomes that often accompany inappropriate relationships.

Organization Structure

Several aspects of organization structure affect the kind of reward system-control system relationship that is appropriate for an organization. Size is a crucial variable. Another is the degree of centralization. Small organizations can do things that large organizations cannot. They can, for example, use bonus pay plans that are based on organization-wide performance. In a small organization, most employees feel that their behavior affects the performance of the total organization. In a large organization this is not likely to be so (except at the very top), and as a result a plan that rewards on the basis of organization-wide performance is not likely to motivate performance. For example, American Motors Corporation has a company wide profit-sharing system that seems to have little impact on motivation while Donnelly Mirrors, a company of 500 employees, has one that seems to have a significant impact.

The degree of centralization-decentralization is relevant because it affects the kind of performance data that can be meaningfully gathered by the control system. In a centralized organization, for example, the performance of a subpart, or a particular part, is often difficult to measure unless a decentralized responsibility-based accounting system is used. Even if it is possible to measure an individual plant's performance, this is often not a good criterion on which to base rewards because the plant employees may not make many of the decisions that influence the performance of the plant. If substantial decision-making power is vested in the central office and local plant management is evaluated and rewarded on the basis of how the plant performs, the motivational impact on the local management will be minimal. Motivation is more likely to occur when decision making is decentralized and
accounting data are gathered on subparts of the organization.

Human relations climate	Authoritarian	Need objective hard criteria; pay clearly tied to performance
	Democratic	Can use participative goal setting and softer criteria
Production type	Mass and unit	Can usually develop hard criteria; rewards on individual or small group basis
	Process	Need to encourage cooperation; individual performance not highly visible or measurable
	Professional organizations (i.e., hospital, school, consulting firm)	Individually based plans; soft criteria; high individual involvement in own evaluation
Size	Large	Organizationwide bonuses poor for all but a few top-level managers
	Small	Organizationwide bonuses possible in some situations
Degree of centralization	Centralized	Hard to base performance on subunit (i.e., plant) performance
	Decentralized	Pay can be based on profit center or subunit performance for members of management

From E.E. Lawler, *Pay and Organizational Effectiveness: A Psychological View*, (New York: McGraw-Hill, 1971), p. 280.

TABLE 4-2
Relevance of Four Organizational Factors to Pay Plans

Table 4-2, which is adapted from Lawler (1971), summarizes the relevance of organization factors to pay plans. It shows how organizational factors limit the possible types of performance-based pay plans that can be successfully used. In order to determine what kind of plan can be used in a specific organization, one must classify the organization according to each of four variables listed in the table. An organization might, for example, practice authoritarian management, engage in mass production, and be large and centralized. Since each of the factors (being of a certain size, having a highly centralized administration, etc.) rules out some kinds of pay plans, in some organizations there is simply no appropriate performance pay plan. In these organizations it is advisable not to try to tie the pay system to control system measurements of performance. Instead pay should be determined on other bases and other rewards should be used to motivate performance. Usually these other rewards have to be intrinsic because in most situations when it is difficult to tie pay to performance, it is difficult to tie other extrinsic rewards to performance.

SUMMARY

Table 4-3 summarizes what has been said so far about the conditions that lead to high extrinsic motivation. They are all condi- **63**

Characteristics of Sensor Measure	A. Complete
	B. Objective
	C. Influenceabie
Nature of Standards	D. Joint process between person and supervisor
	E. Moderate achievement difficulty
Source of Discrimination	F. Joint process between person and other trusted person or persons
Recipients of Communication	G. Person with reward power as well as person being measured and others doing similar work.
Speed of Communication	H. Fast
Frequency of Communication	I. As fast as allowed by the time span of discretion
Type of Activity	J. Not a crucial factor
Source of Motivation	K. Rewards that are important

TABLE 4–3
Characteristics of
Control Systems that
Produce High
Extrinsic Motivation

tions that help individuals see a close connection between important rewards and performance. In practice, it is difficult to create an operational system that incorporates all these characteristics. To the extent they are absent, extrinsic motivation will be difficult to create and at some point it becomes useless to try to use extrinsic rewards as motivators of performance. It is difficult to generalize about when that point occurs but, as will be seen in Chapter 6, whenever a few of the conditions suggested in the table are not present, tying rewards to performance can have more negative consequences than positive. This discussion also suggests that organizations should try to make sure these conditions are present rather than try to influence the importance of extrinsic rewards since these are relatively fixed. Organizations can probably best assure that valued outcomes are tied to performance by first determining which rewards are important to employees and then tying them to performance.

INTRINSIC MOTIVATION 5

Evidence abounds that people are motivated by intrinsic rewards, yet this often isn't taken into account when organizations, jobs, and information and control systems are designed. As a result, this powerful form of motivation is often absent in organizations. In some ways this is not surprising since the approach that must be taken to affect intrinsic motivation is very different from that which must be taken to affect extrinsic motivation. It is much less of a "common sense" approach to motivation. This stems from the fact that, unlike extrinsic rewards, intrinsic rewards cannot be given by the organizations, they must originate and be felt within the person. They are controlled by individuals and can only be given to individuals by themselves. It is possible, however, for organizations to influence when and how people will experience intrinsic rewards. They can do this by how they structure the work environment. Herein lies the key to how organizations can influence intrinsic motivation.

Just as with extrinsic rewards, intrinsic rewards will motivate performance only if they appear to depend on it. Since organizations cannot directly control the reception of intrinsic rewards in the same ways they can control extrinsic rewards like pay, they must determine how to create an environment where individuals will give themselves intrinsic rewards when they perform effectively. They must create a situation where performing well is a rewarding experience to the individual even though no pay raise or promotion is involved. Like a good golf shot or a graceful ski run, good job performance must lead to feelings of accomplishment and satisfaction.

65

But before we discuss in detail the conditions that lead to individuals rewarding themselves for good performance, we need to discuss how individuals differ with respect to intrinsic motivation. Just as not everyone can be motivated by most extrinsic rewards, not everyone can be motivated by intrinsic rewards. Thus, no matter how good the conditions for intrinsic motivation are in an organization, it is unlikely that everyone will be motivated to perform well. Only individuals with strong higher-order needs can be motivated to perform well by intrinsic rewards. These rewards satisfy the needs for competence, achievement, and self-realization, and unless these needs are important to individuals, outcomes that satisfy them will not be rewarding and there will be no intrinsic motivation.

A study on the effects of job design on intrinsic motivation illustrates the point that intrinsic motivation can be present only in individuals who have strong higher-order needs (Hackman and Lawler, 1971). The study first showed that intrinsic motivation will be present when jobs are designed in certain ways. It then went on to look separately at those employees who had strong higher-order needs and those who didn't. Those with strong needs were highly motivated when they had well-designed jobs and were not motivated when they didn't. However, no matter how jobs were designed those with weak higher-order needs had little intrinsic motivation.

Several other studies have looked at the issue of what kind of individuals can be motivated by intrinsic rewards. One study found that individuals who have grown up in rural settings are easier to motivate intrinsically than individuals who have grown up in urban environments (Turner and Lawrence, 1965). The reason for this seems to be that rural people value the kind of intrinsic rewards that jobs can provide (Hackman and Lawler, 1971). They are less alienated from middle class norms about the virtues of hard work and the importance of having a "good job" (Blood and Hulin, 1967; and Hulin and Blood, 1968).

This is not to say that all people who are raised in urban environments cannot be motivated by intrinsic rewards while all who aren't can be. The relationships found have not been large but they do exist and it is important to note why, since it provides some insights into how people react to work. Hulin and Blood (1968) offer one explanation that rests on the kind of socialization experiences people encounter in different environments.

One could argue that the dominant norms and values that all children learn in school and at home are those brought by the Anglo-Saxon Protestants from Europe in the 17th and 18th centuries. These norms and values have become the standard in American middle-class society. Children are taught these values in school by the middle-class teachers and attempt to reach goals defined in terms of these values by means of behavior consistent with these values. However, children raised in slums, where the cost of living is higher, or where there is a great deal of migration are more likely to be frustrated in these attempts. Also, the lower-class American city dweller is less likely to be Anglo-Saxon Protestant (Turner and Lawrence, 1965) and less sympathetic to American middle-class values. Therefore, the acquisition by the lower-class city dweller of goals consistent with the Anglo-Saxon Protestant value system is likely to be met with criticism from his peer group (Whyte, 1955). Such frustrations or negative reinforcement should extinguish behavior and beliefs consistent with American middle-class ideals (Hulin and Blood, 1968, p. 52).

There is some evidence that individuals with more education can be motivated more easily by intrinsic rewards than can others. The explanation here seems to be cultural, as is the explanation for the urban-rural differences noted above. The educational process exposes individuals to people who hold strong beliefs about the importance of intrinsic rewards. It also helps individuals attain an income level that allows the luxury of a strong concern with higher-order need satisfaction. The evidence showing stronger higher-order needs among top level managers also seems to be partially explained by income level (Porter and Lawler, 1965).

The evidence on job level, education level, and urban-rural background suggests that the degree to which individuals can be motivated by intrinsic rewards is at least partially determined by cultural factors. This raises the question of whether individuals can be "turned on" to intrinsic rewards as a result of their job experiences. Some psychologists have suggested that people who previously haven't been intrinsically motivated can be if they are given properly designed and challenging jobs (e.g., Argyris, 1971). The argument essentially is that the reason many people aren't intrinsically motivated at work is that they have never had a job where it was possible to experience intrinsic rewards. Thus, the logical way to motivate these people intrinsically is to place them in a situation where they can experience intrinsic rewards. Presumably, once they spend time in an intrinsically rewarding job, they will begin to be motivated intrinsically.

Unfortunately, there is no strong evidence that job characteristics can dramatically affect the degree to which people value intrinsic rewards and higher-order needs. In terms of our model presented in Chapter 2, this means that job and organizational characteristics are not likely to affect the valence (V) of intrinsic outcomes. This is in direct contrast to the strong research evidence that shows that job and organization characteristics can affect people who value intrinsic rewards are motivated to perform effectively because they affect Effort $\rightarrow$ Performance (E $\rightarrow$ P) and Performance $\rightarrow$ Outcome (P $\rightarrow$ O) beliefs (Lawler, 1973).

It is safe to conclude that a properly designed job situation will motivate those individuals who already value intrinsic rewards. **67**

It is not safe to conclude that it will increase the degree to which individuals value intrinsic rewards although there is the possibility that it may. This conclusion is important because it means that no organization, unless it is populated by people who value intrinsic rewards, can depend on intrinsic motivation. Since it is unlikely that any organization will ever be populated entirely by such people, most organizations will probably have to rely to some extent on extrinsic motivation.

Even though not everyone can be motivated by intrinsic motivation it can be a powerful determinant of behavior for many when the right conditions exist. These right conditions involve building certain characteristics into information and control systems and jobs. Thus, the remainder of this chapter will be devoted to considering how information and control systems and jobs need to be designed to cause individuals to be intrinsically motivated.

CHARACTERISTICS OF SENSOR MEASURES

The kind of sensor measures collected has an important influence on the amount of intrinsic motivation present. Just as with extrinsic motivation, measures that are complete, objective, and can be influenced will lead to the greatest intrinsic motivation.

Completeness is important because when measures are incomplete the behaviors that are not measured are not rewarded and, therefore, they tend to be ignored. Lack of completeness probably has different effects on extrinsic and intrinsic motivation. When extrinsic rewards are tied to incomplete measures, individuals usually try to perform well on these measures even though they are incomplete, because doing so leads to extrinsic rewards. But if measures are obviously incomplete, individuals may not see a connection between performing well and intrinsic rewards such as feelings of competence and achievement and thus they may not be motivated. In other words, individuals cannot be expected to reward themselves for performing well in terms of measures that are obviously poor. In terms of our model, when a measure is incomplete it is unlikely that a strong P → O belief concerning good performance and intrinsic outcomes will exist. There is evidence to support this conclusion in a recent study that showed that managers seem to be motivated to perform well only in areas measured *accurately* (Cammann, 1974a).

As with extrinsic motivation, objectivity is an important determinant of intrinsic motivation. The reason is the same. Unless the measure is objective, it may not be trusted and felt to be a fair and reasonable one. For people to reward themselves for good performance on a measure they must believe their behavior **68** is actually reflected in the measure.

An apparently uninfluenceable measure of performance cannot contribute to intrinsic motivation. It causes the E → P belief to be low and thus, motivation must be low. It also causes those P → O beliefs associated with good performance and intrinsic rewards to be low because it is impossible for individuals to feel good and reward themselves with feelings of competence for results that they do not influence. In fact, much of the research on job design stresses just this point. It shows that unless employees have enough control over how the job is done to feel responsible for the results they will not be intrinsically motivated to perform well (Hackman and Lawler, 1971). This finding has obvious implications for how jobs are designed and emphasizes the importance of having measures that are influenceable by the job holders.

NATURE OF STANDARDS

How standards are set is an important determinant of intrinsic motivation because it is one factor that determines the difficulty level of standards and the degree to which employees accept the standards as their performance goal (Vroom, 1964; Dunbar, 1971). In order for standards to be intrinsically motivating, employees must accept the standards and they must be moderately difficult (Locke, 1968).

Acceptance has an important influence on motivation because when individuals are committed to achieving a certain standard of performance, outcomes like feelings of self-esteem and competence are related to goal achievement. In a sense individuals put their self-esteem on the line when they say they can perform at certain levels (even if they say it only to themselves) and thus, it is important to them to reach the standard and maintain their self-esteem. Strong support for this point comes from a recent study of participation in budget setting (Searfoss and Monczka, 1973; Searfoss, 1972). This study found a strong relationship between the amount of participation managers had in setting budgets and the amount of motivation they demonstrated to achieve their budgets. A weaker but still significant relationship was found in another recent study that focused on the motivation of eighty-eight foremen (Milani, 1975).

Vroom (1964) has explained how participation can influence a person's commitment to a decision and how this in turn can influence motivation.

> . . . people become 'ego involved' in decisions in which they have had influence. If they have helped to make a decision it is "their decision," and the success or failure of the decision is their success or failure (p. 228).

An impressive series of studies by Locke (1968; Locke and Bryan, 1969) has shown that goal difficulty has a direct affect **69** on performance. Easy goals produce low performance. Hard goals produce high performance *if* they seem *achievable.* This finding follows directly from our earlier discussion of how $E \rightarrow P$ beliefs influence motivation. There it was pointed out that when $E \rightarrow P$ beliefs are so low that individuals feel they cannot perform well, motivation will always be low. This strongly suggests that it is dysfunctional to set very difficult standards unless it is clear that they will be perceived as achievable.

Research suggests that in most situations individuals perform best when they feel they have a 50/50 chance of achieving a goal (Atkinson, 1964; McClelland, 1955, 1961). Goals more difficult than this are rejected as too difficult and goals easier than this are seen as so easy that they do not challenge individuals and produce intrinsic motivation. However, giving people an even chance arouses feelings of achievement and accomplishment, and individuals feel that when goals are achieved they have accomplished something worthwhile. In short, it seems that the maximum intrinsic motivation is present in a work situation when there is a roughly 50/50 perceived chance a standard can be met because at that level employees expect to experience a feeling of achievement and accomplishment when they perform well.

Three studies have considered the relationship between the perceived difficulty of attaining a given budget and the motivation of people to achieve that budget. The first was a laboratory study involving 108 students (Stedry, 1960). Later Stedry and Kay (1964) did a field experiment designed to test some of the ideas developed in the lab study. Neither study provides strong support for the view that goal difficulty impacts on motivation. In the laboratory study Stedry used a complicated design that varied budget level and aspiration level. So far as budget difficulty was concerned only difficult-to-achieve budgets (achieved 39 percent of the time) seemed to have a positive influence on performance. This finding fits with the work of Locke (1968) on the motivating power of goal setting and comes close to the 50/50 success probability suggested by Atkinson for maximum achievement motivation.

The field experiment of Stedry and Kay (1964) is inconclusive because of the small number of subjects (17 foremen divided into 4 groups). The data do suggest, however, that where difficult goals are perceived as impossible performance tends to be lower than when either normal goals are given or difficult goals are given that are perceived as challenging. The data also suggest that the worker's acceptance or rejection of the goal has a strong influence on his performance.

Hofstede (1967) has done a questionnaire study that also looks at the effect of goal difficulty on performance. Based on his study he concludes that Budgets and Standards "will have a more positive effect on motivation when they are tighter and less easily attained. This works up to a certain limit: beyond this limit, tightening of standards reduces motivation (p. 160)." Thus, Hofstede's data support the view that goal difficulty is important and that goals can be both too difficult and too easy. Unfortunately, Hofstede's study has substantial methodological difficulties. For example, he lacks independent measures of motivation and budget tightness and the measures he does have (particularly those of motivation) are open to question.

Despite the methodological problems with the studies on goal difficulty and motivation, they do seem to be in substantial agreement. As is shown in Figure 5–1, they all suggest that intrinsic motivation is most likely to be present when standards or budgets are set that have somewhat less than a 50/50 chance of being attained. Very difficult goals seem to have a positive effect on performance only when they are accepted. Easy goals seem to have little positive effect, because even if they are achieved, individuals do not feel they have accomplished anything.

In most work situations a number of individuals can potentially be involved in setting the standard, but, as noted in Chapter 4, the process typically is handled by the boss of the job involved and/or by some staff member of the organization. The individuals doing the job are not involved despite the fact that much behavioral science knowledge suggests that they often should be. Having the person whose performance is being measured involved in the standard setting process is likely to facilitate standards being accepted, and it helps assure that moderately difficult standards are

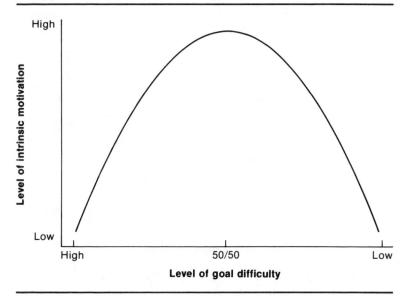

Figure 5–1
Relationship of
Goal Difficulty
to Motivation

set. Hofstede (1967) states that where participation exists moderately difficult goals are particularly likely to be set. There seems to be two reasons for this. First, in most situations individuals have relevant information about the level at which standards should be set, and this information contributes to standards being set at the proper level of difficulty. Further, when individuals participate actively in the decision process they are not likely to allow goals they perceive to be too difficult (Hopwood, 1973). Participation can also contribute to individuals accurately perceiving the difficulty of goals because it requires a high level of superior-subordinate communication that can lead to subordinates (and superiors) getting a clearer picture of what is involved in reaching a goal. This is a crucial point since individuals are motivated by the perceived difficulty of a goal, not the actual difficulty. Just because a superior feels a goal is of moderate difficulty does not mean it will be motivating. The person who must reach the goal has to have the same perception.

A recent study by Swieringa and Moncur (1975) suggests that participation in budgeting may have positive effects that extend beyond intrinsic motivation. Managers who felt that they were consulted on their operating budgets and that their suggested changes were accepted reported higher need satisfaction. Since one of the expected outcomes of high satisfaction is low turnover, it appears that participation can help motivate employees to both work hard and remain members of the organization.

Although it is usually desirable to have the employees being measured participate in setting standards, it is not always necessary. Some employees will accept standards set by the superior or someone else who has the information necessary to set reasonable standards. Further, some individuals simply prefer not to participate in the setting of standards for themselves. For example, one study showed that employees' reactions to participation were determined by a personality trait (Vroom, 1960). Only employees low on a measure of authoritarianism preferred to participate. A recent study on budget setting (Searfoss and Monczkas, 1973) found results that were in this direction but were not as strong. Thus, to decide who should be involved in setting standards one must consider two issues: who has the information needed to set standards and do the employees involved respond favorably to participation.

SOURCE OF DISCRIMINATION

A discrimination process must be credible to the person being measured for that person to see a relationship between performance and intrinsic rewards. If the person doesn't trust the comparison he or she will not act (reward himself or herself) upon it. Intrinsic rewards are simply too important to many individuals to be given out based upon questionable data. They require clear, trustworthy feedback and comparison to standards.

One way to guarantee that the discrimination process will be a reasonable one in the eyes of the person whose behavior is being considered is to have the person involved in the process. This involvement can take forms ranging all the way from the individual being one of several individuals involved to the individual being solely responsible for the discrimination. An example of the latter possibility is having employees test out the products they have made and having them make the decision alone as to whether it is an acceptable product. As a general rule, the more involvement the person has the more the discrimination process will be trusted, consequently, who makes the discrimination is a crucial issue. However, it may not be quite as important to intrinsic motivation as is the issue of who sets standards.

In many cases the discrimination functions can be handled in rather objective, trustworthy ways and in this case the individual need not be involved (e.g., measuring performance in track and field events or in managing a mutual fund). This is less often true for setting standards. It is rarely a rather objective, simple, mechanical counting process. For example, setting a fair budget is a difficult process that may require high levels of participation and openness. However, often someone in the accounting department can accurately and with great credibility to all concerned report on whether or not it was achieved. The same is true for production quotas. Recording production and comparing it to a standard are rather mechanical tasks that can be done satisfactorily in a number of ways that do not involve employees. However, setting production standards can be very difficult to do and often can only be done if the person being measured is involved.

RECIPIENTS OF COMMUNICATION

Intrinsic motivation depends on individuals receiving feedback about their performance (Vroom, 1964). Without feedback, it is impossible for individuals to reward themselves for good performance. Since intrinsic motivation depends on the expectation that good performance will lead to intrinsic rewards, it is important not only that individuals receive feedback but that they know they will receive it. The expectation of feedback and the good feelings associated with positive feedback are the essence of intrinsic motivation. A number of studies have shown that subjects will work longer and harder when provided with knowledge of their results **73**

(Arps, 1920; Locke and Bryan, 1969; Manzer, 1935; Johnson, 1922; and Smode, 1958).

Feedback can come from two sources: the work itself or some outside agent such as the person's boss or a formal information and control system. Either source can provide data on which to base rewards. However, it is preferable in many situations that the feedback comes directly from the task or some automated system that eliminates the superior. As a recent study pointed out individuals seem to find feedback from the task and from themselves to be the most useful (Greller and Herold, 1975). Unfortunately, supervisors tend to be poor and unreliable givers of feedback (Porter, Lawler, and Hackman, 1975). They are uncomfortable giving it and they often don't give it when they should. This causes havoc with intrinsic motivation because it means that the performer cannot count on receiving performance feedback. When performance feedback is not certain $P \rightarrow O$ beliefs tend to be low because the performer cannot count on good performance leading to intrinsic outcomes.

In addition to being necessary for intrinsic motivation, feedback or knowledge of results seems to be crucial because it gives individuals the information they need to correct their behavior when it deviates from the standard or desired behavior. Thus, feedback makes it possible for people to exercise self-control because it gives needed information, and it provides the motivation to exercise such control. A number of early psychological learning studies have shown that good feedback is necessary to improve task performance. For example, Thorndike (1927) found that subjects showed no improvement in drawing lines of specified lengths unless they were told whether they were right or wrong. Elwell and Grindley (1938) found no improvement in subjects' attempts to hit a bull's eye unless they could see what they hit. Finally Bilodeau, Bilodeau, and Schumsky (1959) found no improvement in performance on a level-displacing task unless subjects were told the kind of errors they were making. More studies could be cited, but the point seems obvious: Feedback is necessary for self-control to operate because without it the person will not know how to correct his or her behavior.

In some cases it may be important that more than just the performer receive information about performance. Indeed, there is reason to believe that intrinsic motivation may be highest when all people doing similar work receive information about each other's performance. This is particularly likely to be true in situations where performance measures have meaning only in terms of how others are doing. Intrinsic motivation depends on people knowing they have performed well, otherwise they will not experience feelings of competence and achievement. To decide whether they have performed well they need to know how others are doing who are performing the same task. They may not need to know exactly how well all others did on an individual basis but they clearly need some information about such things as the average performance of others and the high and low scores of others. Batting averages in baseball and profits in business only have meaning when they are related to the performance of others. For baseball players to know they have performed well they need to know how well others have performed.

The research on achievement motivation also shows that intrinsic motivation is highest when individuals know they will be evaluated against a known standard or against others who are performing the same task (Atkinson, 1964). Festinger (1954) in his social comparison theory also points out that individuals seek out information on how their performance compares to that of similar others. This is hardly surprising since in many cases only if they have this information can they experience feelings of competence, self-esteem, and achievement. Despite the potential positive effects of releasing performance information, many organizations keep information secret about such things as who has made their budget or production standard.

SPEED OF COMMUNICATION

As with extrinsic motivation it is vital for intrinsic motivation that the results of performance be communicated as soon as possible so that there is a close relationship between performance and intrinsic rewards. For individuals to reward themselves for good performance they have to find out about it quickly, any delay weakens the connection between the performance and the reward.

Communication delays may also affect the value of intrinsic rewards. There is reason to believe that the value of intrinsic rewards changes over time more than that of extrinsic rewards. Money, for example, tends to retain its value even when its receipt is delayed, but it is not clear that feelings of achievement and competence have the same value when they come long after the performance. One of the reasons that sports, like tennis and golf, are so motivating is that they provide immediate feedback, and therefore good performance leads quickly to valued rewards. It is hard to imagine that people would feel as satisfied about doing well if the results were not known for several weeks.

All too often the information and control systems in organizations operate so slowly that the performer finds out how well he or she performed only after a long delay. Small corporations that report their earnings long after the end of the time period being **75** measured are a good example of this as are the performance appraisals held long after the performance is over.

FREQUENCY OF COMMUNICATION

To maximize intrinsic motivation, communication should be as frequent as the time span of discretion allows. More frequent communication is meaningless, and there will be no intrinsic motivation because individuals will not reward themselves even though the measure indicates satisfactory performance has been achieved. As we mentioned in Chapter 4, organizations often measure the performance of their top people too frequently and end up giving them feedback that does not accurately reflect their performance and that they feel is meaningless. If performance is measured and communicated too infrequently then all the delayed feedback problems mentioned above will occur. One example of this kind of problem is monthly quality reports to employees who turn out hundreds of products a day. Another example is quarterly production reports for a highly automated process production facility.

TYPE OF ACTIVITY

The discussion of extrinsic motivation stated that type of activity is not an important direct determinant of extrinsic motivation. If an important enough extrinsic reward is used any kind of activity can be motivated extrinsically. Nothing can be further from the truth for intrinsic motivation. Only certain limited kinds of activities can be motivated intrinsically. Much research has been done to determine just what kinds of activities can be motivated intrinsically. One line of research has focused on how the performer sees a particular activity in terms of his or her self-concept. Another has focused on how the objective nature of the task influences motivation. Both of these research approaches have produced significant findings for understanding the impact of information and control systems on intrinsic motivation.

Vroom (1964) was quoted earlier to make the point that when people participate in decisions they become identified with the decision and, therefore, are motivated to prove that the decision is an effective one. The same paragraph goes on to make another point about an additional factor that influences people's intrinsic motivation:

> . . . the extent to which they pride themselves on their ability to make that kind of decision. If a person who conceives himself to be a brilliant scientist shares in the making of a decision which he believes requires scientific judgment the outcome of that decision is a test of the adequacy of his self-

conception. A successful decision confirms his self-concept; an unsuccessful decision threatens it. On the other hand, when he helps to make a decision on an administrative matter he has less "at stake." Neither a successful nor an unsuccessful decision would be greatly inconsistent with his self-concept (p. 228).

This quote clearly points out that intrinsic motivation is difficult to generate for activities that are not relevant to an important part of a person's self-concept. As Vroom notes the scientist who makes administrative decisions may well not be motivated to carry them out if making good administrative decisions is not important to him. Similarly employees may be measured in an area like cleanliness of office or courtesy, but unless being clean and courteous are important to them, measuring their activities in these areas by means of a well designed information and control system is not likely to increase their motivation to perform well.

A number of studies of achievement motivation have shown that it is not aroused unless a person is engaged in an activity where achievement is important to the person. For example, studies have shown that when people are asked to complete a well-validated test of intelligence, they perform much better than when they are asked to complete a new test that is being developed (Atkinson, 1964). When an activity is seen as related to an important part of the person's self-concept, intrinsic motivation is high because performing well leads to feelings of achievement and confirmation of one's positive self-concept. When the activity is seen as trivial and is not valued, intrinsic motivation is not aroused.

The research on job design has concentrated on trying to specify just what objective characteristics of tasks are likely to make them intrinsically motivating. The research has established that there are certain characteristics that lead people to feel that a task or job is important and that performance on it is intrinsically rewarding. The early research in this area distinguished between enriched and unenriched jobs.

Unenriched jobs are those designed in accordance with the principles of scientific management: standardization, specialization, and simplification. Jobs designed according to these principles usually end up being highly repetitive and machine paced. The assembly line job is perhaps the best example.

The job enrichment approach argues for expanding jobs on both the vertical and horizontal dimensions (Davis and Taylor, 1972). Horizontal enlargement means designing jobs so that they include a number of activities. Vertical enlargement refers to designing jobs so that workers have considerable control over both how and when the job is done. The term vertical is used to emphasize that in many cases, the person does things that a supervisor normally does (e.g., inspection, deciding on work methods and **77** procedures, setting production rates). Perhaps the best example of a totally enriched job is where a single individual assembles an entire complex electronic instrument, tests it, packages it, and ships it to the customer.

In a classic book, Walker and Guest (1952) pointed out that when employees work on jobs designed according to scientific management principles, they often are not motivated to perform well and in fact sometimes are motivated to perform poorly (Hackman and Lawler, 1971; Lawler, 1973). The jobs are so simple and unchallenging that most individuals do not feel they have done anything meaningful when they perform well. However, not performing well and not getting caught can be very challenging. Stories abound in the auto industry about the ingenious things workers do to make their jobs intrinsically rewarding. These range from welding coffee cans into doors so that they will rattle to arranging names of cars in new orders (e.g., DORF) on hoods and trunks.

During the 1950s and 1960s a number of experiments were done in which jobs were enriched (for a review see Lawler, 1969). Almost without exception these studies showed that job enrichment leads to higher levels of satisfaction and better product quality. In some instances, it also leads to higher productivity. Apparently, enriched jobs motivate employees to do higher quality work because high quality performance is intrinsically rewarding. This is in contrast to repetitive, simplified jobs that anyone can do well and where employees feel no sense of satisfaction from doing high quality work.

Two studies have tried to describe the objective characteristics that make a job enriched and intrinsically motivating (Turner and Lawrence, 1965; Hackman and Lawler, 1971). These studies suggest that at least three characteristics need to be present for a job to be motivating.

1. *The job must allow a worker to feel personally responsible for a meaningful portion of his or her work.* What is accomplished must be through the individual's own effort, and the individual must believe that whatever successes and failures occur are a result of his or her work. Only if what is accomplished is seen as one's own can an individual experience a feeling of personal success and a gain in self-esteem. This does not mean that feelings of personal responsibility for work outcomes cannot occur in team projects; all that is required is for team members to feel that their own efforts are important to accomplishing the task at hand. Autonomy seems to be the key job characteristic that causes workers to feel personal responsibility for their work. In jobs high on measured autonomy, workers tend to feel that they

78 own the outcomes of their work; in jobs low on autonomy, workers more often feel that successes and failures are due to the good work, or the incompetence, of other workers or the supervisor.

2. *The job must be meaningful or otherwise worthwhile to the individual.* If workers feel that their efforts are not being applied to a very meaningful or important task, it is unlikely that they will feel especially good if they work effectively. They must achieve something that they personally feel is worthwhile and important if they are to experience positive feelings about themselves as a result of their efforts.

There are at least two characteristics that work needs to have to be experienced as meaningful by most employees. Both of these have to do with what a task must be like for people to take pride in performing it well and for it to arouse their achievement and competence motives. First, the job must be a sufficiently whole piece of work that workers can perceive they have produced or accomplished something of significance. We would expect this to be the case when a job is high on task identity. According to Turner and Lawrence (1965), jobs high on task identity are characterized by (a) a very clear cycle of perceived closure—the job provides a distinct sense of the beginning and ending of a transformation process, (b) high visibility of the transformation to the workers, (c) high visibility of the transformation in the finished product, and (d) a transformation of considerable magnitude.

The second characteristic jobs must have is variety. Jobs high on variety provide opportunities for workers to experience meaningfulness on the job, since high variety jobs typically tap a number of different skills that may be important to the employee. It should be noted, however, that only variety that does in fact challenge the worker will be experienced as meaningful by workers with desires for higher-order need satisfaction; screwing many different sizes of nuts on many different colors of bolts, if this could be considered variety, would not be expected to be experienced as meaningful. Variety is desirable only if it increases the complexity of the job and therefore the skills required to perform the job. It is also possible for jobs to have too much variety. Activation theory (e.g., Scott, 1969) suggests that when variety is too high, employees may experience a general state of muscular and mental hypertension that greatly handicaps effective performance. In addition, Lawler and Hall (1970) found that among research scientists, very high job variety was associated with low job satisfaction, apparently because jobs with high variety often tended to require employees to do things they do not value.

To summarize, jobs are experienced as meaningful by employees to the extent that they involve doing a whole piece of work of some significance, i.e., have high task identity, and to the extent that they give employees the chance to use their valued skills **79** and abilities, i.e., to be challenged, in doing the work. In many cases the latter condition may be met on jobs with high variety.

3. *The job must provide feedback about what is accomplished.* Job design theory stresses, as did our earlier discussion of feedback, that employees cannot experience higher-order need satisfaction when they perform effectively unless they obtain some kind of feedback about how they are doing. Such feedback may come from doing the task itself, e.g., when a telephone operator successfully completes a long distance person-to-person call, but it may also come from some other person or from an information and control system. The crucial condition is that feedback be present in a form that is believable to the worker, so there is a realistic basis for the satisfaction, or frustration, of higher-order needs.

For all of the job characteristics discussed above, it is not their objective state that affects employee attitudes and behavior, but how they are experienced by the employees. Regardless of the amount of feedback (or variety, or autonomy, or task identity) employees really have in their work, it is how much they perceive they have that affects their reactions to their jobs. Objective job characteristics are important because they affect the perceptions and experiences of employees. But there are often substantial differences between objective and perceived job characteristics, and it is dangerous to assume that simply because the objective characteristics of a job seem good, there will be intrinsic motivation.

The data from one study (Hackman and Lawler, 1971) suggest that an intrinsically motivating job must be high on all four core dimensions (autonomy, task identity, variety, and feedback). At this point it is not clear just how high a job must be, however, it seems safe to conclude that a complete absence of any of these dimensions would produce low intrinsic motivation. For example, a job without feedback simply cannot be intrinsically motivating because it makes intrinsic rewards impossible to obtain.

The research evidence also shows that when employees work on jobs high on the four core dimensions they tend to see a strong connection between performing high quality work and receiving intrinsic rewards. There is a less strong connection between producing at a high rate and experiencing intrinsic rewards. The research data further show that employees who work on enriched jobs typically are higher on job satisfaction and lower on turnover and absenteeism because they receive intrinsic rewards.

In summary then, we have argued that the characteristics of jobs can establish conditions that will enhance the intrinsic motivation of workers who desire higher-order need satisfaction. In particular, we have suggested that four core dimensions of jobs are

80

important: autonomy, task identity, variety, and feedback. Further, we have argued that the harder and better individuals perform on jobs they perceive as high on these dimensions, the more intrinsic satisfaction they will feel. The research on job design also makes two very important points about the impact of information and control systems on motivation. The first, which was mentioned earlier, is that without some sort of feedback, intrinsic motivation is not possible. Thus, if feedback is not present from the work itself, an information and control system must provide it or there will be no intrinsic motivation. The second is that, regardless of how information and control systems are designed, certain kinds of activities (ones that are not important to the people who perform them) do not lend themselves to intrinsic motivation. Simply stated then, a well designed information and control system can help create intrinsically motivating work situations, but it is not the only condition that is needed for intrinsic motivation to exist.

SUMMARY

Table 5–1 presents a summary of the discussion of what makes an intrinsically motivating job situation. As can be seen from the table, it is not easy to produce intrinsic motivation; a very exacting set of conditions must be met. Producing intrinsic motivation is not simply a matter of putting a measurement system into an organization. Many organizations are designed in such a way that no information and control system can be effective from a motivation point of view. Many organization jobs are not designed so that the activities they include are challenging enough to be motivating or significant enough to be measurable. In these

Characteristics of Sensor Measures	
	A. Complete
	B. Objective
	C. Influenceable
Nature of Standards	
	D. Set by Person Being Measured
	E. Moderately Difficult
Source of Discrimination	
	F. Person Being Measured or Other Credible Source
Speed of Communication	
	G. Immediate
Frequency of Communication	
	H. Close to Time Span for Job
Recipient of Communication	
	I. Person Being Measured
Type of Activity	
	J. High Autonomy
	K. High Task Identity
	L. High Variety

TABLE 5–1
Characteristics of an
Intrinsically Motivating
Work Situation

cases, significant job and organization redesign is needed. This may mean organizations going to greater decentralization in decision making and to profit centers so that the responsibilities and authority of employees correspond to what can be measured. Overall, it requires careful coordination among how the organization is structured, the jobs designed, and performance measured. An organization that emphasizes intrinsic motivation must emphasize challenging jobs on which performance is objectively and inclusively measured against moderately difficult standards and it must see that employees receive quick valued feedback on their performance.

DYSFUNCTIONAL EFFECTS OF CONTROL SYSTEMS 6

There is no question that information and control systems often produce dysfunctional behavior. Numerous studies have documented the kinds of dysfunctional behavior that typically occur. Four types have received the most attention: rigid bureaucratic behavior, strategic behavior, the production of invalid information, and resistance. We will discuss these in turn and then try to specify when control systems are likely to produce these behaviors.

RIGID BUREAUCRATIC BEHAVIOR

Control systems can cause employees to behave in ways that look good in terms of the control system measures but that are dysfunctional as far as the generally agreed upon goals of the organization are concerned. This phenomenon, referred to as rigid bureaucratic behavior, has been described by a number of authors (see e.g., Merton, 1940; Selznick, 1949; and Gouldner, 1954). It comes about because certain conditions lead people to act in whatever ways will help them look good on the measures that are taken by control systems. In many cases this is a functional outcome, but in others it is not. In some cases it results in rigid, inflexible, dysfunctional behavior because that is what is "required" by the system. There are a number of examples of this phenomenon in the social science literature.

Blau (1955) analyzed the operation of a department in the public agency of a state government. The agency's "major responsibility is to serve workers seeking employment and employers **83**

seeking workers'' (p. 19). The tasks performed by the department included interviewing clients, helping them to fill out application forms, counseling them, and referring them to jobs. The organization saw these activities as instrumental to the accomplishment
of its objectives, and instituted a control system to be sure they
were done. To evaluate the individual interviewers, managers kept
statistical records of such things as how many interviews a particular interviewer conducted. The effect of this control system was
to motivate the employees to perform those kinds of behavior that
were measured by the system (e.g., interviewing). Unfortunately
this did not always contribute to the organizational goal of placing
workers in jobs. As Blau points out:

> An instrument intended to further the achievement of organizational objec-
> tives, statistical records constrained interviewers to think of maximizing the
> indices as their major goal, sometimes at the expense of these very objectives.
> They avoided operations which would take up time without helping them to
> improve their record, such as interviewing clients for whom application forms
> had to be made out, and wasted their own and the public's time on activities
> intended only to raise the figures on their record. Their concentration upon
> this goal, since it was important for their ratings, made them unresponsive
> to requests from clients that would interfere with its attainment (p. 43).

Babchuk and Goode (1951) have provided an interesting case
study that highlights how control systems, when combined with
rewards, can cause employees to behave dysfunctionally. They
studied a selling unit in a department store where a pay incentive
plan was introduced to pay employees on the basis of sales volume. Total sales initially increased but the pay plan was not functional as far as the long term goals of the organization were concerned. There was considerable ''sales grabbing'' and ''tying up
the trade'' as well as a general neglect of such unrewarded and
unmeasured functions as stock work and arranging merchandise
for displays.

It is possible to cite a number of other examples of situations
where employees in large organizations respond to control systems with rigid control-system-oriented behavior that is dysfunctional from the point of view of the organization. In fact, the negative connotation that has become attached to the initially neutral
term, bureaucracy, stems from just this kind of behavior. Each
of us has probably had many experiences where people representing formal organizations have dealt with us in ways that all the
parties acknowledged were dysfunctional for both the organization
and ourselves. For example, one of the authors recently tried to
rent a car from a large car rental company only to be told that
it would be 30 to 60 minutes before one would be ready. Further
questioning revealed that there were cars available but they had
to be washed because ''we never rent cars that aren't washed''

84 The author then asked that an exception be made because he

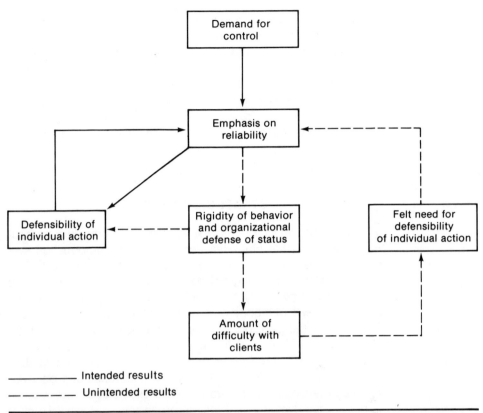

Intended results

----- Unintended results

Adapted from J. G. March and H. A. Simon, *Organizations.* (New York: Wiley, 1958.)

FIGURE 6–1
The Simplified
Merton Model

was in a hurry and needed the car immediately. The salesperson, however, stuck to the rule despite the fact that it lost the company business and goodwill and failed to serve the needs of a customer. The rule, of course, is basically a functional one since it probably does help business to rent clean cars.

The views of a number of sociologists about the bureaucratic behavior phenomenon have been summarized by March and Simon (1958). Merton's explanation for why it occurs is contained in Figure 6–1. It shows that rigidity stems from the emphasis on reliability; and from the need to defend individual actions. However, Merton does not explain why *all* individuals do not respond this way to the emphasis on reliability, nor does he say anything about the conditions that favor people responding this way. Clearly, everyone does not respond to control systems with rigid behavior all the time. People are often willing to break the rules to get things done. Frank (1959) in discussing Soviet management practices has noted that managers often violate some standards and even laws in order to keep their organizations functioning effectively. This occurs so much that it has become socially legitimate. **85**

It is also interesting that one form of labor bargaining is a work-to-rules action. What this means is that, unlike normal times, the employees follow the rules closely, observing the letter of the law, and as a result the organization functions much less effectively. It is also obvious that organizations differ widely in the degree to which the members rigidly respond to the rules and measures set up by the control system (Burns and Stalker, 1961). Part of the explanation for this difference rests in the nature of the control systems that are used in different organizations and part of it rests in the nature of the individuals that work in different organizations.

STRATEGIC BEHAVIOR

In addition to producing the kind of long-term rigid bureaucratic behavior that has been described so far, information systems can cause employees to engage in what Cammann (1974a, 1974b) has called strategic behavior. Strategic behavior involves actions designed solely to influence information system results so that they will look good or acceptable for a certain time period. This kind of behavior does not involve feeding false data to the systems; rather, it usually involves altering behaviors for a period of time to make the control system measures look acceptable. In this respect it is like the kind of rigid bureaucratic behavior that has been discussed so far. Like bureaucratic behavior it also is not always dysfunctional for the organization. However, unlike bureaucratic behavior it only involves a short-term behavior change. For example, if a manager needs to buy a piece of equipment and it's near the end of a budget period, he or she may make a strategic choice. If money is left in the budget, he or she probably will buy the equipment to use up the budget. On the other hand, if the budget has been spent, the purchase probably will be deferred until the next budget period to keep from overspending the budget. From the point of view of organizational effectiveness, it probably won't make much difference if the equipment is bought at the beginning of one period or the end of another and in either case valid data are being reported. Still, the budget system is clearly influencing the behavior of the manager in the sense that he or she is behaving in a strategic way in order to look good on the information system measures.

On several occasions top management has been accused of a particular kind of strategic behavior: smoothing out reported income over a period of years. Gordon, Horowitz, and Meyers (1967) reported that the income of the U.S. Steel Corporation appeared to be tempered through the judicious application of income smoothing accounting techniques. In a similar manner, Schiff (1966) indicated that the management of the Chock Full

O'Nuts Corporation appeared to even out reported income by deciding to either immediately expense or capitalize for expenses in future years the advertising costs of new products. This income alteration may result, as Lewin and Seidler (unpublished) propose, because the discretionary use of accounting methods is seemingly painless to apply and is, therefore, preferred by top management to the difficult alternative of correcting internal problems rationalized as temporary. No matter what the factors are that motivate financial decision makers to perform income smoothing, one thing is certain—it does occur.

Some strategic behavior can result in organizational ineffectiveness. An analysis of Soviet Union management practices has described what can happen when a certain kind of strategic behavior called storming occurs (Berliner, 1956).

> In February 1941, G. M. Malenkov delivered to the Eighteenth Party Conference a report which, as it turned out, proved to be a summing up of the state of industry at the end of the prewar period. Among the many matters which he considered important enough to call to the attention of the assembled party leaders was the following:
>
> Now, Comrades, matters stand thus—in most of our enterprises the output of finished production is carried out unevenly, in spurts, and is concentrated as a rule at the end of the month. Enterprises lack a firm, previously worked-out schedule of production. Here are some typical examples.
>
> The Kolomensk Machinery Works in Moscow County worked this way in 1940: In the first ten days of every month it produced 5 to 7 per cent of the month's output, in the second ten days, 10 to 15 per cent, and in the third ten days, 75 to 80 per cent.
>
> The Karl Marx-Leningrad Plant, in December 1940, produced 2 per cent of monthly output in the first ten days, 8 per cent in the second ten days, and 90 per cent in the third ten days.
>
> In Moscow Pump and Compressor Plant, in December 1940, 3.4 per cent of the month's output was produced in the first ten days, 27.5 per cent in the second ten days, and 69.1 per cent in the third ten days.
>
> We must put an end to this lack of planning, to this uneven rate of production, to this storming in the work of enterprises. We must achieve a day-by-day fulfillment of the production program according to a previously worked-out schedule, by every factory, mill, mine, and railroad.
>
> This practice of "storming" leads to a number of uneconomic consequences. States of emergency constantly arise; men and equipment are subject to periods of unnecessary idleness; during the days of storming the rate of spoilage increases, overtime pay mounts up, the machines suffer from speed-up, and customers' production schedules are interrupted. It is certainly a practice which the state would wish to eliminate if it could (Berliner, 1956, p. 87–88).

An interesting example of managers engaging in strategic behavior to keep their facility open occurred in a gold mine. In this particular company, mines were shut down after the yield **87** per ton of ore dropped below a certain level. One old marginal mine managed to stay open for several extra years because of the strategic behavior of its management. It happened that the mine contained one very rich pocket of ore. Instead of mining this all at once the management used it as its reserve. Everytime the yield of the ore it was mining fell below an acceptable level, it would mix in a little high grade ore so the mine would remain open. This was dysfunctional as far as the company was concerned since maximum cost effectiveness would have been achieved by mining all the high grade ore and then closing the mine.

There are numerous other examples of strategic behavior in the literature where employees develop JIC (just in case) and CYA (cover your ass) files in order to defend any decisions they have made. Jasinski (1956) and Hopwood (1972, 1973, 1974a, b) have written about how control systems have lead to dysfunctional maintenance and production schedules. Thus, the evidence is overwhelming that strategic behavior is fostered by information and control systems.

INVALID DATA REPORTING

All control systems need valid data about what is occurring in the organization to be effective, yet behavioral science research shows that often false data are obtained (see, e.g., Wilensky, 1967). As Argyris (1964, 1971) points out, control systems tend to be effective and to produce valid information only for the unimportant and programmed problems.

Evidence suggests that control systems produce two kinds of invalid data: invalid data about what can be done and invalid data about what has been done. The first kind of invalid data, of course, makes planning difficult, while the second makes the control of day-to-day activities difficult. The research on budgets and on piece rate payment systems provide a number of good examples of situations where organizations are given invalid data about what is possible. Much of the available research data is from case studies and thus it is difficult to establish how widespread the production of invalid data is. To understand how and why invalid data are reported it is worth reviewing a few of the case studies that have illustrated this phenomenon.

Whyte (1955) has provided some graphic case examples of how individuals distort the data that are fed into production measuring systems. Most of Whyte's examples are cases where individuals under pay incentive systems distort data about the kind of production possible on a given job. The following quote illustrates one worker's attitude toward the measurement system and the time-study men who run it.

> "... you got to outwit that son-of-a-bitch! You got to use your noodle while you're working, and think your work out ahead as you go along! You got to add in movements you know you ain't going to make when you're running the job! remember, if you don't screw them, they're going to screw you! ... Every movement counts! ...
>
> "Remember those bastards are paid to screw you," said Starkey. "And that's all they got to think about. They'll stay up half the night figuring out how to beat you out of a dime. They figure you're going to try to fool them, so they make allowances for that. They set the prices low enough to allow for what you do."
>
> "Well, then, what the hell chance have I got?" asked Tennessee.
>
> "It's up to you to figure out how to fool them more then they allow for," said Starkey.
>
> "... when the time-study man came around, I set the speed at 180. I knew damn well he would ask me to push it up, so I started low enough. He finally pushed me up to 445, and I ran the job later at 610. If I'd started out at 445, they'd have timed it at 610. Then I got him on the reaming, too. I ran the reamer for him at 130 speed and .025 feed. He asked me if I couldn't run the reamer any faster than that, and I told him I had to run the reamer slow to keep the hole size. I showed him two pieces with oversize holes that the day man ran. I picked them out for the occasion! But later on I ran the reamer at 610 speed and .018 feed, same as the drill. So I didn't have to change gears—And then there was a burring operation on the job too. For the time-study man I burred each piece after I drilled and reamed, and I ran the burring tool by automatic feed. But afterwards, I let the burring go till I drill 25 pieces or so; and I just touched them up a little by holding them under the burring tool" (Whyte, 1955, pp. 15–18).*

Gardner (1945) has also pointed out that employees often give invalid data in industry and provides an example of how it can occur.

> In one case, a group, who worked together in assembling a complicated and large sized steel framework, worked out a system to be used only when the rate setter was present. They found that by tightening certain bolts first, the frame would be slightly sprung and all the other bolts would bind and be very difficult to tighten. When the rate setter was not present, they followed a different sequence and the work went much faster (pp. 164–165).

Argyris (1951, 1964), Hofstede (1967), Hopwood (1973), and others have pointed out that employees also often provide misleading data when they are asked to give budgetary estimates. Not surprisingly, they tend to ask for much larger amounts than they need. On the other hand, in instances where a low budget estimate is needed in order to get a budget or project approved (e.g., under some Program Planning and Budgeting systems, Lyden and Miller, 1968), a low estimate is submitted. Managers submit high budget requests because they realize that their budget request will be cut and to play the game they must come in with a high initial budget figure. The bargaining process they go through

---

*By permission of the publisher.

is not too dissimilar from the one that goes on between the time-study man and the blue collar employee. Both the time-study man and the manager try to get valid data about what is possible in the future and the employees who are subject to the control system often give invalid data and try to get as favorable a standard, or budget, as they can. Budget setting sessions can degenerate into a game of seeing how much slack can be placed in the budget by the subordinate and how little slack is allowed by the superior. As Schiff and Lewin (1970) have cogently stated, slack in budgets, the process of underestimating revenues and overstating costs, exists because many managers prefer to operate in a slack environment. It makes sense for managers to opt for slack since the negative sanctions for missing a tight budget are likely to have more impact than the rewards for making a tight budget (Onsi, 1973).

How frequently do employees consciously provide invalid data when standards and budgets are being set? It is impossible to come up with any hard figures but the research on standard setting suggests that it happens much of the time (Lawler, 1971). There is less evidence on how often it occurs in budget setting but what data there are suggest it happens much of the time there too. In this situation as in the standard setting situation there is usually low trust, and, as a study by Mellinger (1956) shows, when there is low trust people are likely to conceal data or to communicate invalid data (see also Rosen and Tesser, 1970).

There are also a number of examples in the behavioral science literature of cases where employees have fed invalid information about what has happened into a control system. Again it is difficult from the literature to determine just how often this overt falsification occurs, but it seems likely that it is not as common as the practice of making consciously invalid estimates of what is possible. Undoubtedly one of the reasons for this is that it is easier to catch and punish an employee who has misreported what has happened than it is to punish one who has consciously given an erroneous estimate of what can happen.

Roethlisberger and Dickson (1939) in their classic study of the Bank Wiring Room point out how employees can manage the kind of production reports that go outside their work group. In the Bank Wiring Room the employees were on a pay incentive plan and they wanted to show a consistent daily production figure. They did this by not reporting what they produced on some days and on other days reporting things as having been produced that were never produced. Similar examples have been cited by others who have looked at the way employees react to financial incentive systems (e.g., Whyte, 1955; Lawler, 1971).

There are also data that suggest employees will consciously feed invalid information into management information systems (e.g., Argyris, 1971; Mumford and Banks, 1967; Pettigrew, 1970, 1972, 1973). One reason for such falsification seems to be to cover up errors or poor performance. Employees also feed invalid data to the management information systems to make the system look bad and to discourage people from using it. Invalid data are also sometimes fed into a control system simply because control systems occasionally demand data that simply are not and cannot be collected. Faced with this situation an employee may choose to estimate the data rather than admit that it does not exist or give up on the system. This would seem to be a particular problem where computer-based management information systems are being installed. They often call for historical cost, production, and other data that simply are not available (Argyris, 1971).

RESISTANCE

Every discussion of the behavioral problems associated with control systems points out that they often meet strong resistance from the people who are subject to them. Rarely, however, do these discussions show, as we have in the preceding chapters, that control systems can also fulfill some important needs people have because they provide feedback and structure and that for this reason many people want a control system. Virtually every author who discusses control systems tends to explain the resistance to them in terms of their being perceived as a threat to the need satisfaction of employees (e.g., Argyris, 1971; Caplan, 1971; Mumford and Banks, 1967; Pettigrew, 1970; and Whisler, 1970a, 1970b). They then go on to emphasize how control systems can threaten the satisfaction of a number of different needs. Lawler (1971) and Whyte (1955) have shown how the imposition of a pay incentive, performance measurement system can threaten the satisfaction of social, esteem, and security needs. Argyris (1951) and others have shown how budgets can do the same thing. Along similar lines, Argyris (1971), Gibson and Nolan (1974), Mumford and Banks (1967), and Whisler (1970b) have pointed out how computer-based management information systems can threaten the satisfaction of social, security, esteem, autonomy, and self-realization needs. Pettigrew (1970, 1972) has pointed out that control systems also often significantly change the power and status relationships in an organization.

The questions that remain concern why control systems are generally seen as such significant threats to the satisfaction of **91** so many needs and why they significantly change the power relationships in organizations. There are a number of reasons, the most significant of which will be discussed next.

Control systems can automate expertise.   Control systems can automate or computerize jobs that presently are considered to require expertise (Carroll, 1967; Pettigrew, 1970, 1973; and Gibson and Nolan, 1974). The effect of this can be to make superflous a skill that a person has developed and has been respected for having. This phenomenon seems to occur most frequently when management information systems (MIS) are installed. Such systems can have a tremendous impact on the nature of middle- and lower-level management jobs. For example, they can make costing, purchasing, and production decisions that previously were the essence of many management jobs. Because of this, Leavitt and Whisler (1958) have pointed out that the potential is present for the elimination of many management jobs. This has not happened, and it may not ever happen, but there is still the potential for automating or computerizing many jobs. Even if systems don't lead to the elimination of managerial jobs, they may make managerial jobs less desirable because they lead to a "rationalization" and "depersonalization" of managerial work (Carroll, 1967).

The elimination and depersonalization of jobs certainly is not restricted to managerial jobs. Pettigrew (1973) has provided an example of how stock order clerks saw computerization as potentially making unnecessary the skills they had developed to do their jobs. It didn't turn out that way, but the point is they feared it would happen. A study on the impact of computerization on white collar jobs in a bank also found that computerization was seen as making useless the expertise that was required to do some jobs (Mumford and Banks, 1967). A crucial factor in understanding the impact of computerized information systems seems to be the stage of their development. Gibson and Nolan (1974) have suggested that there are four stages. During the first stage (installation) computers have a tendency to produce strong job displacement anxieties. This problem is particularly likely to occur at the lower levels of organizations. It is only when the systems reach stage four (maturity) that they are likely to be in a position to displace middle-level managers. At this point they are devoted to applications touching on critical business operations and the head of the system is a member of top management.

To the extent that control systems can automate, standardize, and rigidify work, people will see them as threatening their need satisfaction in a number of areas. Particularly relevant would appear to be satisfaction in the status, autonomy, and security need areas. Security because the person may feel more expendable, status because what the person is respected for can become valueless, and autonomy because the new system may seriously restrict the person's freedom to perform the job (Argyris, 1971).

Control systems can create new experts and give them power. Pettigrew (1970, 1973) gives an excellent example of how the installation of a computerized MIS created a new power elite in one organization. There was considerable jockeying for position within the organization and some groups' power and status were reduced. The individuals who ended up in control of the system, however, gained in power; they not only didn't resist the system, they pushed for its expansion and development into a stage four system. In another paper, Pettigrew (1972) stresses how information can be a source of power in an organization and how the individuals who run MIS can find themselves in the sometimes powerful and satisfying role of gatekeeper even though they are in staff positions. This is particularly likely to occur as the systems approach stage four.

It is probably safe to assume that no matter what control system is involved, there is some group that will gain as a result of its installation and another that will lose. In the case of budgets the winners typically are the accountants that run them, in the case of incentive systems it is the time-study experts, and in the case of MIS it is the computer experts and staff people who run them. These people favor installation of the system because the system helps them. However, there are usually others who lose power to these people. They typically see their power, status, and job security threatened as a result of the new control system and resist it.

Control systems have the potential to measure individual performance more accurately and completely. Certain kinds of control systems can increase the validity of performance measurement in an organization by improving both the accuracy of the performance data collected and its inclusivity. For example, moving from a simple superior's rating of performance to a performance evaluation system based on both quantitative responsibility accounting data and production data can increase the accuracy of the available performance data. Some employees welcome this since it reflects positively on their performance and increases their own position in the organization. Others feel that such objective data will put them in a less favorable light than they are in presently. In fact, they might see the installation of such an objective evaluation system as threatening their job security, their status, and their power in the organization. Thus, while one group will favor better measurment, another group is likely to resist it.

Argyris (1971) has talked about how an MIS can lead to leadership based more on competence than on power. In many ways **93** this point is similar to the one being made here. Both are pointing out that with better performance data the highest level of need satisfaction is more likely to go to the more competent. This is a positive outcome for some but it may be resisted by those who doubt their own competence but have achieved reasonably satisfactory positions in organizations.

Control systems can change the social structure of an organization. Changes in a control system can produce major changes in the social relationships in an organization (Mumford and Banks, 1967). They can break up social groups, pit one friend against another, create new social groups, and, as was pointed out earlier, by creating new experts they can change the status and power of organization members. This is dramatically illustrated in studies where pay incentive plans, work measurement systems, and computerized MIS have been installed or altered. Changes in these control systems almost always have a strong impact on the social relations in the organization. Some people have less opportunity to form friendships after the changes have been made, others have more. Some people end up pitted in a competitive way against people with whom they formerly had cooperative relationships. Because of the potential impact of control systems on social need satisfaction, it is not surprising that some employees see control systems as threats to their social need satisfaction and for that reason resist the installation of such systems.

Control systems can reduce opportunities for intrinsic need satisfaction. Information systems can help provide feedback about performance, thus they can help create opportunities for psychological success and intrinsic satisfaction. However, they can also reduce the opportunities available for experiencing psychological success if, as often happens, they reduce the amount of autonomy employees have by specifying in considerable detail how jobs have to be done. This has already happened in many jobs where incentive pay and budget systems are in effect and it appears to be about to happen in many jobs because of the installation of automated information systems. If, as Carroll (1967) says, real time decisions will soon be made by centralized management information systems, then it certainly appears that many lower level jobs in organizations will lose their autonomy.

The fact that control systems can provide feedback may not compensate for the fact that they may decrease autonomy since this often is enough to prevent people from experiencing intrinsic satisfaction from task accomplishment. Naturally when people see that the control system will reduce their autonomy and thereby their opportunities for experiencing psychological success and intrinsic satisfaction, they will resist the system if they value these feelings.

94

CAUSES OF DYSFUNCTIONAL BEHAVIORS

So far we have discussed four kinds of dysfunctional behavior information systems can produce: rigid bureaucratic behavior, strategic behavior, invalid data reporting, and resistance. Now we need to consider in detail when control systems are likely to lead to these kinds of behavior. Dysfunctional behavior is not a necessary result of the existence of an information and control system; it only occurs when the system has characteristics that produce dysfunctional behavior.

Characteristics of Sensor Measures

As far as producing dysfunctional behavior, the completeness of measures is a mixed picture. Complete measures seem to produce less rigid bureaucratic behavior and strategic behavior but typically produce more resistance and perhaps more invalid data than incomplete measures. Let us look at each of these in turn so that we can understand the mixed impact of completeness.

By definition, rigid bureaucratic behavior should not exist when complete measures are used. It results when people perform only a limited part of their job because that is all that is measured. Several examples were given at the beginning of this chapter. The study by Babchuk and Goode (1951) provides a good example of a control system that failed to measure all the necessary or relevant behavior while the study by Blau (1955) shows what can occur when systems measure activities rather than results. Another example is the case of a trailer company that decided to measure their salespeople on how many trailers they sold. The result was a dramatic increase in trailer sales, a number of sales to poor credit risks and a sales lot full of over-priced trade-ins. The dysfunctional behavior in all of these examples occurred for one simple reason: An incomplete measure of individual performance was used. It was incomplete either because it measured only activities and not results or because it measured only some of the results necessary for organizational effectiveness.

Completeness leads to resistance because it often is a threat to individual need satisfaction. As was noted earlier, the use of better performance measures can make some individuals look better and others worse. It can also reduce the autonomy of individuals by making it impossible for them to ignore performing well in unmeasured areas.

The installation of an MIS or a budgeting system can, for example, measure an aspect of a manager's performance that has not been measured before. Again, some managers might want this while others resist it. Specifically those managers who see themselves as doing poorly in the area about to be measured **95** would be expected to resist the installation of the new control system. Other managers might also resist it because it would restrict their freedom to perform. The more that is measured the less freedom there is to disregard certain aspects of performance in order to do well in those areas that are measured.

Human resource measurement systems like the ones we will discuss in Chapter 9 (Likert and Bowers, 1969; Brummet, Flamholtz and Pyle, 1968) provide an interesting example of a new control system that many managers might be expected to resist. When working properly they purport to be able to measure how a manager handles the human assets for which he or she is responsible. Thus, they can tell whether a manager has liquidated them in order to obtain short-term profits or built them up in order to help the organization grow. At the moment organizations rarely measure managers' performance in this area and managers often liquidate human assets to look good on dimensions that are measured (Rhode and Lawler, 1973). If human asset values were measured, it would pose a severe threat to those managers who tend to manage without regard to these values (see Argyris, 1953, for an example of this type of manager). Their performance might suddenly not look so good and their esteem, security, and autonomy needs would be threatened. Thus, human resource accounting or any measurement system that makes performance measurement more inclusive will be supported by some, but will be resisted by those whose need satisfaction it threatens.

Completeness is unlikely to have a strong impact on the tendency of individuals to produce invalid data. There are situations where it might, however. As has been mentioned when more complete measures are generated, individuals often find performing well more difficult because they have to be concerned about more performance areas. They can no longer ignore unmeasured X to look good on measured Y. This pressure for performance can force individuals to provide false data and lead them to resist information and control systems.

Objectivity is also a mixed blessing as far as dysfunctional behavior is concerned. It can lead to rigid bureaucratic behavior because it can make it obvious that measures are not complete. One of the advantages of subjective measures (like a superior global performance rating) is that they can potentially include everything. When measures are objective, it is clear what they include and what they don't include. This is fine if the measures are complete; it is not fine if they are incomplete. Objectivity can encourage strategic behavior in the same way. Strategic behavior is only effective if there are clear ways to influence measures.

It is difficult to say whether objective or subjective measures **96** are likely to be resisted more. When superior-subordinate trust is low, subjective ones probably will be resisted more for obvious reasons. Individuals do not like to be measured by systems they cannot trust. Some individuals, however, may resist objective measures because they often allow for better measurement and for potentially embarrassing comparisons among individuals. Individuals who will not look good on objective measures resist them because they have little to gain and much to lose from better measures. Thus, both objective and subjective measures are resisted but usually for different reasons.

Individuals provide invalid data to both objective and subjective measurement systems. Earlier in this chapter, there were a number of examples of how employees provide false data to their bosses and to time-study experts. Another clear example of workers providing false data, to an objective system, occurred recently in an automobile plant. A telemetric system was set up to count the number of parts that went through a certain machine. At the end of one week, the production engineers found that the system showed the employees had produced almost twice as many finished products as they had received parts for. It seems that the workers found out how to fool the counter and decided to see how many parts they could run up.

Overall, employees probably are more likely to try to distort subjective measures than objective ones. For one thing, providing false data to subjective measures is easier and the possible repercussions are less serious. Also, it seems to be true that biasing is most likely to occur where there is uncertainty (March and Simon, 1958; Pettigrew, 1970). This means that a manager is more likely to report that morale is high when it is low and that a group of subordinates is working well when they are working poorly than he or she is to report false data about whether the budget was made. Or in the case of a commander in Vietnam, he was more likely to report invalid data on enemy casualties than his own. One implication of this, of course, is that organizations need to mistrust measures of subjective dimensions, particularly when the sensor is the person responsible for the measure and extrinsic rewards are involved.

Uninfluenceable measures tend to produce invalid data and resistance but not rigid bureaucratic behavior or strategic behavior because, if measures are truly uninfluenceable, these behaviors will not accomplish their objective—making the person look good on the measures. Uninfluenceable measures are resisted because, when individuals cannot influence measures, they don't get valid feedback on their performance and they are unable to influence the kind of extrinsic rewards they receive.

Individuals seem to feel justified in feeding systems invalid data when they are being evaluated and measured based on mea- **97** sures they cannot influence by normal job performance. The unfairness of the situation the organization has placed them in seems to justify their presenting false data. Of course, in some cases when individuals cannot influence the measures by normal job behavior, they cannot do it by presenting false data either. Corporate profits sometimes fit into this category. They are often influenced by factors beyond the control of most employees and, because of the way they are audited, they are difficult to falsify. There are, of course, famous cases (e.g., Yale Express, Penn Central, Equity Funding) where the top officers of the companies have presented false data and for a while have even influenced profits in the direction they wanted. These are the exceptions rather than the rule, however.

Nature of Standards

When standards are seen as unreasonably difficult, they tend to produce rigid bureaucratic behavior, strategic behavior, invalid data, and considerable resistance. A clear illustration of this point is provided by Berliner's (1961) description of the situation faced by plant managers in the Soviet Union. The managers are typically placed on a production-based pay incentive plan and are assigned unreasonably high production goals on the assumption that this is best for the overall economy.

> . . . the bonus system is an effective device for eliciting a high level of managerial effort, but in the context of excessively high production targets, it induces management to make certain types of decisions that are contrary to the intent of the state. The production of unplanned products, the concealment of production capacity, the falsification of reports and the deterioration of quality are the unintended consequences of the system of managerial incentives.
>
> . . . the incentives that motivate managers to strive for the fulfillment of their production targets are the same incentives that motivate them to evade the regulations of the planning system. Because of the tightening of the supply system . . . managers are compelled to defend their enterprise's position by overordering supplies, by hoarding materials and equipment and by employing expediters whose function it is to keep the enterprise supplied with materials at all costs, legal or otherwise (p. 369).

Berliner also points out that difficult standards cause storming.

It is not difficult to understand why individuals often resort to rigid bureaucratic behavior, strategic behavior, and reporting invalid data when they are faced with unreasonable standards. These are the only ways they can achieve the standards. Unreasonable standards also provide psychological justification for reporting invalid data: "If they are going to do that to me then I can deal with them dishonestly."

Standards set by others are less likely to be understood and **98** more likely to be seen as unreasonable and difficult to achieve.

Because of this they tend to cause more dysfunctional behavior than participatively set goals. Participation in setting standards reduces dysfunctional behavior because it reduces the chance that too difficult, poorly understood standards will be set. When people participate, they simply don't allow this to happen. The major reason that employees are not allowed to participate in the standard setting process seems to be the fear that they will try to have standards set too low. This may happen in some instances, but it happens anyway as is illustrated by the studies of piece rate situations cited earlier. Further, there are studies that suggest it may not happen when the standards are set by the employees. For example, Gillespie (1948) has reported on a situation where workers were allowed to participate in setting rates.

> When a new job was to be quoted, the job description was sent to the shop and the men got together and worked out methods, times and prices; the result went back via the foreman to the sales department in order that a quotation could be sent. I was . . . surprised and horrified at this unplanned, nonspecialized and dishonesty-provoking procedure and set out to improve organization and method. As I went deeper into the study of department economics, I found:
>
> a. The group's estimates were intelligent.
> b. The estimates were honest and enabled the men, working consistently at a good speed, to earn a figure LESS THAN THAT COMMON TO SIMILAR SHOPS IN ORGANIZED PIECEWORK.
> c. The overhead costs were lower than they would have been if the shop was run on modern lines (p. 95).

Much of the literature on the effects of participation suggests that under certain conditions participation can reduce the amount of resistance toward change. In the classic study on this topic, Coch and French (1948) found that participation reduced the motivational and morale problems associated with a change in work procedures. Mann and Williams (1960) found in a company they studied that resistance to the introduction of a computer was greatly reduced by participation. This firm had managers meet and discuss the changes for several years before they took place. Somewhat similar results have been found in a recent study of a Danish bank (Winther, 1974). Seventy-eight percent of the employees in the study felt that the new system was better for the employees.

Miller (1960) and Mumford and Banks (1967) have reported on studies where participation was not used in the installation of a control system and where resistance was high. They concluded that participation probably would not have reduced resistance. Others (e.g., Strauss 1963) have seriously questioned the value of participation in reducing resistance to change and some later studies have shown (French, Israel, and As, 1960) that participation does not always reduce resistance to change. **99**

As we mentioned earlier, one reason for this seems to be that certain individuals are not comfortable with participation and do not respond to it favorably (Vroom, 1960). It also seems that partic- ipation is effective only when it involves areas or topics on which employees feel there should be participation.

Finally, it seems that participation in something like standard- setting is likely to be effective if it is part of an overall strategy of participative management and employee-management trust. When it isn't, employees seem to use participation to get slack standards set and to manipulate management (Hopwood, 1973).

A number of explanations have been offered in the literature for why participation reduces resistance under some conditions, but three of the reasons seem to be the most valid. The first is that with participation individuals have a chance to shape the nature of the change being instituted. Presumably because the individuals will be motivated to protect their need satisfaction, they will influ- ence the change in ways that will make it less threatening than a change designed by someone else might be. Thus, because of participation the change may actually be less threatening to the satisfaction of their needs and for this reason be resisted less. This explanation is directly relevant to the issue of standard setting, since participation should reduce the likelihood that unreasonable standards will be set.

The second reason is suggested by a number of studies that have pointed out that some of the resistance to control systems is irrational (e.g., Mumford and Banks, 1967; Pettigrew, 1970, 1973). It is irrational in the sense that it is based on misinformation. Most major organizational changes tend to produce a tremendous number of rumors. Not infrequently these rumors have only a small basis in fact and make the change look worse than it is. This is not surprising since it follows from some of the early research on rumors. Rumors are particularly likely to occur on important topics where there is ambiguity about what is occurring (Allport and Postman, 1947). Control systems certainly are important and when there is little participation, there is often a great deal of ambiguity about what is going on. People also tend to fill out rumors to make them fit their own organization of the world. They elaborate on facts, make inferences, etc., until the rumor no longer resembles the fact that started the rumor. In situations where peo- ple are anxious because a major change is anticipated they often fit the rumor to their anxieties and as a result the rumor paints a much more threatening picture than the real one. This leads to resistance because people see the control system as threaten- ing their need satisfaction.

One obvious way to reduce resistance based on erroneous information is to communicate valid information. This often is done by organizations on a top-down, one-way basis. Unfortunately people don't always hear or believe one-way communications and even if they do, the communications may not answer the questions they are concerned about. The obvious point is that good communication in sensitive areas must be two way, hence the relevance of participation to the issue of communication and resistance to change. One thing participation encourages is good communication. Thus, where participation takes place one would expect people to be better informed about the nature of any change. In some cases, this should lead to less resistance to change because the valid picture is less threatening than the invalid one. If, however, the valid picture is a threatening one, then obviously, participation will not eliminate resistance and may increase it.

Earlier it was suggested that participation can lead to employees feeling that decisions are theirs. This sense of ownership is the third reason why participation may reduce resistance. When decisions are theirs, people's self-esteem and feelings of competence get tied to their success. Thus, not only are people unlikely to resist changes, which are associated with decisions they make, they are motivated to carry them out.

The three explanations we have given for the fact that participation can reduce resistance to standards and control systems are not mutually exclusive; all can and probably do operate at the same time. Also they probably are not equally powerful. There is relatively little data to indicate how important the various explanations are and how often they operate to reduce resistance, but it is still possible to speculate a little about their relative potency. Probably the major reason participation reduces resistance is that it allows individuals to shape the change to better fit their needs. Probably less important is the fact that with participation the change is owned by the people, and least important is the informational effect. If the information effect were strong, it would seem that better communications alone should be able to reduce resistance, yet there is little evidence of this. Power equalization seems to be necessary for resistance to be significantly lowered. There are no strong, data-based reasons for stating that ownership of the change is a less important factor than restructuring the change to better fit the needs of the people. It does seem, however, that the latter is more likely to occur and to make a concrete, easily noticeable difference.

Source of Discrimination

It is not clear who should act as the discriminator to minimize dysfunctional behavior. A brief review of the impact of having different individuals serve as the discriminator will illustrate this point.

Based on our discussion of extrinsic motivation, it would seem that if the discrimination function is performed by someone other than the person being evaluated, the control system is more likely to be adhered to and thus there is a greater potential for rigid bureaucratic behavior. Once an outsider becomes involved, there is the possibility that rewards can be given on the basis of how the person performs the behavior measured by the control system. The rewards may be formal (e.g., pay, promotion) or they may simply be approval or disapproval as shown by the discriminator. Once valued rewards become involved, the person's behavior is going to be influenced by what he or she feels must be done to obtain them. The person may develop the idea that rewards depend on the control system measures if someone with reward power acts as the discriminator. Based on this reasoning, if the discriminator function is performed by a person's superior, the chances of rigid adherence to the system will be greater than if it is performed by a staff person, some other outside agent who lacks reward power, or the person performing the job.

The more the individual whose behavior is being measured acts as discriminator and sensor for his or her own behavior, the greater the possibility there is for invalid data. If the individual reports the data and compares them to the standard, it is easier for him or her to distort them. Whether the individual will distort data under these conditions is influenced by how the data will be used, who receives them, and the relationship between the individual and the organization. As was noted in the discussion of standard setting, individuals don't always try to cheat the organization. However, as will be discussed later in this chapter, they are particularly likely to produce invalid data when extrinsic rewards are involved.

If the individual acts as the discriminator, there is usually less resistance to the control system than if another person acts as the discriminator. There are two reasons for this. First, if the individual acts as the discriminator, then he or she will receive performance feedback and people want to receive feedback about their performance. Second, when people act as discriminators, they may feel that they can control the data that are passed on to their superiors or to the rest of the system. This can be important if the individuals feel that the system is likely to produce data that will threaten their need satisfaction. If the individual acts as the discriminator, there is the possibility of distorting or withholding negative data. This may allow the individual to avoid many of the negative repercussions that might come from a control system. A control system that has an outside agent acting as the discriminator makes such distortion more difficult and thus the

102 person is likely to see it as potentially more threatening to his or her need satisfaction. If performance is poor under these conditions, there is little the performer can do to prevent this information from being passed on to the rest of the organization.

In summary, having the individual act as the discriminator tends to reduce rigid bureaucratic behavior and resistance. However, when extrinsic rewards are involved, it can increase the tendency for invalid data to be produced. This suggests the advisability of having the individual be one of several individuals who act as the discriminator in most situations. A good joint process developed by the person and whoever else is involved should lead to the lowest overall level of dysfunctional behavior.

Recipients of Communication and Source of Motivation

The amount of bureaucratic behavior, strategic behavior, resistance and invalid information present in an organization are all influenced by who receives information from the control system. When information goes to someone (e.g., a superior) who either has or potentially has the power to give extrinsic rewards, rigid bureaucratic behavior, strategic behavior, and invalid data are much more likely to be present. The reason for this is when extrinsic rewards are involved, employees become concerned about looking good on performance measures. Behaving in a rigid bureaucratic or strategic manner and giving invalid data are ways to look good. This follows directly from the motivation theory presented in Chapter 2 and has been shown by a number of studies (Argyris, 1951; Dalton, 1959; Stedry, 1960; Becker and Green, 1962; and Tannenbaum, 1968). It occurs because in some situations individuals perceive that the only way (or best way) to receive the rewards they want is to distort the data used to evaluate them. In these situations, people tend to withhold and distort data that go to individuals who can give them rewards. For example, Read (1959) has documented the tendency of subordinates to withhold information from their superiors. According to his study, managers tend to withhold information about such issues as fights with other units, unforseen costs, rapid changes in production, insufficient equipment, and so on. Read also reports that the tendency to restrict information was most severe among managers who would be classified as being high upward mobiles.

A dramatic example of individuals presenting false data to obtain money is present in the research on the giving of blood (Titmus, 1971). In the United States many blood banks pay donors for blood. In large cities there is also a high incidence of patients coming down with hepatitis after they have received transfusions. The research shows that the incidence of hepatitis is much higher among patients receiving commercial blood than among those receiving free blood. Apparently the blood of paid **103** donors is more likely to be infected than the blood of voluntary donors because blood banks have to rely on their donors to give accurate medical histories to avoid collecting infected blood. And, as Titmus points out:

> . . . it has been repeatedly shown that paid donors—and especially poor donors badly in need of money—are, on the average and compared with voluntary donors, relatives and friends, more reluctant and less likely to reveal a full medical history and to provide information about recent contacts with infectious disease, recent inoculations, and about their diets, drinking and drug habits that would disqualify them as donors (p. 151).

Two recent studies have shown that when superiors use information to create pressure for better performance and to punish poor performance, it is particularly likely to produce dysfunctional behavior (Cammann, 1974b; Hopwood, 1972, 1973, 1974a). In his research, Hopwood has distinguished three distinct ways superiors use budgetary information for appraising the performance of their subordinates.

1. *Budget Constrained Style*

> . . . performance is primarily evaluated upon the basis of ability to continually meet the budget on a short-term basis. This criterion of performance is stressed at the expense of other valued and important criteria and the manager will receive unfavorable feedback from his superior if, for instance, his actual costs exceed the budgeted costs, regardless of other considerations.

2. *Profit Conscious Style*

> . . . performance is evaluated on the basis of ability to increase the general effectiveness of [the] unit's operations in relation to the long-term purposes of the organization. For instance, at the cost center level, one important aspect of this ability concerns the attention which [is devoted] to reducing long-run costs. For this purpose, however, the budgetary information has to be used with great care in a rather flexible manner.

3. *Nonaccounting Style*

> The budgetary information plays a relatively unimportant part in the . . . evaluation of . . . performance (Hopwood, 1973, p. 85).

Hopwood's research shows that:

> While both the Budget Constrained and Profit Conscious styles result in a concern with costs, only the Profit Conscious supervisor achieves this concern without the costly dysfunctional decision making and manipulation of the data. [There were] decisions taken in Budget Constrained departments which resulted in higher processing costs, less innovative behavior and a poorer quality service to the customer, and where the manipulation of the data reduced their usefulness for analytical purposes (Hopwood, 1972, p. 176).

This did not tend to happen in other situations. He also reports that tensions and mistrust are much higher when the Budget Constrained style is used.

Another study has shown that the leadership styles of managers seem to be influenced by the kind of budget pressure they are under from their superiors (DeCoster and Fertakis, 1968). The negative effects of control system pressures are emphasized by Carmichael (1970), who notes how it may actually motivate embezzlement (the ultimate form of invalid data!). This position is supported by Cressey (1953), who relates the following story of a convicted embezzler:

> After one day's business he was approximately $1,000 short in his cash account and was told at the time by . . . the cashier to find the $1,000 before he left the teller's cage of he would lose his job. Defendant says that he checked and rechecked his accounts but was unable to locate the missing money. Consequently, the defendant states he withheld deposit tickets for the day to make up the $1,000 shortage. It was necessary then that he continue withholding deposit tickets at various times to cover the first shortage. After he discovered it was so simple he began withholding deposit tickets and pocketing the difference between the deposit tickets and the actual cash (p. 62).

A further danger created by the idea that strong punishment oriented internal control systems are necessary because employees are immoral, dishonest, or prone to fraud is that the supposition may become a self-fulfilling prophecy. If employees are treated as if they are dishonest and must be constantly watched, they may become motivated to challenge the system and do whatever they can to work around the tight internal control. This may also be counter-productive because the employees are pitted against the organization. McGregor (1967) has concluded that pressure for accountability can easily provide some justification for dishonest behavior. He stated that:

> One fundamental reason control systems often fail and sometimes boomerang is that those who design them fail to understand that an important aspect of human behavior in an organizational setting is that noncompliance tends to appear in the presence of a perceived threat (p. 8).

It is not hard to see why people present invalid data when the information goes to individuals involved in giving extrinsic rewards. They have something to gain. It is not as clear why this happens even when such obvious extrinsic rewards as pay are not directly on the line. The explanation for this lies in the motivation model presented in Chapter 2. It was stressed that behavior is influenced by expectations about what will happen. Any time information goes to someone else there is the potential that it will be used for reward and punishment purposes.

An example is an incident that occurred in a coffee company. For years, corporate headquarters requested weekly production data from its plants. A newly hired operations research analyst decided to use these data to calculate the yields of the different coffee beans the company had been buying. A careful analysis **105** revealed that if the company shifted its bean purchasing pattern, it could decrease its costs. The company followed the advice of the analyst only to find that this caused an immediate production drop at the plants. It seems that for years the plants had been sending headquarters invalid production data to keep from being bothered. Even though there were no pressures on them in this area, they were afraid that there might be, so they reported invalid data. When the data were used to decide which beans to purchase, the result was the purchase of inferior beans.

The amount of resistance to information and control systems is also strongly influenced by who receives information about the results of the discrimination. It has already been stressed that individuals are more likely to accept control systems if they receive the feedback from them. If they act as the discriminator, they will get the feedback directly, but even if someone else acts as the discriminator, they can still give the employees feedback and reduce their tendency to resist. If individuals do get the feedback their need to know can be satisfied by the control system, providing the data are presented in meaningful terms. Naturally, if the installation of a control system offers people something they value (e.g., feedback about performance) they are less likely to resist its installation than if it offers nothing of value. If social comparison theory and psychological success theory are correct and people do value feedback about their performance, then control systems that provide it should be resisted less than those that do not.

Likert (1961, 1967) has pointed out that the amount of resistance to a control system is very much determined by who gets the information. He correctly notes that when the data go to the individual's superior or to others in the organization, resistance to the system is likely to be increased. It is particularly likely to be high if the information is used to determine the level of reward an individual will receive. When rewards are involved, there is the greatest threat to a person's need satisfaction level. However, if the control system does not provide performance data to the superior or to higher levels in the organization, the system may fail to fulfill some of its most important functions, e.g., providing higher levels with the information they need to coordinate and plan the future activities of the organization. Likert, recognizing this dilemma, suggests that superiors be given data only on the performance of the group of people who report to them. Thus, no data on an individual's performance is passed on to a superior; such data go only to the individual, and superiors receive combined data on the performance of all their subordinates.

Likert suggests that a similar pattern could be followed up the hierarchy so that no superior would receive individual data on the performance of his or her subordinates. This should reduce many people's resistance to control systems. However, it also would prevent the use of control system data to reward and punish on an individual basis and this could damage extrinsic motivation. Some sort of individual performance measures are needed to produce extrinsic motivation, unless the organization decides to use a group or company-wide incentive plan. It is also important to note that some people prefer to have their rewards based on their performance (Lawler, 1966) because they feel it allows them to control the rewards they receive and to receive a high level of rewards. They, of course, are likely to resist the kind of approach Likert suggests. Finally, group performance data cannot be used for individual problem solving and career development unless, of course, the individual is willing to share the uncombined data with his or her superior. Thus, Likert's approach should reduce resistance to control systems among some individuals, but with significant costs.

There is evidence that frequently a majority of the workers in an organization prefer to work where pay is based on performance (Lawler, 1971). When asked why they prefer this type of pay system, many of them talk in terms of the kind of control it gives them (Viteles, 1953; Whyte, 1955). Evidence also suggests that the reason many employees do not favor pay incentive plans is that they don't trust management to administer them fairly. It is not that they don't like the control it could give them, rather, they seem to believe that because of the way the plan would be run, it would not give them that control. Thus, it appears that control systems tied into reward systems may, under certain conditions, be sought by most employees rather than resisted by them.

Speed and Frequency of Communication

It is doubtful if either speed of communication or frequency of communication influence the frequency with which rigid bureaucratic behavior, strategic behavior, or the reporting of invalid data occur. One qualification is probably necessary here, however. When rewards are involved it may have an effect. The example of storming by Soviet factory managers cited earlier in this chapter shows that too infrequent use of communications can cause strategic behavior if rewards are involved. In that case, managers tried to correct poor results near the end of the reporting period. The resulting crush was dysfunctional in many ways. More frequent reporting might well have led to a smoother level of work effort and less costly products. Thus, it seems that when communications are too infrequent they can produce strategic behavior if they are used for reward purposes.

Ironically, if communication is very slow and the frequency very inappropriate, it may, under some conditions, decrease the **107** frequency of dysfunctional behavior. The reason for this is that when communication is poor, there is less potential for using the results to give rewards and punishments, and less reason for individuals to behave dysfunctionally.

Frequent rapid communications can lead to reduction in the resistance to information and control systems under certain conditions. As has been stressed, many individuals want valid feedback on their performance and they want it when it is useful to them. An information system that measures their performance quickly and at appropriate time intervals can fulfill this need. Thus, rather than resisting it, they want it.

Type of Activity

The more important an organization considers an activity the more likely measures of it are to be distorted. This relates to Argyris' (1964, 1971) point that organizations have their greatest difficulty gathering data when important issues are involved. It also follows from the fact that organizationally important activities are more likely to make a difference in a person's rewards, and there is greater pressure to look good on those particular measures. This pressure may be generated internally by the person or externally by the organization's reward system. In short, measures of important dimensions are more likely to be distorted because they can make a difference to a person, and therefore, according to motivation theory, there should be more motivation present to distort the measures. The same line of reasoning led to the prediction that important activities are more likely to produce rigid bureaucratic behavior and strategic behavior.

Because they are more likely to be used for reward and punishment purposes, measures of important activities will be resisted by some and supported by others. Those who feel they will gain in terms of extrinsic rewards will, of course, be inclined to support them. Measures of important activities may be sought for other reasons as well. As has been continually stressed, people want feedback on their activities. They particularly want it on the important activities. Thus, an information and control system that gives people information on how they perform an important activity is likely to be welcomed rather than resisted.

In Conclusion

A summary of the major causes of dysfunctional behavior is presented in Table 6–1. This summary is different from those presented at the end of the last two chapters in one important respect. In the cases of intrinsic and extrinsic motivation, there was little doubt about the effects of each of the characteristics. Thus, it

	ALL DYSFUNCTIONAL BEHAVIORS	BUREAUCRATIC BEHAVIOR	STRATEGIC BEHAVIOR	INVALID DATA	RESISTANCE
Characteristics of Sensor	a. Incomplete b. Subjective c. Uninfluenceable	Incomplete Objective Influenceable	--- Objective ---	--- Subjective Uninfluenceable	Complete Subjective Uninfluenceable
Nature of Standard	d. Set by others without participation	Set by others	Set by others	Set by others	Set by others
Source of Discrimination	e. Very difficult f. Superior or Other	Very difficult Superior/Other	Very difficult Superior/Other	Very difficult Self	Very difficult Superior/Other
Recipients of Communication	g. Superior or Other	Superior/Other	Superior/Other	Self	Superior/Other
Speed of Communication **Frequency of Communication**	h. Fast i. Frequency inappropriate	Fast Frequent	Fast Too infrequent	Fast Frequent	Slow Too infrequent
Type of Activity	j. Important	Important	Important	Important	---

TABLE 6-1   Characteristics of Control Systems that Produce Dysfunctional Behavior

was quite clear what was best in terms of motivation. The situation is much more complicated with dysfunctional behavior. As you can see by looking at the last four columns in Table 6–1, the same characteristic that tends to cause one kind of dysfunctional behavior sometimes tends to reduce another. This conflict was taken into account in producing an overall summary of the characteristics that produce the greatest amount of dysfunctional behavior. In constructing the first column in Table 6–1, we considered all the effects of a certain characteristic and reached a decision on what characteristics are likely to produce the greatest amount of dysfunctional behavior. For example, sensors that are incomplete, subjective, and uninfluencable are likely to produce more dysfunctional behavior than ones that are complete, objective, and easy to influence. Completeness and objectivity can, in fact, lead to resistance, but they tend to strongly reduce bureaucratic behavior and thus the conclusion is that overall they lead to less dysfunctional behavior.

BEHAVIOR IN CONTROL SYSTEM JOBS 7

To understand the behavioral impact of information and control systems, it is important that we understand the attitudes and behavior of the individuals who design, maintain, analyze, and perpetuate these systems in organizations. The systems used reflect the nature of these individuals, their jobs, and their feelings about their jobs. Thus, in this chapter we will first consider the nature of the jobs that the individuals have who develop and maintain these systems. Then we will review what is known about the type of people who perform these jobs and finally we will consider the feelings that individuals have about working in jobs that involve information and control system design and maintenance.

CHARACTERISTICS OF THE JOBS

Individuals both inside and outside organizations have jobs that involve working on information and control systems. We will first consider what the internal jobs are like and then we will look at a particular external job, the work of the certified public accountant (CPA), because of its great importance in shaping the nature of internal control systems and the information outsiders receive about the organization. CPAs have this impact for two reasons. First, CPA firms must audit and approve the financial information system in all large business organizations. Second, many information systems are designed by a management specialist from a CPA firm or by someone working closely with the organization's CPA. Thus, the influence of CPAs on information and control systems is significant.

111

Internal Jobs

Internal jobs that involve working on information and control systems normally are part of the staff positions in an organization. The distinction between line and staff jobs is an old one in organization theory but it has never been completely clear. The traditional distinction between line and staff functions is that individuals in line jobs are concerned with the main operations of the organization and function within the direct chain of command from which they derive their authority. Staff jobs are concerned with auxiliary services and provide advice, expertise, and assistance to the line workers and managers. Staff jobs are outside the chain of command and therefore, typically lack formal authority and the power that goes with the authority. The line-staff distinction has led to a great deal of conflict in organizations. There is probably no other area of management which in practice causes more difficulty, friction, and conflict (Koontz and O'Donnell, 1968).

The staff concept has been used by military organizations throughout history. The use of staff in armies dates back to 1500 B.C. when Thothmes set up a form of intelligence service and an administrative system for his command in Egypt. As far back as Thothmes' command, "the military mind had discovered that not even the mentality of a god-descended Pharaoh could successfully command an army without some help in executing the responsibilities of command" (Dale and Urwick, 1960, pp. 78–79). The staff concept continued to be used by other armies, notably the Roman legions and the Crusaders; however, it was not until the latter part of the eighteenth century that the size and complexity of modern armies forced the evolution of a complete staff system. Frederick the Great of Prussia laid down the intellectual foundation for the system around 1765, but it was not until after Napoleon defeated the Prussian army at Jena in 1806 that the Prussian General Staff was reorganized and the movement truly got started. The general staff was originally used to aid and supplement the activities of the army in the field, but it eventually developed into a pool of well-defined staff groups responsible for operations, intelligence, supply, administration, and training.

At first, the staff was used mostly to help the generals handle the vast amount of communication that came to them so that the clearinghouse principle could be maintained. It also helped collect the kind of information the generals needed to make decisions. Next, specialized staffs were formed to provide services to the regular army, and then general staffs were created to help organize the large modern-day armies. Finally, the staff position was seen as a valuable training ground where young officers could see, first hand, the problems of higher command and how these problems were handled by the best leaders.

Today, most organizations have a large number of staff positions because specialized services are needed to keep complex organizations functioning. In this discussion we are primarily concerned with those staff jobs that involve the collection, processing, analysis, and distribution of financial or management information. Keep in mind, however, that these functions represent just one type of staff job. Much of the research has not distinguished between the different types of staff jobs.This creates a problem in describing the kinds of staff jobs we are interested in, but not a serious one. In many ways all staff jobs are the same because they all have the same kind of relationship to the line, one of service. This is true for staff positions in business as well as in the military and government.

It is almost axiomatic that when two groups are created, problems will appear in their relationship with each other. Argyris (1951) provided one of the best examples of a staff/line conflict relative to an information system when he investigated behavioral reactions to budgets. Among other results, Argyris noted that budget pressure may unite the line against the staff and that the finance staff can obtain feelings of success only after finding fault with factory (line) people. Most of the line/staff problems stem from the fact that the staff must work through the line to get their suggestions implemented because they have no formal authority. Their suggestions often are not welcomed by the line and, as a result, the staff people often feel unappreciated and under-utilized. The conflicts between line and staff personnel have led some organization theorists to suggest the virtual elimination of the distinction (Drucker, 1964). At the present time, however, most organizations continue to maintain large staff groups.

The nature of the conflict between line and staff people is clearly shown by the type of criticism they often level at each other. According to line managers, staff people:

1. Are not happy unless they are making changes;
2. See only their little narrow area of expertise and, as a result, make unrealistic recommendations;
3. Are too concerned with techniques and not concerned enough with getting the work done;
4. Often try too hard to sell their ideas;
5. Try to steal credit for things when they go well; and,
6. Often are simply spies for top management.

The other side of the coin is that staff people see line people as:

1. Resistant to change;
2. Overly concerned with their own prerogatives;
3. Unwilling to provide proper recognition;
4. Unwilling to give the staff enough authority; and,
5. Trying to use them as policemen.

113

Finally, line and staff managers often criticize each other for failing to provide adequate and accurate information to one another.

As these points illustrate the relationship between the line and staff usually involves tension. As a result of this tension, staff jobs typically involve dealing with conflict and political behaviors. This aspect of staff jobs seems to be reflected in a research study done by Porter (1964) on the nature of staff jobs. He had 1,786 managers describe their jobs. They were then classified as holding line, combined line-staff, or staff jobs. Each manager ranked ten traits in terms of how important they were for determining success in his or her position. Table 7–1 presents the results. As can be seen from the table, staff managers said that other-directed behavior was more important than did line managers although both rated inner-directed as most important. These ratings probably reflect the fact that staff people have to get things done through the line organizations and that this requires them to be cooperative.

A recent study by Browne and Golembiewski (1974) has also collected data on the differences between line and staff jobs. The results show that, as might be expected from our discussion so far, staff jobs are seen as lower in esteem and power and higher in centrality. Research studies on communication in organizations (Davis, 1953; Bruns, 1965) provide further data on the centrality of staff positions. These studies show that staff people receive information sooner and spread it faster. This result was attributed to the staffs' greater physical mobility and to its contacts all along the line from top management to the first line of supervision. A

TABLE 7–1
Mean Importance of Traits for Job Success by Type of Position

Trait	TYPE OF POSITION		
	Line (N = 507)	Combined Line-Staff (N = 492)	Staff (N = 684)
INNER-DIRECTED			
Forceful	4.55	3.90	3.70
Imaginative	6.62	6.67	6.76
Independent	2.38	2.50	2.61
Self-Confident	5.70	5.57	5.43
Decisive	6.49	5.84	5.49
TOTAL FOR CLUSTER	25.74	24.48	23.99
OTHER-DIRECTED			
Cooperative	5.45	5.77	5.73
Adaptable	4.98	5.05	5.03
Cautious	1.06	1.42	1.45
Agreeable	2.53	2.79	2.95
Tactful	5.26	5.51	5.85
TOTAL FOR CLUSTER	19.28	20.54	21.01

Note: Higher numbers indicate greater importance.

L. W. Porter and M. M. Henry, "Perceptions of the Importance of Certain Personality Traits as a Function of Line Versus Staff Type of Job," Journal of Applied Psychology, 48 (1964), p. 307. Copyright 1960 by the American Psychological Association. Reprinted by permission.

good illustration of this point and of the role of staff jobs is provided by the controller's function. In most organizations it is large and impacts on all parts of the organization. A recent study reports that in an organization with sales of $375 million a year, the controller function had an operating budget of $20 million and in another organization with sales of $200 million a budget of $12 million (Livingstone and Sathe, 1975). A good guess is that, in most organizations, just the operations of the controller function take about 5 percent of every sales dollar. Thus the controller function is an expensive operation in its own right, but perhaps its biggest impact on costs comes through its influence on the behavior of line members.

Accountants in the controller function perform several different tasks concerned with the timely processing of financial information. Their duties may include accumulating and processing financial data into the information system, auditing as internal auditors some of the expense reports and work of others, developing cost accounting standards, preparing financial budgets, and controlling and analyzing the accounting reports that emerge from the information system. These staff positions may be titled accountant, chief accountant, comptroller, treasurer, or financial vice-president. Although accountants in industry are not required to be certified public accountants, the individuals in the most important financial positions—the comptrollers, treasurers, and financial vice-presidents—are often CPAs. This is due to the tremendous amount of personnel migration from CPA firms to industrial accounting. Accountants usually migrate to an internal accounting position after approximately three to six years of public accounting experience. A similar trend also often occurs among information system specialists who work for consulting firms.

Because of their frequent contacts with external auditors, internal accountants experience considerable conflict. Studies of role conflict have found that positions deep within an organizational structure are subject to less conflict than those near the boundary (Katz and Kahn, 1966). Thus, individuals who have the greatest amount of public contact representing the organization in such activities as selling or preparing accounting reports for distribution outside the organization, face more conflict than do, say, the manufacturing foremen.

Often the emphasis on control and asset surveillance in the controller's function has a decided impact on the nature of the jobs that individuals inside the system have. The procedures for handling financial information in most organizations are designed primarily to provide information and prevent fraud and theft. The result is that people may end up with boring, highly repetitive jobs. For instance, a study of a large company's purchasing de- **115** partment showed that the jobs had been designed in a way that was low on variety, autonomy, feedback, and task identity in order to satisfy the requirements for internal control. In this situation the employees who handled payments to vendors were not allowed to talk to the vendors and each employee handled only a small part of the operations necessary to pay vendors for their materials. When the jobs were redesigned by the employees to make them more interesting (a single employee handled all work for a given vendor) errors dropped by over 30 percent. In another group doing similar work, the jobs were redesigned by the manager and errors dropped by about 10 percent. This study shows the advantage of employee participation in job redesign, and it shows that sometimes preoccupation with internal control procedures can lead to an increase in the number of errors. It may make theft more difficult, but if the side effect is poor employee performance, the cost may be too high.

In summary, the research that has tried to define the nature of staff jobs presents a picture congruent with how the jobs are usually described by organization theorists. Staff jobs appear to have little formal authority attached to them, to require good political skills, to be a center for information and communication, to involve intergroup conflicts with the members of the line organization, to require expertise in speciality areas that are important to the functioning of the organization, and to provide access to a number of different parts of the organization.

External Jobs: The Certified Public Accountants and Management Advisory System Specialists

The kinds of information and control systems organizations have are influenced by people outside as well as by those inside the organization. In the financial area, certified public accountants play a particularly crucial role. The kind of auditing procedures they set up have much to do with how the internal systems in organizations must operate and the kind of decisions they make influence the kind of information outsiders receive. The CPA's audit checklist, for example, can strongly influence the flow of financial resources and information in a business organization. External auditors like internal accountants also have a kind of staff position, but it is a different kind of job. The nature of their work involves both stewardship and surveillance. This presents conflicts for the CPA. The model presented in Figure 7–1 indicates four forms of pressure for CPAs: financial, regulatory or legal, personnel, and professional.

The financial pressure must be first satisfied or else the CPA, for want of revenues, will no longer be able to operate. If the CPA doesn't have clients to audit, then he or she is soon out

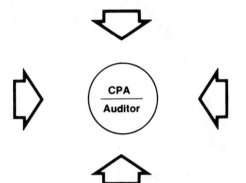

Regulatory or legal forces:

Internal Revenue Service; Securities and Exchange Commission; state, county and municipal reporting authorities; Cost Accounting Standards Board.

Financial forces:

Client preservation

CPA
Auditor

Personnel forces:

Staff maintenance

Professional and Ethical Forces:

AICPA; Accounting Principles Board opinions; Financial Executives Institute; Financial Accounting Standards Board; State Boards of Accountancy.

FIGURE 7-1
The Accountant's
Pressure Sources

of business. This means that, although the CPA should be primarily concerned with an independent appraisal of the control system and resulting financial reports, the CPA has more than a casual interest in seeing that his or her clients are financially successful. Ideally, the client should be a success and the CPA should be independent. However, these attributes may be in conflict, and this can create pressure-laden problems for the CPA.

The CPA may also experience pressure in maintaining clients. Clients may prefer to state their accounting reports differently than the CPA would like to state them. Does the CPA hold a professional line and demand that the client give in—especially at the possible loss of the client to a more compliant CPA? Or, does the CPA acquiesce and give in to the client? The question will probably be decided as a function of two variables; the personal ethics of the CPA and the financial importance of keeping the client. The CPA's pressure really doesn't end here though, because legal and professional forces still exert a considerable amount of influence. These financial forces can potentially create

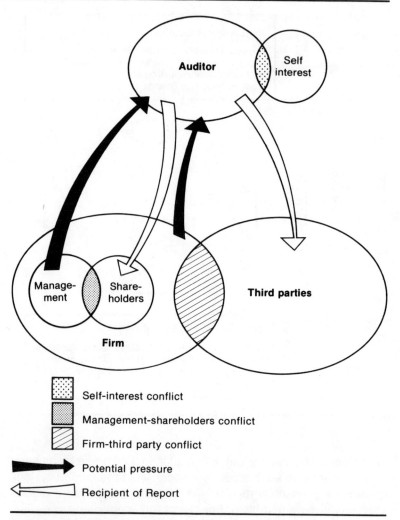

Self-interest conflict

Management-shareholders conflict

Firm-third party conflict

Potential pressure

Recipient of Report

FIGURE 7–2
Diagram of a
Conflict Model

From A. Goldman and B. Barlev, "The Auditor—Firm Conflict of Interests: Its Implications for Independence," *The Accounting Review,* 49 (4) October 1974, p. 710.

a severe conflict of interest in the auditing role of a CPA. As part of their extensive analysis of the auditor's conflict situation, Goldman and Barlev (1974) diagramatically describe a conflict model (Figure 7–2) and also present a behavioral model of a CPA's independence (Figure 7–3). Goldman and Barlev conclude that there is a power asymmetry in favor of the client and that pressures to violate the professional rules of conduct for CPAs are inherent in the client-CPA relationship. Under the present system whereby management selects and compensates the CPA who audits its records, the inherent pressure and conflict described by Goldman **118** and Barlev is likely to continue.

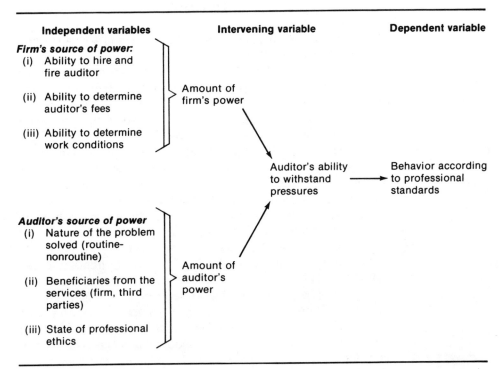

Independent variables	Intervening variable	Dependent variable

Firm's source of power:
(i) Ability to hire and fire auditor

(ii) Ability to determine auditor's fees

(iii) Ability to determine work conditions

Amount of firm's power

Auditor's ability to withstand pressures → Behavior according to professional standards

Auditor's source of power
(i) Nature of the problem solved (routine-nonroutine)

(ii) Beneficiaries from the services (firm, third parties)

(iii) State of professional ethics

Amount of auditor's power

From A. Goldman and B. Barlev, "The Auditor—Firm Conflict of Interests: Its Implications for Independence," *The Accounting Review*, 49 (4) October 1974, p. 712.

FIGURE 7–3
Behavioral Model of
Independence

The regulatory or legal forces also exert a pressure to be professionally or educationally current with professional accounting's guidelines and rules. These guidelines, once mastered, reduce somewhat the client-generated pressures for other than ordinary accounting reports since CPAs can stand firm on the basis of the law and attendant reporting requirements from regulatory authorities. There really is only one way to satisfy the regulatory reporting requirements and that is by strict adherence to the law. Any deviance, if detected, is highly detrimental to both the CPAs and their clients. Consequently, legal compliance can become a highly forceful form of assistance in reducing client pressures for inappropriate accounting or reporting.

While not having the impact of a statute or law, the reporting recommendations of the CPA's professional and ethical organizations, like the American Institute of Certified Public Accountants (AICPA), still present an important source of pressure or influence. The most severe punitive measure that the AICPA can exert against a member CPA for failure to follow professional reporting and auditing guidelines is to terminate membership in the AICPA. There are no fines, no restrictions on practice, just simply a delisting of membership. Nonetheless, this potentially embarrassing situation will cause most CPAs to remain highly aware of AICPA **119** reporting requirements and recommendations and will cause them to ensure that their clients comply with them.

If a CPA should find that a major client does not comply with a ruling of the Accounting Principles Board (APB) or of the Financial Accounting Standards Board (FASB), the SEC may issue an order for that client's corporate securities to be taken off the active trading lists at the various stock exchanges. This possibility is an extremely powerful force in bringing about compliance, and again serves to keep clients with unsanctioned alternative reporting intentions in line. The remaining professional and ethical forces, the Financial Executives Institute (FEI) and the State Board of Accountancy, are either sanctionless (FEI) or serve to legally monitor the admission and continuing licensing requirements for practice as a CPA. The state boards of accountancy follow, for the most part, the guidelines of the AICPA but differ from the AICPA in that the boards can take away a CPA's license to practice.

These groups represent the primary external forms of pressure on CPAs. There is a fourth and highly impactive internal pressure—that of personnel or staff maintenance. CPAs must be attentive to the needs of their staff accountants since it is the staff that performs the audit work that generates the revenues necessary to maintain the economic vitality of the CPA firm. Stories and rumors abound about long hours for staff during the winter months of the accounting busy season, travel on one's own time, and CPA firm preference for client concerns before those of the staff.

A CPA who continuously audits the financial affairs of others must maintain an impeccable set of social and financial credentials because to do otherwise would cast doubt on the validity or thoroughness of the audit and professional accounting work. To be above reproach and so pure of personal or financial inquiry requires, for the most part, very cautious and conservative personal behavior.

Another factor that needs to be understood in looking at the role of CPAs is the nature of the reward system for their work. When they do their job well it is an expected result. Consequently, the immediate reward is seldom substantial. Indeed, most major CPA firms administer at most one major review of performance each year. As a result, the amount of feedback on performance may be less than desired. Yet, if the accounting work is not done particularly well, the punishment is rather immediate. Non-partners may, at the extreme, be discharged, and at a minimum, receive a verbal dressing down. Consequently, the CPA firm employee operates within a negative sanction environment. Auditors hear more frequently and much louder about what they have done wrong than what they have done well. A system like this is more likely to produce defensive, or do-the-job-as-it-was-done-last-year behavior than it is to motivate imaginative or progressive behavior. This conditioned negative sanction reward system may even stay with CPAs when they leave public accounting for positions in industry. Consequently, they encourage a defensive or conservative work atmosphere if they supervise industrial internal control systems.

While performing their audit work, CPAs have little contact with the general public. Their personal contact usually is limited almost entirely to a few staff people within the organization they are auditing and, for the partners, to members of a board of directors. Also, other then presenting the outcome of the Oscar balloting, CPAs typically have extremely limited exposure through national media. For example, the F. Lee Bailey or Christian Barnard of the CPA profession does not readily come to mind. As professional persons, CPAs unlike lawyers and especially doctors, never have much personal contact with many of the people directly affected by their work.

For example, contrast the contact that a person who wants to invest in General Motors Corporation would have with the CPA partner responsible for the audit of General Motors with the contact that person would have with his or her doctor. The doctor and CPA both perform a useful function for the investor, in the form of health, property and investment protection, yet contact with the CPA is rarely made. People regularly see their doctors but the CPA auditing their financial holdings, is, for the most part, unknown.

The depersonalized professional relationship with shareholders who receive CPA's financial statements also permeates through to the financial control systems they audit. The primary concern of most information systems is control and asset surveillance, not the reactions of individuals to the control system. This means that the CPA, often designated as a management information system specialist, who designs a control system is no closer to the persons subjected to the system than CPAs are to the people who receive certified annual reports based on the audit of their corporate holdings. This contact removal allows the CPA a certain amount of charisma because the persons subject to the control system know very little about the CPA who set the system into operation.

While a CPA always audits the control system to ensure that it is operating correctly, the design of the system is likely to come from a management information system specialist who is often a CPA and may be a member of the CPA firm auditing the system. Information systems are usually designed by specialists in systems design. These individuals are typically MIS experts who work in **121** close association with the corporation's chief financial person-nel—the comptroller, treasurer, and financial vice president. The MIS specialists, since they frequently are employed by CPA firms, experience many of the same work pressures and possess most of the same traits and characteristics as CPAs who audit the sys-tems.

One additional pressure that leans CPAs toward conservative behavior follows from the nature of their practice. If a CPA certifies an incorrect financial statement and third parties suffer financial hardship as a result of relying on the statement, the CPA, together with the corporation, is subject to a law suit from the damaged parties. And, since all of the large CPA firms are organized as partnerships rather than as corporations, the CPA partners are liable for considerably more in damages than the total of their investment equity in the CPA firm. They can be sued for their personal estates if the judgment so determines. This virtually unlimited professional liability can be a strong motivating factor toward conservative behavior. Cautious auditing becomes not only a virtue, but a necessity. Most importantly, a CPA cannot be shield-ed from the jeopardy of a suit if a junior staff member missed the error rather than a partner. All financial statements are attested to in the name of the partnership and all partners are liable for the fairness of the financial statements. Staff members may be dis-charged for improper behavior, but the partnership cannot escape the legal liability for the work of its staff accountants. An article in The Wall Street Journal (1975) revealed that the Securities and Exchange Commission (SEC) emphasizes that lawyers, accoun-tants and others hired to advise corporations must serve as the first line of defense against management fraud. Consequently, the SEC believes that even if a company's management deceives brokerage firms, accountants, and outside directors, the act of deception will not remove their legal jeopardy. Liability of this nature will likely promulgate conservative behavior among CPAs. To act otherwise could be financially disastrous.

Small CPA firms have recently started to incorporate them-selves as professional service corporations rather than as part-nerships. This form of business structure does not lessen the potential liability for principals of the firm since limited liability with respect to professional issues lawsuits is not available to profes-sional service corporations. It may, however, provide for more flexible organization (Buckley and Buckley, 1974), and that could have the effect of reducing the pressure on CPAs to engage in conservative behavior. But it may not. The work role of a CPA may be so powerful a motivation for conservative behavior that legal form for the business of being a CPA may make little difference.

122

CHARACTERISTICS OF INDIVIDUALS

Now that we have looked at the nature of the internal and external jobs associated with information and control systems we are in a position to consider what kind of individuals take these jobs. Fortunately, some research has focused on this issue. Much of it has been concerned with the accountant. The accountant is an ideal focus for our purposes since as has been noted he or she has a central role in the establishment and maintenance of the financial information and control systems in organizations. Based on Bureau of Census (1970) data, there are some 714,120 accountants in the United States. CPAs comprise approximately 119,000 of the total as indicated in Table 7–2.

Occupation	Number	Percent
Public Accounting	73,304	61.6
Business and Industry	37,247	31.3
Government	4,522	3.8
Education	3,972	3.3
TOTALS	119,045	100.0

TABLE 7–2
Jobs of
Accountants

We will be concerned primarily with certified public accountants because of the important jobs they hold. Their careers are usually a matter of staying in public accounting and auditing control systems or leaving public accounting primarily for financial executive positions in industry where they design, maintain, and interpret control systems. With the possibility that the two years public accounting experience requirement for a CPA license may be dropped (AICPA, 1969) and since the National Association of Accountants has established the Certified Management Accountant certificate (CMA, 1973), it is likely that in the future, accountants seeking careers in industry will no longer go through CPA firms for a period of years. Yet, until these developments become effective, the primary financial positions in organizations will likely be staffed by former practicing CPAs. The accountants who gather and process financial data into the information system are not usually CPAs, but the comptrollers and treasurers who analyze the information reports and determine what sort of reports the information system should produce are typically CPAs and probably will be—at least in the near future.

Characteristics of Staff Employees

A few studies have found background differences between line employees and staff employees. They are informative in that some of the differences help to explain the conflicts that often exist **123** between line and staff employees. Three studies have compared line and staff employees in terms of how important they say various job factors are to them. Rosen and Weaver (1960) found that managers in line and staff positions did not differ in their ratings of the importance of twenty-four desirable working conditions. Another study found no differences between line and staff managers in the importance attached to pay. Porter (1963) found that there were no line-staff differences in the importance attached to four of five need areas studied. However, staff employees rated the fifth need area, autonomy, more important.

In a classic study, Dalton (1959) compared the attitudes of line and staff employees. The results were interesting and congruent with the finding that staff employees value autonomy more than do line employees. The data showed that the staff managers, assistants, and specialists had higher levels of education, were younger, and had spent less time with the company. Dalton also found that the staff people came from a different socioeconomic background. They tended to come from families of higher class and more wealth. It is important to be cautious in drawing conclusions from Dalton's work since it is based on only one company; however, the results do fit nicely with previous studies. For example, the younger age and higher education levels of the staff employees fits well with and helps explain the finding of stronger autonomy needs. Younger and particularly better-educated people do have stronger autonomy needs. The results also help to put the stress between line and staff members into clearer perspective. It is not hard to see that in many cases conflicts involving business decisions might be fueled by the background difference of the two groups. The line-staff situation is ripe for some conflict because of the way the jobs are defined; differences in such important things as age, educational level, and background can only serve to increase the chances of conflict. Dalton, for example, talks of line managers referring to staff employees as college punks, naive, and impatient. Line managers on the other hand were referred to as conservative old men and uninformed.

What Are Certified Public Accountants Really Like?

What sort of image does a CPA have? Becker (1969), in a light mood, described them as most likely to straighten a picture in a house as a visitor. A survey of manufacturing executives once described CPAs as having lots of ability—in a very limited direction (Roper and Associates, 1963). While this is primarily a positive assessment, not all evaluations of public accountants are so complimentary. From a survey of 1,000 randomly selected Chicago and Cleveland citizens, Solomon (1970) reports that 91 percent of the women and 96 percent of the men considered medicine and law to be professions while only 23 percent of the women and 27 percent of the men considered CPAs professionals. Moreover, a noted psychologist (Maslow, 1961) further reduced the accountants' image by labeling them as obsessional, interested in small details, tradition bound, and noncreative.

A study of attitudes describing the accountants image at private and public arts and science colleges found that the private school students label accountants as low in status, conforming, lacking social skills and aesthetic sensibilities, passive, weak, shallow, cold, submissive, and evasive (O'Dowd and Beardslee, 1960). Although the attitudes of state university students were somewhat kinder to accountants, the image description remained relatively unattractive. Moreover an anthology by Newgarden (1969) presents an interesting literature-based summary of accountants that tends to corroborate the image statements of the undergraduate students surveyed.

Perhaps the most widely quoted description of accountants is one originally written for buyers, not accountants, but it has been so often used to describe the typical auditor it is worth mentioning for its contribution to the image of CPAs.

> . . . a man past middle life, tall, spare, wrinkled, intelligent, cold, passive, noncommital, with eyes like a codfish, polite in contact but at the same time unresponsive, cool, calm, and as dammably composed as a concrete post or a plaster-of-paris cat; a human petrification with a heart of feldspar, and without charm of the friendly germ; minus bowels, passion, or a sense of humor. Happily they never reproduce, and all of them finally go to Hell (Hubbard, 1922).

As Newgarden (1970) has noted, this image of buyers—extrapolated to describe auditors—appeared recently in a leading AICPA publication to indicate that CPAs lament, but have not abandoned, the idea that the green eyeshade is still worn by professional auditors (Rea, 1968).

In summary there is considerable evidence that the public has a stereotype of accountants. This stereotype contains several attributes connoting a negative demeanor like coldness, aloofness, nonsociability, submissiveness, shallowness, weakness, and insensitivity. This stereotype, whether accurate or not, is of concern to CPAs because it may be detrimental to recruiting the sort of person to the CPA profession who is most capable of dissipating the negative image of CPAs (Ashworth, 1968, 1969a, 1969b).

While it is beneficial to know that there is a stereotype for CPAs and what their image is, it is more meaningful, when attempting to understand the characteristics of CPAs, if we separate the data-free or rumor-based images of CPAs from research findings on their personal characteristics. In an attempt to determine the stereotypes' validity, DeCoster and Rhode (1971) compared the **125**

personality test scores of CPAs with other professional and occupational groups. Their sample included partners, managers, and
staff accountants from the largest national CPA firms. The comparisons revealed that CPA firm employees had higher, or more desirable personality profiles when contrasted with salesmen, bank
managers, business executives, city school superintendents, ar-
chitects, and military officers. These findings partially deny the
validity of the accountants' stereotype as dull, wary, cold, and
aloof. When compared to the practicing dentists and research
scientists, the CPA firm employees scored somewhat lower. These
scores demonstrated a slightly less desirable personality set that
might be accounted for by the considerably more extensive education of dentists and scientists. The CPA firm employees scored
considerably higher than their comparison groups on the sociabi-
lity, self-acceptance, socialization, self-control, good impression,
psychological-mindedness, and flexibility scales. Thus, the study
results indicate that the accountants' stereotype may not only be
unwarranted, it may also be completely inappropriate—at least for
the group studied.

While this study did not find data-based support for the negative image of CPAs, it did identify substantial differences between
the staff accountants, managers, and partners of the CPA firms
surveyed. The staff accountants and managers had higher, or
more desirable personality scale mean scores than the partners.
This may be due to the partners having entered public accounting
years ago when CPAs were more introverted and conservative.
Or, the CPA profession and its younger members may have simply
moved in a more liberal direction. Whatever the reason, the fact
is that the personality test score data indicate that the partners
are considerably different personality types—more conservative
and inflexible.

Since the partners, not the staff accountants and managers,
are the CPA firm representatives who make the major policy decisions that affect how the public views the accounting profession
and how control systems are established and utilized in organizations, we should pay particular attention to the inflexible and conservative partners' personalities. They hold the decision-making
power in the CPA firm—both for audit and management advisory
service work. In addition, because the major public accounting
firms adhere to an internal promotion policy of up or out, the
only permanent positions are those of partner. All staff accountants and managers have temporary positions. Either they become
partners or they eventually leave the CPA firm. And since the
partners displayed a lower variability of personality test scores
when contrasted with the staff accountants and managers, there

is some evidence to support the notion that to become a partner you have to be like a partner—particularly in terms of personality, demeanor and ability.

In many ways this difference in personalities is consonant with the findings of Sorensen (1967). He contrasted the bureaucratic and professional orientations of partners and staff accountants in several national CPA firms. While not explicitly defining bureaucratic and professional orientations, Sorensen offers examples of the values and beliefs that characterize the two orientations. These are reproduced in Figure 7–4.

The data in Table 7–3 also show that partners are the most bureaucratic and the least professionally oriented of any of the groups Sorensen analyzed. Their profile, in a personality sense, appears to emphasize control and inflexibility rather than authority from competence or initiative based on creativity.

Given that partners are the only persons in CPA firms holding tenured positions, it is likely that the findings of Sorensen will apply for some time if not increase in intensity over time. There is already some evidence that the bureaucratic orientation of junior accountants has decreased and their professional orientation has increased while the orientation for partners has remained the same over time (Sorensen, 1970; Sorensen and Sorensen, 1972). This means that the differences in attitudes that existed between partners and staff in Sorensen's (1967) early study have now increased. The partners held on to their bureaucratic and professional orientations while the junior staff accountants became less bureaucratic and more professional. Further evidence of a generation gap between public accounting partners and staff was presented in a more recent study (Sorensen, Rhode and Lawler, 1973).

Some indication of how the personality types of financial executives affect their financial decision making is provided by a study of how corporate personality is reflected in accounting decisions (Sorter and Becker 1964). To test their thesis that a corporate

Position	Average Orientation Scores*,**	
	Bureaucratic	Professional
Partners (N = 37)	151.3	144.0
Managers (N = 48)	148.1	148.0
Seniors (N = 95)	139.4	150.5
Juniors (N = 84)	133.7	152.6

TABLE 7–3
Professional and Bureaucratic Orientations by Position

*Higher score means higher orientation.
**F ratios were statistically significant (P<.01); t tests between non-adjacent positions were statistically significant (P<.01).

From J. E. Sorensen, "Professional and Bureaucratic Organization in Large Public Accounting Firms," *The Accounting Review*, 39 (3) July 1967, p. 558.

BUREAUCRATIC		PROFESSIONAL
High ◄─────► High		High ◄─────► Low

I. AUTHORITY

A. Basis of Authority

BUREAUCRATIC	PROFESSIONAL
1. Rules sanctioned by organizational hierarchy	1. Rules sanctioned by powerful and legally created professions
2. Authority from office	2. Authority from personal competence

B. Use of Knowledge in Decision Making

BUREAUCRATIC	PROFESSIONAL
3. Decisions applying rules to routine problems	3. Decision relating to professional policy and unique problems

C. Direction of Loyalty

BUREAUCRATIC	PROFESSIONAL
4. Loyalty to organization and superiors	4. Loyalty to professional colleagues, clients, and community

II. STANDARDIZATION

A. Approach to the Problem

BUREAUCRATIC	PROFESSIONAL
1. Emphasis on uniformity; client's problems; personnel	1. Emphasis on uniqueness; client's problems; personnel

B. Latitude of Rules

BUREAUCRATIC	PROFESSIONAL
2. Rules stated as categoricals/specifics	2. Rules stated as alternatives/multiples

C. Initiative in Work

BUREAUCRATIC	PROFESSIONAL
3. Emphasis on stability (e.g. records and files)	3. Emphasis on creativity (e.g. research, change)

III. SPECIALIZATION

A. Functional Objective

BUREAUCRATIC	PROFESSIONAL
1. Efficiency of technique for specific task	1. Satisfaction of specific client needs

B. Depth and Breadth of Knowledge

BUREAUCRATIC	PROFESSIONAL
2. Specific tasks based primarily on practice of narrow range of technical skills	2. Variety of activities based primarily on generalized knowledge

From J. E. Sorensen, "Professional and Bureaucratic Organization in Large Public Accounting Firms," *The Accounting Review*, 39 (3) July 1967, p. 555.

FIGURE 7–4 Professional and Bureaucratic Organizational Models Contrasted

personality exists that influences corporate decisions on accounting and financial reports, Sorter and Becker administered a psychological test to the chief financial officer in some 150 of the U.S. corporations listed in *Fortune's 500* (1961) and *Accounting Trends and Techniques* (1961). The results were rather interesting in that the psychological attitudes concerned with rigidity and tolerance for ambiguity were all in the direction predicted by whether or not a corporation used conservative (intolerant of ambiguity) policy decisions for reporting depreciation on financial statements. Financial decision makers with conservative personality scores were found to be employed by corporations with conservative depreciation reporting policies. This means that the financial control system for a corporation is demonstrably not isolated from the personality of the CPAs or financial officers who design, maintain, and use the system. While we have touched on selected aspects of the CPA's working environment, a more intensive summary of the accounting profession is given by Buckley and Buckley (1974).

In Conclusion

The studies reviewed show some clear differences between staff and line employees and between CPAs and the rest of the population. The studies do not clearly establish why these differences exist but it is a good bet that one reason is because staff jobs and public accounting jobs attract and select a certain kind of employee. For example, the finding that staff employees are younger and better educated can best be explained by the kind of selection and placement decisions organizations make. The differences are also probably due to the impact of the jobs on the people. As was pointed out, the pressures generated by jobs are very strong and do shape the people who take them. For example, the job of a CPA has tremendous pressures toward conservatism and thus it is not surprising that the personality data suggest that senior CPAs tend to be conservative and bureaucratic. Unfortunately, we lack studies that compare the personalities of individuals who work for CPA firms with those who work in staff jobs, so it is difficult to draw any strong conclusions about the differences between them. However, they do seem to be somewhat different. The more senior CPAs appear to be conservative and bureaucratic, while the staff employees value autonomy and are young and impatient. One thing seems clear, they both hold jobs that are low on line authority, that require interpersonal and political skills in order to make things happen, and that demand considerable education and technical information to carry out their assignments. **129**

ATTITUDES AND BEHAVIOR IN CONTROL SYSTEM JOBS

Now that we have considered the nature of the jobs associated with information and control systems as well as the nature of the people who fill these jobs, we are in a position to consider what the people in these jobs do, think, and feel. We will start by looking at those people who work within organizations and then turn to a consideration of CPAs.

Staff Employees

Several studies have looked at the kind of satisfaction staff jobs provide. The results are not surprising now that we know the nature of the jobs and the people who fill them. It follows that staff employees should be more dissatisfied than line managers in their jobs given that they have less power and status but similar needs. The results of studies by Porter (1963) and Rosen (1961a,b) show just this. In Rosen's study, for example, staff managers report particularly high dissatisfaction in the areas of decision making and implementation; they felt frustrated because they could not make decisions and get them implemented. Porter found that staff managers in comparison to line managers were particularly dissatisfied with respect to esteem.

It seems quite likely that staff people who work with financial information and control systems may be even more dissatisfied than other staff employees. They have the same problems as other staff employees (e.g., low formal authority) plus some others. They have more outside pressures to deal with because they are subject to audits by outside CPAs. This puts severe limitations on the kind of internal practices they can adopt and it means that most changes they make have to be approved by an outside group. This, of course, makes change very difficult—particularly when the outside group tends to behave conservatively.

One somewhat positive effect of the conservatism of the CPA profession for the staff person is that he or she is seldom forced to revise the company's system because of some outside requirement. The negative effect, which may outweigh the positive, is that it places the internal people in a difficult position when they want to introduce change unless the change is designed to bring the internal system in line with generally accepted internal control procedures.

It also seems likely that staff people who hold jobs involving financial matters probably behave more conservatively than people in other staff jobs. Like the CPA, they are in a stewardship position and all the rewards in their positions are tied to not making an error and to preventing fraud. This leads them to build systems full of checks and balances that are not easily changed. Change

130

often is the enemy of an effective system because it may open a loophole for either fraud or error. As a result, every change needs to be carefully scrutinized.

How do staff employees deal with the lack of formal authority in their positions? As may be predicted, one thing they do is quit. Dalton (1959) in his study looked at the relative turnover rates of staff and line managers. He found that staff employees had more than twice the turnover rate of line employees. This is not surprising given their lower satisfaction level and the casual relationship between satisfaction and turnover.

Those who don't quit or resign themselves to impotency use power other than that derived from formal authority. Social psychologists have identified five types of power (see French and Raven, 1959):

1. Reward Power, based on the ability of the person to administer valued rewards;
2. Coercive Power, based on negatively valued rewards;
3. Legitimate Power, based upon a role or position that has been established as having authority;
4. Referent Power, based on becoming close to or maintaining a closeness with an attractive person; and
5. Expert Power, based upon information.

People in staff positions have relatively little legitimate power and the organization usually does not give them many rewards and punishments to administer. This is not always true since some staff employees are able to control rewards and punishments through their membership in top management. When this occurs, as it does with advanced computerized MIS, staff people can be quite powerful, but this is rare. They also can sometimes influence rewards by how they set up their systems and process the data in them. In some cases different variations of the same system can make line employees look better or worse. Referent power is difficult for them to use because they are often different from line managers and not particularly attractive to them. Here, too, there are exceptions. Some staff people succeed quite well in presenting a very attractive image of the bright young person on the way up in the organization. Still, if most staff employees are to get things done they usually have to rely on the expert power they have because of their unique access to information. Even the use of this kind of power can produce conflict. As was noted earlier in this chapter, the relationship between line and staff employees in most organizations is one characterized by mistrust, stereotyping, and conflict.

Pettigrew (1973) has done an interesting study of the way employees with information system jobs in one organization used their expert power to influence decisions. The particular decision **131** he focused on was the purchase of a new computer. The experts in this case were divided on which kind of computer to buy. The different factions used all kinds of strategies to influence top management's decisions. They withheld information, they stressed the technical advantages of some machines over others and they even relied on friendship and referent power. Much of this was possible because top management was not technically competent to evaluate the different machines and had to rely on their staff people.

This study also points out how the expert power of people in staff positions can influence many decisions. The staff people in this situation were charged with building computer information systems to do such things as maintain inventories. Because they designed the systems and were the only ones who knew how they operated, these staff people had a lot of influence over what kind of decisions were made and indeed over how the organization was run.

The situation studied by Pettigrew is not an unusual one. In most situations employees who work on information and control systems have influence because of their expertise. As will be discussed in the next chapter, they influence many decisions by the kind of systems they develop, by the kind of information they report and do not report, and by the form in which they report information. The problem from their point of view is that they only influence decisions, they don't make them.

CPAs

The data on the personalities of CPAs as well as our analysis of the pressure in a CPA job point to a common prediction about what their behavior should be. In a word it should be conservative. It is hard to cite quantitative data to support the conclusion that the behavior of CPAs is conservative, but most people who have studied the field conclude it is. The emphasis in most CPA firms seems to be on holding on to all clients even if they compromise the practice. Although firms sometimes change their auditors, an analysis of audit-client concentrations (Rhode, Whitsell, and Kelsey, 1974) indicates that these concentrations are quite stable over several years. Most CPA firms follow a pattern of treating their staff as they always have, few have a well-developed personnel function nor have they tried using paraprofessionals, job enrichment, or other innovations in organization and job design. Furthermore, the emphasis in all CPA firms is on following the same work pattern that has been followed in the past. Stated succinctly, the emphasis is on consistency not innovation. New and authoritative accounting principles are rarely formulated and **132** indeed dissatisfaction with the lack of progress in this area eventually led to the elimination of the Accounting Principles Board. Finally, most firms have maintained a low personal profile and have done everything they can to avoid public exposure. For example, tradition has argued against CPA firms issuing public annual statements on their own firms and taking positions on public issues and this tradition has been maintained by most large CPA firms.

The conservatism of CPA firms and of their senior members, of course, has its costs. One of these seems to be a high turnover among the younger employees. The figures vary but somewhere around 50 percent of all newly hired CPAs leave their original job before five years are over. Part of this is due to the traditional and rigidly maintained up or out policy of most firms. However, some of it is due to dissatisfaction of the employees. In a study to determine causes of professional staff turnover in public accounting firms, Rhode, Hamlin, Lawler, and Sorensen (1973) gathered data on what staff accountants like best and least about their professional work. The responses, obtained from a national survey of entry-level staff accountants and reproduced in Tables 7–4 and 7–5, give an indication of how they feel about their jobs.

Reading Tables 7–4 and 7–5 gives a good picture of what the jobs are and are not like. The CPAs most enjoy the learning experiences, contact with different accounting systems, challenge of their work and accompanying responsibility together with the opportunity to work with high calibre colleagues and clients. They do not like the dull work and long hours they must endure.

When examining the tables it is important to note that the work experience reported on by the respondents is from one and one-half to two and one-half years of auditing business systems. Because CPA firms usually assign audit tasks involving a consider-

TABLE 7–4
Rank-Ordered Tabulation of Responses to the Question: What Have You Liked *Best* About Your Work in Public Accounting?

Category of Responses

1. Contact with a wide range of people, firms accounting systems—diversity or variety of work situations
2. Personal development—learning and work experience—training
3. Challenging work—enjoyable work
4. Responsibility—recognition
5. Professionalism
6. Working with high calibre, intelligent, competent, interesting colleagues and clients
7. Salary
8. Opportunity to use technical skills and personal abilities, e.g. those learned in school
9. Freedom and independence
10. Opportunity for advancement
11. Prestige
12. Feelings of accomplishment

From J. G. Rhode, R. Hamlin, E. E. Lawler, and J. E. Sorensen, "Pre-Employment Expectations Versus Actual Work Experience in Public Accounting," Accounting and Information Systems Research Program, Los Angeles: University of California, Graduate School of Business Administration, 1973, p. 20.

Category of Responses

1. Dull work—work that does not require brains or education
2. Long or irregular hours
3. Time constraints and budgets—pressures
4. Firm attitudes toward personnel—attitudes required of personnel—unprofessionalism
5. Salary and salary increases
6. Travel
7. Job insecurity
8. Lack of proper personal development opportunities—inadequate supervision and training by seniors and above—supervisors who will not listen to problems or are insensitive
9. Off-season uselessness—too much unassigned time—any unassigned time
10. Office politics and rules
11. Client lack of understanding, appreciation and helpfulness—client attitudes toward public accounting personnel
12. Lack of feedback

TABLE 7-5
Rank-Ordered
Tabulation of
Responses to the
Question: What Have
You Liked *Least*
About Your Work in
Public Accounting?

From J. G. Rhode, R. Hamlin, E. E. Lawler, and J. E. Sorensen, "Pre-Employment Expectations Versus Actual Work Experience in Public Accounting," Accounting and Information Systems Research Program, Los Angeles: University of California, Graduate School of Business Administration, 1973, p. 22.

able amount of detail work during the early years of an auditor's career, it is not surprising that the respondents stated that they most disliked the dull work, long hours, budget pressures, salary, travel, job insecurity, and lack of personal development opportunities. The problems have been mentioned for years by junior accountants and little has been done by CPA firms to solve them. Just the same, these concerns often result in professional staff turnover—an expensive and often unpleasant prospect. This means that the CPA firm will lose the time, money, and effort expended for training and recruitment.

The conservatism of CPA firms also has its advantages. In addition to minimizing the risks the firms are exposed to, it seems to create rather satisfying jobs for the higher level managers in the firm. Those few accountants who are able to obtain senior positions seem to end up with relatively high paying, powerful, and satisfying jobs (Strawser, Ivancevich, and Lyon, 1969). A good guess is that in many ways, they are better off than are their counterparts in industry.

Summary

A single word seems to characterize the behavior of individuals who develop and maintain information and control systems: conservative. In the case of external auditors, this seems to be the only way individuals can behave if they want to survive. For them, innovative behavior tends to involve many risks and few rewards. Individuals inside the organization face a somewhat dif-

134

ferent situation. They too face a number of pressures toward conservative behavior, particularly if they are concerned with financial matters. Their attitudes and behavior, however, are also strongly influenced by their relationship to the line organization. Since they lack formal authority they often engage in political and other behavior designed to influence the decisions made in the organization. They also tend to be less satisfied with their jobs than are line managers and find themselves in frequent conflict with line employees.

8 CONTROL SYSTEMS AND DECISION MAKING

The information produced by control systems can potentially impact on the behavior of two types of decision makers: managers inside the organization and individuals outside the organization (e.g., bankers and investors). Unfortunately, little research has been done on how and when the information provided by control systems affects the behavior of either of these groups. Much of the research has taken a simulation approach. Subjects have been asked to imagine that they are managers or investors, and then have been given information and asked to respond. These studies will be reviewed since they provide some insights into how decision makers use information, but they must be interpreted cautiously because it is not certain that individuals will behave the same in a laboratory situation as they will in an actual decision-making situation. Thus, we don't know in great detail what kind of characteristics an information and control system should have in order to influence decisions in a constructive way. This is an important deficiency because, as Hopwood (1974) has stated, ". . . decision making can be viewed as the very fabric of which organized activity is made . . . and an understanding of how decisions are made is essential for anyone concerned with the design and operation of accounting systems (p. 121)." Hopwood identifies three main stages in a decision-making process:

1. Finding occasions for making a decision
2. Searching for and analyzing alternative courses of action
3. Choosing among the alternatives

To illustrate how a control system can influence each of these decision stages, consider an example of an information system that provides information that a manufacturing process is generating a product whose cost is beyond the tolerance levels of the budget. This is a standard use of accounting data, as noted by Katz and Kahn (1966), "The simplest type of information input found in all systems is negative feedback. Information feedback of a negative kind enables the system to correct its deviations from course (p. 22)." In this case, the excess product costs must be controlled for the organization to remain profitable. It may be necessary to increase employee productivity, materials' prices may have to be reduced, or perhaps a new decision should be made on the fairness of the overhead allocation. Whatever remedial action eventually results, the accounting system, by indicating that product costs were out of line, highlighted the occasion for making a decision.

The second and third decision stages—searching for alternatives, and choosing among the alternatives—can also be assisted by the information and control system. To extend our example, suppose that the manufactured product that is costly and out of budget could be purchased rather than manufactured. Assume also that it is one of several parts of a large product, like an automobile. If the quoted purchase price from an outside vendor for this make-or-buy part is less than the organization can ever manufacture if for, then the part should obviously be purchased. The accounting system, based on historical experience, can tell us the lowest price at which the organization can expect to manufacture this part. The decision about which vendor to select if two are bidding the same price for the part can also be aided by the control system because it should have information on the ability to meet delivery dates and the credit terms of each of the competing vendors. Although this is a hypothetical example, similar events take place every day in organizations. Accounting reports and information of this nature are frequently utilized. However, just how frequently and in what manner is a subject of some debate.

UTILIZATION OF DATA FROM SYSTEMS

Most individuals who maintain information and control systems like to believe that the reports they prepare are useful for decision making by managers and external parties. But some have argued that they often aren't used. For example, it has been stated that accounting reports are prepared only for legal reasons and are not used for planning or controlling the economic affairs of a business or, at the extreme, are not even useful for external decision making. Kenneth Boulding, a leading economist, maintains that the complete process of preparing, sending, receiving, and using accounting reports may be better understood as a cir- **137** cumscribed ceremonial ritual than in terms of decision-making usefulness (Simmons and Barrett, 1972). This point hits at the very heart of the value of information and control systems. If they are not attended to at all by decision makers then they obviously cannot effect decision quality—the major reason for their existence.

There is evidence to support the point that information system data are not always used. In a study designed to identify variables that may help to explain and predict how much middle managers use internally generated routine accounting reports, Simmons and Barrett were unable to determine if these reports were regularly read, what conclusions were made from reading them, and what utility the reports had for decision making.

A study by Khemakhem (1968) provides some interesting data suggesting that management decisions in the short run are influenced by financial information, and that they are more concerned with maximizing working capital funds than with maximizing the ratio of cash, accounts receivable, and inventory relative to current or thirty-day liabilities. Although a policy of maximizing funds flow may eventually lead to higher profits, it primarily results in organizational liquidity and fosters a smooth operating cycle. In his study, Khemakhem used an experimental group comprised of students and financial executives. He also determined that the financial executives, acting as management decision makers, often use new working capital funds flow data rather than net income data for their decisions. The accounting decisions involved selecting inventory and depreciation methods, determining investments for idle cash, calculating a cash dividend to shareholders, selecting capital budgeting alternatives, and developing an acceptable performance measure.

The Khemakhem study does not recommend that funds flow statements should replace the traditional income statement for internal managerial decisions. Rather, we may infer from Khemakhem's work that funds flow statements, valuable in their own right, are a necessary accounting statement that can beneficially accompany the income statement and balance sheet. And, in the short-run period of three months or less, it may be the most important accounting statement for decision making, particularly for managers faced with determining how best to allocate working capital resources. Thus, it seems that some, if not all, accounting reports are utilized. Monthly analyses of budgeted versus actual performance, balance sheets, profit and loss statements, and, as determined by Khemakhem, funds flow statements, all play an important role in managers' decision making.

Studies that have looked at whether accounting data influence investors' decisions have generally concluded that they do (Hopwood, 1974b). For example, Ball and Brown (1969) found a significant relationship between the reported profits of 261 organizations and the price movement of their shares. Companies with higher earnings definitely had higher share prices. Interestingly, investors seemed to anticipate the earnings of the companies since some of the price movements took place before the earnings were announced. Overall, the evidence is convincing that the simple existence of information does not assure its use but that sometimes the data from information and control systems are used by decision makers and that they can increase decision quality. We now need to investigate what factors influence whether information will be used and how effectively it will be used.

FACTORS AFFECTING DATA UTILIZATION
AND DECISION QUALITY

In reviewing the factors affecting data utilization and decision quality we need to consider the same issues that we considered earlier in our analyses of motivation and dysfunctional behavior. In addition, we need to consider the problems of information overload and how effectively individuals can handle data based on complex computations.

Characteristics of Sensor

The characteristics of a sensor measure strongly influence whether it will be utilized and its impact on decision quality. Decision quality and utilization are likely to be highest when the measures are complete and objective. Several studies have pointed out that complete, objective measures are likely to be utilized because they are seen as valid (see e.g., Cammann, 1974a), and decision makers search for valid measures. The degree to which measures are influenceable is also an important factor in data utilization because it contributes to validity. The important thing for validity is that the sensor be influenced by whatever it is supposed to measure in a manner that seems to be reasonable.

Completeness, objectivity, and influenceability are also characteristics measures must have to contribute to decision quality. Without these characteristics the measures will be invalid at worst and incomplete at best. In any case, they are likely to present a distorted view of reality; one that will not lead to effective decisions because they will be based upon false premises.

Who Sets Standards and Acts as Discriminator

Data utilization is likely to be highest when standards are set by the decision maker or by some individual who has reward power for the decision maker. The reason for this is the same as was **139** given in our discussion of motivation. People attend to measures related to rewards and intrinsic rewards are likely to be involved when individuals set their own standards and extrinsic rewards are likely to be involved when power figures set standards.

Decision quality probably is not directly affected by who sets the standard. It may be indirectly affected, however, in two ways. First, by how standard setting affects utilization and second by how it influences the quality and understanding of the standards. Valid standards are needed because without them the data from a measure will be difficult to interpret. As we noted earlier, valid standards are most likely to be set when all the knowledgeable parties engage in an open and frank discussion of what standards should be. Usually this means involving the person or persons being measured as well as others. If the decision maker is involved in setting the standard he or she is more likely to understand its difficulty and what went into it. This should help the decision maker understand the data and thus encourage its effective use. As Bower (1970) has noted, managers who are not involved in setting up information and control systems often don't have the expertise to interpret them and thus all they can do is rubber stamp the decisions of those who have the knowledge. In most cases this means that top level managers end up simply rubber stamping such things as capital budgets.

Decision quality and utilization probably are not strongly affected by who acts as the discriminator, but to the extent that the person who makes the decision is the discriminator it may encourage him or her to utilize the data more and in a better manner because of familiarity. In addition, utilization and decision quality are affected by the apparent and real validity of the data and this in turn is affected by who acts as the discriminator. The real and apparent validity of the measure may well suffer if the person being measured acts as the discriminator since, as was discussed in Chapter 6, individuals do give invalid data under certain conditions. Thus, the more trustworthy and knowledgeable the discrimination, in the eyes of the decision makers, the more likely data are to be used and to lead to high quality decisions.

Frequency and Speed of Communication

Based on our earlier discussion we would expect frequency of communication to have a strong affect on both decision quality and data use. Just as with motivation and dysfunctional behavior, the desirable practice is to provide feedback at an interval that approximates the time span of discretion. In a pioneering study to determine the effect of receiving accounting reports on a quarterly versus yearly basis, Cook (1968) reported that the degree of success or failure in performance (at the end of the fourth quarter that was the end of a business game simulation) was directly related to the frequency of feedback. This makes intuitive sense when extrapolating to the real world for both internal managers and outside investors. The managers, if they need to take corrective action because costs of product and resulting net income are out of line, are most likely to be able to act decisively if they receive the accounting report of operating net income on a monthly basis rather than quarterly or yearly. Over a lengthy reporting period the uncontrolled costs may become runaway costs and the situation may be too desperate to salvage. Although the Cook study did not specifically look at the issue of how long a delay should exist between the end of an accounting period and the decision making process, it does suggest some conclusions about those issues.

It seems safe to conclude that a minimal delay is desirable just as are measures that cover an appropriate time period. If either period is too long, then it is impossible for decision makers to respond effectively to the situation, and this may lead to them eventually losing interest in measures that are reported on a delayed basis. In a similar manner, an investor can make a more informed judgment as to buying, selling, or holding a corporate security if accounting data—including at least earnings per share—are received on a monthly or quarterly basis rather than annually. By the time the annual report is received, the time may have passed for taking effective action. The technology of modern computer-based financial control systems certainly allows for timely feedback. Rapid feedback clearly is desirable for the transmission of accounting-based earnings per share estimates to security analysts and stockbrokers from management. And it is no less desirable for the reporting of monthly operating results for decentralized divisions of a major corporation. A manager needs to know which divisions are operating above or below the expected level for net income, since timely reward for good performance and corrective action for nonoptional efforts should be made as soon as possible.

Motivation

Decision makers can be motivated to utilize data by either intrinsic or extrinsic means. It probably doesn't matter which source of motivation is involved as long as at least one is. The crucial point is that people will not utilize data unless they feel it can help them make a decision related to their receiving either intrinsic or extrinsic rewards. The simple existence of the information is not enough. Extrinsic motivation is most likely to be present when the activity being measured is an important one where the data will be communicated to someone who has reward power over **141** the decision maker. It is not clear that decision quality is substantially better under intrinsic motivation than under extrinsic motivation (Hopwood, 1974b). The key, as we noted earlier, is that there must be some motivation to utilize the data and come to a high-quality decision or it will not happen.

Two studies of internal decision makers suggest what may happen when there is no motivation to utilize information (Bruns, 1965; Dyckman, 1964). One of the early behavioral accounting studies was done by Bruns (1965) on the effects of using alternative inventory valuation methods on financial decisions. The choice of an organization's inventory method may have a pronounced effect on reported net income for a corporation because the value of the year-end inventory is one of the determinants of the cost of sales. The higher the year-end inventory, the lower the cost of sales will be for a given level of purchases and beginning inventory. From this it follows that the lower the cost of sales, the higher the net income; or that the larger the year-end inventory valuation, the greater the net income and accompanying income tax. Conversely, the lower the year-end inventory, the lower the net income and attendant tax. Consequently, a change in the inventory valuation method may make the difference between a reported net income or net loss for a corportaion during a particular time period.

An interesting example of the net income effect resulting from a change in inventory valuation occurred when Chrysler Corporation reported an increase in 1970 year-end inventory valuation of approximately $150 million (Briloff, 1972). The added inventory valuation brought about an additional 1970 tax liability of some $75 million to be paid interest free over twenty years. In this situation the top management of Chrysler Corporation decided that an increase in reported net income and an increase in the valuation for the year-end inventory, which increased total assets on the balance sheet, was so important that the corporation would be willing to pay an additional $75 million in 1970 federal income taxes —a tax liability that could have been deferred, perhaps indefinitely, if Chrysler maintained its existing method of inventory valuation.

While attempting to analyze a real world effect in the laboratory, Bruns used the format of a management game with students. They were asked to act as managers to determine if decisions based on accounting reports using one method of inventory valuation differ from decisions that would be made if another method were used. The management decision involved the price of product, the company's advertising expenditure, and the quantity of product to be produced during thirteen accounting periods. Bruns concluded that analysis of the experimental evidence did not sug-

142

gest that the particular inventory valuation method affected the decisions made by the managers.

In another study, Dyckman (1964) also used a computerized business game and tested for the influence of company size, earnings trend, and inventory cost-flow assumptions on financial decision making. For ten periods of simulated business activity, individuals acting as managerial decision makers made decisions on total units to be produced, research and development expenditures, marketing expenditures, product prices, and dividends for the accounting period. All subjects in the experiment received detailed statements of the companies' financial position, prior period earnings, cash inflows and outflows, ten-period summaries of previous decisions and resultant market share, and unit cost data for prior period output levels and production changes of ten percent. The sets of reports for the same company were similar except for the inventory valuation method and a random size factor. After the decision-oriented data were adjusted for assigned random size factors, no relationships could be established between decisions and earnings trends except for a marketing decision. Most importantly, the inventory valuation data, as was found in the Bruns study, had no significant effect on decisions. In both the Bruns and Dyckman studies the subjects were highly motivated to win but they didn't seem to be highly motivated to use the inventory valuation data. This probably came about because they could not change the method of valuation and they felt other factors were more important in influencing whether or not they would win the game and receive the rewards this offered.

Do the results of the Bruns and Dyckman studies mean that Chrysler made a mistake in changing their valuation approach? Probably not. It is unlikely that the inventory valuation decision made by Chrysler had as few effects on other management decisions as the results of Bruns' and Dyckman's studies would indicate. Management bonuses, dividends, stock options, and salary increases were probably all affected by the increased profit and tax liability. In addition, the Chrysler decision was undoubtedly made with investors in mind and these were not relevant in the laboratory studies. The problem is that of adequately portraying the real world in a laboratory situation. When viewed as a whole, investors and managers may treat most inventory valuation changes with the indifference of Bruns' subjects, but the extreme example of Chrysler indicates how potentially important these changes can be. The behavioral reaction of investors and managers to a change in inventory reporting is most likely a function of how much the change affects them. If the change results in higher reported net income, as it did in the case of Chrysler, other **143** studies suggest that investors may hold and not sell their investment in the corporation's common stock. Or, if the change effects the total valuation of assets under a manager's control, the change may cause that manager to increase or curtail investments in other assets so as to stay within the financial operating budget. Thus, the suggestion is that changes in computation methods are likely to influence decisions only when they influence the level of results reported.

Behavioral Effects of Information Overload on Decision Making

An additional influence on the utilization of data from information systems is the effect of information overload. Rosen and Schneck (1967) define information overload as ". . . the amount of information input which is greater than that which the organization or its decision-makers can adequately handle (p. 13)." In Chapter 2 we discussed the important impact of intellectual skills and personality on managerial effectiveness. These individual attributes play an important role with respect to how much information a manager can adequately process. Information overload makes some managers into ineffective decision makers much sooner than it affects other managers. The ability to handle large amounts of information is a function of prior experience, tolerance for the system, and intellectual skills. Unfortunately it is not always possible to predict when a particular individual will become overloaded, although it is possible to make some general statements about how individuals respond to information overload. Miller (1960) has categorized several behavioral reactions to information overload. His expected reactions to overload are generally negative for the organization:

1. Ommission, failing to process some of the information
2. Error, processing information incorrectly
3. Queuing, delaying during periods of peak load in the hope of catching up during lulls
4. Filtering, neglecting to process certain types of information according to some scheme of priorities
5. Approximation, or cutting categories of discrimination
6. Employing multiple channels, using parallel channels; as in decentralization
7. Escaping from the task

Also, information overload can cause a considerable hardship on those executives and creative individuals who need to ponder their decisions and perform their research and writing within the protective shield of large blocks of uninterrupted time. Constant information, particularly an overload, may erode completely that shield. The costs of such information overload, though not subject to ready measurement, are still very real. As Rosen and Schneck (1967) propose, the solution for dysfunctional behavioral reactions to a system with information overload is to alleviate the situation by reducing the information input or by creating multiple channels for handling the overload. This is not often done, however, since the process requires an organization with considerable financial resources together with managerial personnel who are adaptive to change.

An additional negative side effect of information overload is its absolute cost. All information has a cost, therefore, information should only be obtained by the control system if the benefits from its use can be justified as greater than or equal to its cost. This process is simply information economics—a means of defending the gathering of information only on the basis of cost-benefit analysis. In the absence of an information economics analysis the costs of an information overload are double edged. The entire organization suffers from the negative behavioral effects elucidated by Miller (1960), and the preparation of the overload data remains costly in its own right. Information is simply not free.

There is also some evidence that stockholders aren't eager for extra corporate data. A recent article in the *Wall Street Journal* ("A Special Background Report on Trends in Industry and Finance," 1974) indicated that companies now offering the detailed Form 10–K financial statements to stockholders have received very few requests for the data. The 10–K has always been available to the public—generally at no charge. Yet the general investor is apparently not interested in additional financial information, since fewer than 1 percent of the shareholders in some fifty companies surveyed requested the added data. Thus, shareholders are preventing a personal information overload by saying "thanks, but no thank you" to the additional financial information. They evidently already have enough data to make their buy, sell, or hold decisions. In effect, these shareholders have decided that the information benefit of this additional financial data is not worth the cost in terms of their time or money to obtain and process it, even though the cost of these reports was five dollars or less. This finding is consistent with the research to be discussed next on how investors process data from financial statements.

Behavioral Effects of Functional Fixation on Decision Making

Several experiments (Jensen, 1966; Dyckman, 1969; Bonini, 1963) have been concerned with the effects accounting methods have on decision making and investment analysis. Jensen's (1966) study, which entailed a computer simulation with responses from professional security analysts, investigated relation- **145** ships between security evaluation leading to portfolio selection and alternative methods of financial reporting. He determined that the average calculated stock values and the proportions allocated between the two hypothetical companies were always greater for the company reporting higher levels of prior period net earnings. Also, the more favorable the past earnings, the higher the value placed upon the stock despite the existence of earnings differences due solely to accounting measurement techniques rather than economic differences in company performance. Jensen also reported that the accounting valuation and measurement differences studied were either unnoticed by the security analysts or ignored.

As Beaver (1972) has noted, two difficulties obscure Jensen's findings. First Jensen's results ignore the ability of the market to handle different data in an efficient manner, and second, there was no economic or professional motivation for the analysts to make the best investment portfolio selections, Again this study must be interpreted as a further indication of the difficulty encountered when attempting to temporarily establish the real world or even a small portion of it in the laboratory. Nonetheless, it is an important study because it indicates that security analysts, who make investment recommendations to the investing public, place most of their analytic emphasis on only the end-porduct of the accounting process—earnings per share. Thus it seems that the control systems in large corporations concern outside investors primarily in terms of the net income figures they generate.

One of the more interesting studies of the impact of an accounting policy change was done by Bonini (1963) in his computer simulation of an organization's information and decision process. Bonini determined that an entire organization could be considerably influenced by simple changes in the valuation of inventory and the resultant effect on profits. His study, while important for several reasons, indicates that managers and directors do accept accounting reports at face value. Moreover, they will make radical decision changes as a result of the accounting report—even though the changes in profit originate from procedural or accounting changes rather than an actual increase in cash revenues.

The findings of Jensen and Bonini are consistent with the thesis of functional fixation (Ijiri, Jaedicke, and Knight, 1966). Basically, functional fixation exists where decision makers take accounting information at face value, attaching meaning to it as an object rather than as an imperfect reflection of underlying events. An example of functional fixation occurs when investment securities that are alike in all relevant aspects sell for different prices because accountants report the operating results using different measurement and valuation techniques. The functional fixation thesis asserts that when accounting statements are based on different accounting methods that are labelled with the same name, like cost or net income, individuals who do not have a professional background in accounting will neglect the fact that different accounting methods may have been used to prepare the financial statements. In the Jensen study, net income, no matter how determined, became the key variable for investment portfolio decisions and the accounting process that determined net income was largely ignored.

In a later study, Dyckman (1969) investigated the relationship between investment analyses and financial statements cast in a traditional historical cost format and those that include general price level adjustments. There is little doubt that, with all other things equal, the declining purchasing power of the dollar should cause a company with the majority of its assets purchased ten to thirty years ago to be valued differently than a company that purchased most of its assets during the last five years. The purchase price or historical cost for these companies should be distinctly different. Yet, an adjustment for price level changes to the older assets may bring about a comparability of analyses for the two companies.

How then do individuals react to price level adjusted statements? The results indicate that:

> ...a substantial number of traditionally trained financial analysts either do not understand or do not trust (or both) statements which incorporate price-level adjustments. They are unwilling or unable to make such adjustments themselves, and they will simply ignore or distort the information if the adjustments are made for them! Apparently, those who favor price-level adjustments—as well as those who support other modifications in conventional accounting—will need to recognize that obtaining acceptance of proposed improvements in financial reporting is as much a behavioral problem involving the perceptions of the users as it is a technical problem of the preparers (Caplan, 1970, p. 810).

Whether the same result as Dyckman found would be repeated under economic conditions of hyperinflation is subject to speculation. Presumably price-level adjustments might have more impact on the behavior of analysts, but only future experiments on accounting information and its behavioral effect can determine this.

Overall, the research reviewed so far indicates that the same economic data in different forms is often reacted to in the same way as is different economic data in the same form because of functional fixation. In one case the fact that different computational approaches were used is ignored and in the other unfamiliar data are ignored. There seems to be a ready explanation for the existence of functional fixation and the resultant tendency to ignore **147** data and make poor decisions: information overload. As was pointed out earlier, most investors can obtain much more information about firms than they can possibly process; thus they must decide not to process certain information. The selecting process as to which information to use is the critical issue since a decision to ignore crucial data can lead to low quality decisions.

In the case of investment decisions it is hardly surprising that investors focus on earnings. The results of an accounting measure such as earnings per share are perceived by most investors and some managers as relatively objective, inclusive, and responsive to the actual operating effectiveness of the organization. As Cammann's (1974a) research points out, when measures are perceived to have these characteristics, they are particularly likely to be attended to by decision makers. It is important to note that ignoring how accounting figures are obtained probably is dysfunctional for decision quality. As Briloff (1972) so clearly points out, investors often make poor decisions simply because they fail to look at how such things as earnings per share figures are obtained. Thus, as long as earnings are computed in so many different ways investors need to go beyond simply accepting the reported earnings per share data. How realistic is it to expect investors to do this? Probably not very realistic when there is an information overload. As we have already seen, several studies have shown that it often doesn't happen.

There have been some studies on investor reactions to changes in accounting policies that suggest that sometimes investors do base their decisions on more than reported earnings per share. In a study of market responses to changes in depreciation accounting, Comiskey (1971) determined that investors react to accounting information in an informed manner. He noticed that when steel companies attempted to increase profits by switching from accelerated to straight-line depreciation, a somewhat deflated market price for the securities resulted after a temporary increase immediately following the change. Somewhat similar results have been found in another study (Kaplan and Roll, 1972). It showed that the market initially reacted to a change in accounting methods with functional fixity but that later a more analytic approach was taken. A study by O'Donnell (1965) on the relationship between reported earnings and stock prices in the electric utility industry found that investors may make their own estimates of profit rather than accept the organization's reported profits when there are different methods of interperiod tax allocation.

There is some evidence that financial decision makers also look to information outside traditional accounting statements when asked to estimate what a corporation's future earnings per share will be. In a recent study, Hofstedt (1972) sought to find answers to five important behavioral accounting questions:

1. What is the importance of accounting information *relative* to non-accounting information?
2. Is information processing behavior different when analyzing firms with different earnings per share trends?
3. What is the effect on investors when accounting and non-accounting information give conflicting signals?
4. How do investors differ in their information processing behavior when they have varying levels of financial sophistication?
5. What are the interactions and relationships between information processing behavior, earnings per share trend, inconsistent information, and different levels of analyst sophistication?

Hofstedt used three sets of subjects, business executives with active investment experience, second year MBA candidates majoring in accounting and finance, and first year MBA candidates with minimal exposure to accounting, finance, or investing. He also utilized both increasing and decreasing earnings per share trends together with a positively or negatively toned president's letter about the future prospects of the company and asked subjects to predict the company's earnings per share for next year. Some of the major findings from Hofstedt's study revealed that the trend of earnings has an important effect on predictions of future earnings. Also, a decreasing earnings trend made the subjects less certain of their forecasts. In addition, an inconsistency between the president's letter and the accounting statement data on earnings per share led to subjects being more confident about their predictions of future earnings performance. This was surprising, but it may indicate what happens in the real world where the president presents a glowing letter and the earnings are somewhat negative, or just the opposite for both the letter and the earnings.

One of the more interesting results of Hofstedt's experiment is that the students and executives did not differ significantly either in terms of predictions or their confidence in those predictions. This means that expected financial sophistication differences either didn't exist, or the experiment was not sufficiently sensitive to extract these differences from the subjects. From this study, two important conclusions can be made. First, the importance of earnings per share data to financial decision making was again demonstrated, and, second, non-accounting information in the form of the president's letter had a clear impact on the decision-making behavior of the subjects.

Perhaps the best example of how investors typically can be expected to react to financial data is provided in a study by Livingstone (1967). He focused on a period when utilities could use **149** a variety of accounting procedures for recording the interperiod allocation of tax and thereby influence their reported after-tax profits. He found that government agencies accustomed to adjusting for the effects of different accounting methods did not take the after-tax profits figures at their face value. Instead, they adjusted the figures for the purpose of computing rate of return. In contrast, agencies accustomed to dealing with relatively uniform accounting practices did take the new after-tax profits at face value; in other words they demonstrated functional fixity.

Overall the research suggests that not all investors accept the generated accounting reports at face value. Trained analysts who are used to handling complex data do not, presumably because they are not as susceptible to problems of information overload. Even so, because the majority of investors do not have a sophisticated financial or accounting background, they are likely to use profit or earnings per share data without making additional profit calculations for their buy, hold, or sell decisions. This has some important implications for how financial data should be reported. The most significant of which is that accountants and others should assume that functional fixity will exist and do everything they can to make such things as earnings comparable from one company to another.

OVERVIEW OF WHEN INFORMATION WILL BE EFFECTIVELY USED BY DECISION MAKERS

Bruns (1968) has developed a model of when accounting information will be used in decision making. His model, reproduced as Figure 8–1, provides a framework for the analysis of any kind of information. Bruns developed his model around the premise that accounting information may or may not be *perceived* to be relevant to a given decision. He hypothesized that "... if accounting information is perceived as irrelevant for the set of decisions to be made, accounting information will not affect decisions"; and "if accounting information is perceived as relevant to the set of decisions to be made, it may affect decisions (p. 472)." According to Bruns, financial information may or may not be perceived as relevant, because for many decisions only non-economic data are very important.

Bruns model argues that once it has been determined that information is relevant to the decisions it will affect the decision if the accounting results have goal properties because they influence the reception of rewards. This point is in agreement with our discussion of extrinsic motivation, which showed that people will attend to measures that are related to important extrinsic re-

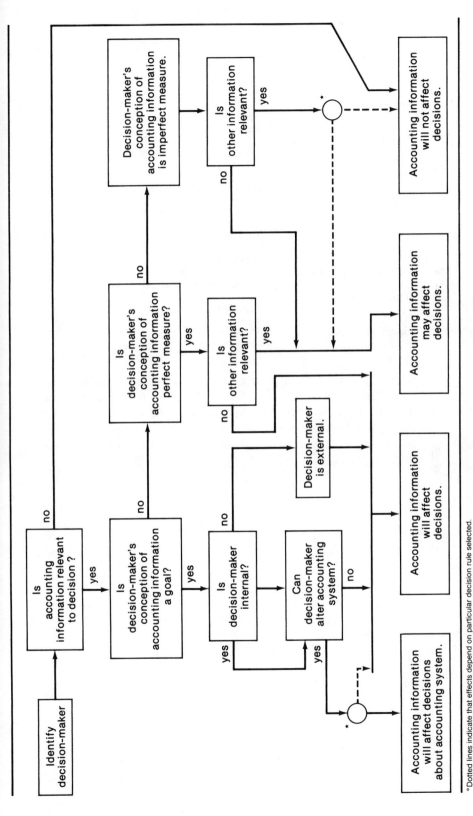

*Dotted lines indicate that effects depend on particular decision rule selected.

From W. J. Bruns, Jr. "Accounting Information and Decision-Making: Some Behavioral Hypotheses," *The Accounting Review*, 43 (3) July 1968, p. 476.

FIGURE 8–1   Accounting Information and Decisions

Characteristic of sensor measures	
	A. Complete
	B. Objective
	C. Influenceable
Who sets standard	
	D. Decision maker or other source of valid standard
Who acts as discriminator	
	E. Decision maker or other knowledgeable individual
Source of motivation	
	F. Either extrinsic or intrinsic
	G. Decision maker and if extrinsic motivation needed someone with reward power
Type of activity	
	H. Important
Speed of communication	
	I. Immediate
Frequency of communication	
	J. Appropriate to activity being measured
Amount of information	
	K. Appropriate to processing capability of decision makers
Form of information	
	L. Standardized across situations

TABLE 8–1
Characteristics
Associated with
Effective Utilization for
Decision Making

wards. Bruns model also argues that information is more likely to be used if it is seen as perfect than if it isn't. Based upon the Bruns model and the research reviewed in this chapter, it appears that when the conditions listed in Table 8–1 hold, information is particularly likely to influence decision making and make it more effective.

MEASURING THE HUMAN ORGANIZATION 9

Who will buy this wonderful morning?
Such a sky you never did see.
Who will tie it up with a ribbon?
And put it in a box for me.*

Measuring the human side of the organization is somewhat like the wonderful morning in the play *Oliver*. It has been the subject of articles, speeches, and discussions for years without being usefully packaged for decision makers. Behavioral scientists have stressed the importance of human assets and accountants have attempted to quantify these assets. But, in spite of this effort, most management information systems, balance sheets, reports to government agencies, and corporate profit and loss statements contain little or no information on the cost, value, or condition of an organization's human resources. No one has been able to tie up human system measurement and put it in a box in a way that is generally seen as useful. A number of individuals have tried, however, and this chapter will focus on their attempts. We will consider the impact of human system measurement on the individuals being measured and the individuals who run the systems, yet the major emphasis will be on the individuals who make decisions based upon this kind of information.

WHY MEASURE THE HUMAN ORGANIZATION?

It is difficult for anyone to deny the importance of the human system in organizations. As we pointed out in Chapter 3, without an effective human system no organization can operate effectively.

In fact, there is much evidence to indicate that not only does a poor human system cause organizational ineffectiveness, it can be destructive to the people who live and work in it (Porter, Lawler, and Hackman, 1975). Furthermore, many firms spend over 40 percent of their operating revenues on salaries. When the costs of training, selecting, and recruiting personnel are added to this total, it becomes clear that for many firms, most of their money is spent on obtaining, developing, and maintaining the human resources that make the organization operate. Yet most statements about the condition of organizations only provide information about what was spent on salaries and other personnel costs and report nothing about the health of the human system or the value of the human resources.

The omission of information about human resources from financial reports seems particularly serious for service oriented firms. Organizations such as computer software companies, universities, governmental units, law firms, and entertainment agencies often have human resources that are more important than their physical or financial assets. Traditionally, information and control systems have been tailored to manufacturing firms where physical and financial assets predominate. But service firms are currently enjoying tremendous growth, and financial statements need to be changed in some way to accommodate these people resource organizations.

POSSIBLE MEASUREMENT APPROACHES

The behavioral science research on how people react to their work environment, which we reviewed in Chapter 2, suggests the model shown in Figure 9–1. It shows that people's affective, attitudinal, and perceptual reactions to jobs are caused by a combination of the characteristics of the person and the characteristics of the job environment. The relevant characteristics of individuals include their skills and abilities as well as dimensions of their personalities and interests. The affective reactions in turn cause certain observable behavioral reactions. Figure 9–1 also shows that the specific kind of behavioral reactions that result are influenced by the external environment. For example, job satisfaction frequently causes turnover except when high unemployment exists (Lawler, 1971). The model goes on to show that individual behaviors combine to influence organizational effectiveness as measured by such economic indices as profits and sales. The relationship between individual behavior and organizational effectiveness is not, however, a direct one. It is influenced by the structure of the relationships among people and by the characteristics of the external environment.

154

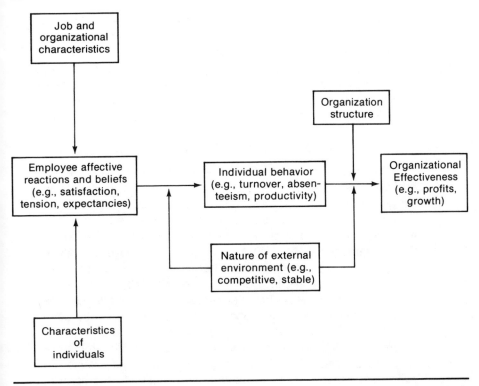

```
┌──────────────┐
│   Job and    │
│organizational│
│characteristics│
└──────┬───────┘
       │
       ▼
┌──────────────┐    ┌──────────────┐         ┌──────────────┐
│Employee affective│ │Individual behavior│    │Organizational│
│reactions and beliefs│──▶│(e.g., turnover, absen-│──▶│Effectiveness │
│(e.g., satisfaction,│  │teeism, productivity)│      │(e.g., profits,│
│tension, expectancies)│└──────────────┘          │   growth)    │
└──────────────┘                                  └──────────────┘
```

FIGURE 9–1
Model of the
Determinants of
Organizational
Effectiveness

Many studies have shown that the same individual behaviors can have very different impacts on organizational effectiveness in organizations that are structured differently in terms of the relationships among people and/or operate in different environments. For example, in some organizations turnover is very expensive, but in others it is not, and, in fact, may be desirable. Similarly, rigid repetitive behavior is just what is needed by organizations that operate in a stable environment but is very dysfunctional in organizations that operate in rapidly changing environments (Lawrence and Lorsch, 1967).

The approach presented in Figure 9–1 suggests a number of different human system variables that could be measured. The problem is to determine which of the variables shown in Figure 9–1 should and can be measured. It is apparent from the discussion in Chapter 8 that there are three characteristics that are desirable for any measure to have. First, the measure should be valid, in the sense that it measures accurately and completely all the important aspects of what is to be measured. Second, it should be influenceable by the people who are involved. Third, it should be objective. Finally, it should have enough face **155** or appearance validity so that it will be seen by all involved as a legitimate measure.

With these points in mind, we will review the four different kinds of measures suggested by Figure 9–1. In each case they will be evaluated in terms of their objectivity, influencability, face validity, and actual validity. At the end of the chapter we will consider their overall usefulness to decision makers.

CHARACTERISTICS OF INDIVIDUALS

There are many psychological tests designed to measure the characteristics of individuals (Guion, 1965). These include tests designed to measure the personalities of individuals as well as ones designed to measure their skills and abilities. Intelligence and other ability tests are used by over 70 percent of the firms in the United States (Campbell et al, 1970). Many organizations have also developed extensive skills inventories that list the work related skills (e.g., typing, bookkeeping) of all employees. The usefulness of this type of information for internal decision making is well established (Dunnette, 1966), and these data are frequently used in making personnel selection and placement decisions. The test scores and skills inventories, however, frequently suffer from poor face validity and relatively low objectivity, and their results are expressed either in terms of abstract non-economic scores or in terms of nonquantifiable descriptions. This limits their usefulness with respect to decision making because many decision makers don't trust the results of tests and prefer to make decisions based upon their own intuition. Further, although it is difficult for individuals to make themselves look unrealistically good on ability tests, many personality, vocational, and attitude tests are fakeable. At the moment, organizations do not, as a rule, provide external decision makers with information about the personalities and abilities of organization members. Occasionally in an annual report an organization will state figures showing how well educated or experienced its employees are but they don't provide information on employees' test results.

For the moment, no one is seriously proposing releasing test data to most decision makers. Their role is typically and appropriately limited to helping with personnel decisions involving specific individuals. It would be useful, however, if some kind of information could be given to decision makers about the overall level of skills that are present in organizations. Unfortunately, like test data, the kind of information stored in organization skill banks doesn't lend itself very well to this purpose. It typically simply lists the skills each individual has. This is useful information for planning, training, and recruitment programs but it fails to provide any overall indication of the human resources in an organziation. For a single measure of the skills present in the organization to be computed, the skills of each individual would need to be quantified and converted to a single score or measure and these combined for the organization as a whole. One possible way to do this is to measure the value of these human resources in economic terms, and this is what Human Resource Accounting (HRA) attempts to do. According to Flamholtz (1974):

> Human resource accounting means accounting for people as an organizational resource. It involves measuring the costs incurred by business firms and other organizations to recruit, select, hire, train, and develop human assets. It also involves measuring the economic value of people to organizations.
>
> The primary purpose of a human resource accounting system is to help management plan and control the use of human resources effectively and efficiently. In addition, some human resource accounting information may also be reported in financial statements for use by investors and others outside the organization (p. 3).

Hermanson (1964) and Brummet, Flamholtz, and Pyle (1968, 1969a, 1969b) have proposed that organizations do HRA. As is well known at this time, one firm, R.G. Barry, began doing HRA in the late 1960s and included HRA data in their 1970 annual report. Recently, many other firms have begun to do work on HRA systems. Flamholtz's (1974) recent book provides a good account of much of this work. As his review makes apparent, there is no agreement in the literature on what human resource accounting measures. Often measurement methods purport to measure some type of value to be placed on the human component of a firm's resources without defining precisely what value they measure. The appropriate value to be measured depends on how the human resource value data are to be used. There are, however, some economic and accounting principles that should be brought to bear on this question.

A definition of what assets represent that is accepted by some accountants is:

> Assets represent expected future economic benefits, rights to which have been acquired by the enterprise as a result of some current or past transaction (Sprouse and Moonitz, 1962, p. 8).

This requires that assets, including human resources, must have been acquired through a transaction, and have future economic benefits. The first of these requirements presents a constraint that is surely not met by human resources. Consequently, either the traditional basis of accounting must be changed to accommodate human resources, or organizations must report information about human resources separate from the traditional accounting reports, as R.G. Barry does. It may be argued that human resources are quasi-assets, that is, they are possessed by a firm despite the fact that they were not purchased, and cannot be sold. For example, **157** a contracted labor force may be close to meeting the definition of an asset, and one might maintain that the economic substance of other situations may well be nearly identical to a contracted labor force. Because a firm can lay off or fire employees, the human resources may be more flexible than other assets. The act of reducing the labor force might be considered an exchange of human resources for money resources (salary savings) in the same way that the sale of a machine is an exchange of one type of asset for another. Whether human resources fit the definition of assets, as the definition currently exists or as amended, must be resolved before it can be decided whether human resource information should be reported within or outside of the accounting statements of an organization.

Another requirement for an asset is that it have a future economic benefit. This is essential if human resource information is reported within the accounting system, and it is important even if the information is only a supplement to traditional reports. For the sake of presenting arguments about economic benefits, assume for the moment that human resources meet this constraint even though there are serious accounting measurement problems concerning the value of that economic benefit.

Traditionally accountants have recognized only assets with a *net* future economic benefit—a greater contribution than future cost. Lately, however, with the advocacy of capitalization of leases by many accountants, it is fashionable to support gross future benefits as the asset value, offset by a corresponding liability for the future cost of that asset. Both net and gross concepts of human resource values have been advocated by proponents of human resource accounting (Flamholtz, 1974). Yet, whether we accept gross or net values, it may be important to distinguish between future economic benefit and future cost to have information that is meaningful for decision making. Lev and Schwartz (1971) contend that "human capital values may be presented on the assets side of the balance sheet and the present value of the firm's liability to pay wages and salaries on the liabilities side. The two values are equal by definition (p. 110)." If we accept these two as equal, however, we cannot distinguish between the human resource values of two companies if one can pay less than the market salaries and wages and the other must pay more.

In analyzing net economic benefit, consider briefly a simplified view of the economic analysis of wage rate determination (Cartter, 1959). Under marginal productivity theory human resources are paid a wage equal to their marginal productivity. As more and more human resources are added to a fixed amount of physical capital, the marginal (and average) productivity of the human resources falls. Therefore, the average product (value in dollars) of the human resources is higher than the marginal product (cost in wages). With conditions of equilibrium and under perfect markets, and assuming that the only relevant exchange is employees' time and effort for monetary remuneration, the difference between average and marginal productivity for human resources represents the appropriate return for the physical capital employed. Under such idealized conditions the gross value of a firm's human resources is equal to the wages it must pay to retain them. As a result the net human resource value is zero.

Such a situation rarely—if ever—exists in real environments. First, due to permanent imperfections in the labor market, a firm may be able to pay employees less than their marginal productivity. Such a firm has a positive *net* human resource value. Second, partial payment to employees may be in the form of non-monetary compensation. The amount by which marginal productivity exceeds actual monetary salaries and wages is a net economic benefit to the firm. Associated with the non-monetary rewards may be some monetary investment such as expenditures on a modern plant to create better working conditions. Yet, as long as the discounted saving in salaries and wages exceeds this investment, there is a new human resource value created. Note that this also creates a decision for which human resource values may be used. If an expenditure creates a net human resource value greater than the expenditure, it is, *ceteris paribus,* desirable. Therefore, any definition of human resource values that ignores the possibility of a *net* human resource value eliminates at least one possible benefit from the reporting of human resource values—decision making for more optimal allocation of human resources.

Perhaps the most critical problem in human resource accounting is that of developing an adequate means of measuring the value of human resources. The first question to be asked in this area is whether each employee has an individual value, or whether value should only be placed on groups of employees. It is easier to measure the value of a group than that of an individual, but information about individual values is potentially more useful in some respects because it allows decisions about specific individuals.

A second question concerns the efficacy of directly measuring value. Since this is nearly impossible, a surrogate measurement must be used. The capitalized historical cost of recruiting and training employees has been espoused as a possible surrogate for human resource values, and it has been used by the R.G. Barry Corporation. This immediately raises the question of why employee value is equated with recruiting and training. The reason may be the professional accounting constraint of historical cost. **159**

But whatever the reason, consider some of the following difficulties with calculating the value of human resources: (1) Because people are personally capable of adding to their package of skills or productivity, their value can increase beyond that of their training and procurement costs. (2) Individuals may experience an increase in their skill level because of personal experience independent of their work place—at home or while on vacation. Moreover, these experiences can occur whether or not their employer has spent any money on training and development. (3) Two individuals experiencing the same training may demonstrate different abilities in implementing their training. One individual may be able to immediately and favorably affect his or her job performance as a result of the training while the other person may demonstrate only partial use of this training. Should historical cost of the training then serve as the valuation base for these two human resources?

Valuing human resources at the historial cost of training also fails to consider technical breakthroughs or individual breakdowns. An individual may develop a product or process for the organization worth considerably more than the training and recruiting costs would ever reflect. Conversely, an employee may return from intense sessions of sensitivity training as a disturbed individual who, because of the effect of the training, begins to destroy the organization. Writing off the historical cost of that person's training may not reflect an amount even close to the total loss the organization has suffered.

Allied with the problem of determining an individual's human resource value is the problem of how, and if, the resource value should be written off. Physically and mentally, individuals grow and deteriorate at different rates in their personal and working environments. Some develop as a result of their work experience, others do not; some leave the organization after a few days, others stay for years. In addition, the skills an organization needs change, so that a valuable employee today may be valueless tomorrow. Developing a means of writing off an individual's value, given the difficulty of predicting changes in the person's ability to effectively contribute to the business organization, presents an enormous measurement problem (Rhode and Lawler, 1973).

Abandoning the notion that the historical cost and current value of human resources can be equated, Flamholtz (1970) argues for the use of compensation, replacement cost, and performance measures as surrogates of individual value. Based on two independent samples of claims, personnel, and sales employees in an insurance company, he determined that replacement cost, compensation, and performance measures possessed convergent and discriminant validity as surrogates of individual value.

Utilization of these proposed measures for improved decision making has not yet, however, been demonstrated.

Continuing his efforts to demonstrate the utility of using surrogates as measures of individual value, Flamholtz (1972) developed an operational replacement cost validation model. Replacement cost, as used in the model, is comprised of the costs of acquiring a new person for an existing position, the cost of training the new person to bring that person to a level of performance expected of the position, and the necessary costs of moving the existing position holder either out of the organization or to a new position within the organization. Again working with insurance company employees, Flamholtz (1973) applied his replacement cost model to both claims and sales personnel. The calculated expected positional replacement costs for claims personnel ranged from $6,000 for a claims investigator to $24,000 for a field examiner. In contrast, the positional replacement cost for sales personnel ranged from $31,600 for salesmen with below average performance to $185,100 for a sales manager.

It would be interesting to ask corporate officials to note the amount for which they would be willing to individually insure their management personnel. Flamholtz's surrogate model may provide the same type of individual value information that valuation on the basis of key-man insurance totals would allow. Using this approach, key-man insurance totals could possibly provide either corroborative or surrogate data for Flamholtz's positional replacement costs.

One obvious problem with Flamholtz's approach is that he used salary data as a measure of value, yet, as has been frequently shown by research, salaries do not necessarily reflect the inputs or value of people (Lawler, 1971). It is also clear that Flamholtz's approach measures only the value of individual employees and does not place a value on their ability to work together as an effective decision-making team, their morale, or their commitment to the organization. This criticism is relevant to any human resource measure that looks only at values for individuals. In sum, his approach will not measure the effectiveness of the human system in the organization. This is unfortunate since in many organizations the ability of employees to work together and their commitment to the organization is the organization's most important resource. Just how valuable a resource some organizations consider this to be is exemplified by the large amount of money they spend on team building and organizational development activities.

Flamholtz's approach does seem to represent an improvement over the cost model and the valuation approach suggested by Likert and Bowers (1969), who propose that the value of a firm's **161** human organization may be conservatively estimated at 15 times earnings. When this formula is applied to the R. G. Barry Corporation's published earnings of $770,222, a human resource amount of $10,503,330 results. The Likert and Bowers estimate exceeds the R. G. Barry Corporation's human resource calculation of $986,094 by a factor of 10. Consequently, the two measures do not appear to be comparable. The Likert and Bowers approach would also seem to have difficulty dealing with a situation where a company suffers a loss. Would this mean its human resources have a negative value?

When we understand more about why individuals make the employment choices they do, we may be able to evaluate the attractiveness of one firm over others and the likelihood that individuals will continue to work for an organization. This may be translated into an assessment of the amount by which a firm's salaries and wages are below (or exceed) the marginal productivity of its employees and into an accurate basis on which to write off investments in training and recruiting. While we presently can make some analyses of changes in attractiveness of a firm over time and we can predict turnover and absenteeism rates from attitude survey data, we are far from being able to quantify the difference between marginal productivity and salaries and wages on the basis of psychological measures.

The problem of measuring human resources is in some ways akin to determining something as abstract as Thorndike's (1949) ultimate criterion of an individual's lifetime contribution to an organization. It has been observed by Guion (1965) that amorphous phrases like "all things considered" and "overall contribution" form elements of the ultimate criterion. Attaching a face value dollar amount to these phrases would undoubtedly result in a very useful measure of an individual's human resource value, but the problems associated with objectively and validly determining an individual's overall contribution in dollars clearly are enormous. At this time human resource accounting is insufficiently developed to expect that an accurate measure will soon be forthcoming. This view is shared by Caplan and Landekich (1974) who, in a book on human resource accounting, conclude that there are formidable problems associated with the evolution of practical methods for measuring the current value of human resources.

Potential Unintended Effects of Human Resource Accounting in an Organization

Forgetting for the moment the difficulties of measuring human resources and assuming proper valuation can be made, additional problems might occur from disclosure of individual values. The area of pay administration, for example, could be significantly affected. Our discussion of individuals in Chapter 2 stresses that people's satisfaction with their pay is a function of the relationship between their inputs and their outcomes. According to this view, employees compare their inputs and outcomes to the inputs and outcomes of similar others. When the comparison is favorable they feel satisfied with their pay, but when it is unfavorable they feel underpaid and express pay dissatisfaction. Pay dissatisfaction tends to lead to, among other things, turnover, absenteeism, and strikes. Indeed, most organizations make an effort to see that as few employees as possible are dissatisfied with their pay. The problem, of course, is that there is no accepted measure of the inputs of an employee. This means that feelings of underpayment may occur because individuals disagree with their organizations about the value of their inputs. Frequently, employees tend to value their inputs more highly than does their organization, and when this happens they question the pay administration practices of their organization.

The issue that now arises is what the impact of human asset data might be on this situation. Its relevance is undeniable, since presumably it will partially measure the inputs of the individual. If the organization decides to ignore this information, they will undoubtedly end up with situations where an employee's human resource value does not match the employee's pay. This will, of course, provide many employees with proof that they are under-paid because, after all, their value is x and they are paid y, while their comparison person is valued at $x - a$, and is paid $y + b$. This situation could make the pay administration job even more difficult than it is now.

Another possibility is that human resource accounting might be a blessing in disguise for salary administrators. It might provide them with the kind of data they have long needed to place salary administration on a more objective footing. Human resource data could become an integral part of an organization's pay plan, such that it would be used as one of the ways a person's inputs are measured. This could lead to a correspondence between the pay of individuals and their human resource values.

Knowledge of individual human resource totals could also affect employee bargaining power both within and outside the company. Employees could go to other department managers, or to the employment office of a rival firm, and bargain for a better position using not only current salary information but also their ascribed resource value as a way of establishing their value. One factor that presently mitigates against turnover in many organizations is that the value of many employees is not obvious to people outside the organization. This can make it difficult for an organiza- **163** tion to know who to recruit from their competitors, and it can make it difficult for the employee who wants to leave to establish his or her value on the outside. Interestingly, this is not true in all professions. In professional sports, for example, it is obvious how well different people perform just as it often is in academic research because of the publications of the researcher. In both of these cases, however, barriers are often established to prevent the free movement of people; universities adopt no-raid policies, and sports teams literally own the right to the labor of their players. If human resource values can be developed and become known, it could dramatically change the job market in those situations where presently people inside organizations are essentially invisible to the outside world.

It is also worth noting that human resource data could have a negative impact on the attitudes of some employees. Particularly troublesome might be the situation of employees whose resource values are declining. If employees see their resource total continually written off with no addition, the reality of a waning or depleted contribution potential may have a strong impact on them. It may cause them to leave the organization or it may cause them to perceive themselves as less adequate since the organization has visibly assigned them a continuously decreasing resource value. Related to this is the point made by many psychologists that people's motivation is strongly affected by their self-esteem. It is quite possible that some individuals' self-esteem could be negatively affected by finding out what their resource value is in comparison to others. Social comparison theory stresses that people evaluate themselves based on how they perform on certain criteria in comparison to others. Thus, a low human resource value could be seen by some as negative feedback and have an unfavorable impact on their self-esteem and desire to remain in the organization.

One possible way of preventing some of the potential negative consequences of an individual knowing his or her own and other people's resource values would be to keep this information secret. Many organizations do just this with managerial salaries. However, the information still seems to get out, though often in a distorted form. This would probably happen if human resource values were kept secret, and distorted information is often worse, from the point of view of the organization, than the actual information.

Again, assuming human resources can be measured in an acceptable way, a further issue may arise, not from employee knowledge of personal asset values but from the manager's knowledge of his or her subordinate's asset values. With human resource accounting, managers would presumably be evaluated on how well they utilize their physical, monetary, and human assets.

Control systems might have to be changed to motivate the proper treatment of human resources since otherwise they might motivate managers to fire or transfer their high-value human resources just before the year-end comparison of profit to human resource total so that the best short-term rate of return is made. Because of their inherent mobility, human resources can be moved about easier than fixed physical assets like heavy machinery or manufacturing plants. A manager may have much more discretion and control over the human resources than the physical assets for which he or she must account. Accordingly, human resources may be more easily manipulated to produce a good current performance rating. The cost of this to the organization may be severe in the long run.

Preventing the managers from knowing the personal resource totals of their subordinates offers a potential solution. But managers might then object to being evaluated on the basis of an unknown criteria, so much of the value of the system would be lost. A more reasonable solution would involve educating managers to look at information on human resources differently than they look at physical asset data. Managers might, for example, be rewarded for increasing the human resource value of their employees, or they might be allowed to sell their human resources to other parts of the organization and realize a profit on the exchange. In addition, the replacement cost of an employee who quits might be charged immediately as an expense. Under the right conditions, reporting human resource values to managers could motivate them to manage better. For one thing it might provide them with feedback about performance in this area.

MEASURES OF JOB AND
ORGANIZATION CHARACTERISTICS

An alternative to measuring the characteristics of individuals is measuring the characteristics of the organization that influence the effectiveness of the human system. This approach would involve measuring such things as how challenging and how stressful an organization's jobs are and what kind of communication channels an organization has. The capability is being developed for measuring some of these conditions reliably and validly (Jenkins, Nadler, Lawler, and Cammann, 1975), and evidence is appearing as to how they are related to a number of outcomes such as absenteeism and turnover. But at this point the measurement technology is at a primitive stage and needs further development to be valid.

Measures of job and organization characteristics cannot take into account individual differences in how people respond to the **165** same objective conditions. The same set of conditions often have a quite different effect on one set of people than on another. Therefore, in order to make known the human effects of a certain design or characteristic it is important to know something about the nature of the people. This is not a serious problem in areas like physical health, but is a problem when the issue is psychological. Exposure to extreme temperatures and noises of greater than 90 decibels are harmful to almost everyone; therefore, it makes sense to measure noise and temperature and to prohibit certain levels. It is not true, however, that repetitive assembly line jobs or authoritarian supervision are necessarily regarded as negative by all workers. Quite to the contrary, some see these factors as part of a high quality of working life. Others, often the majority, see them as negative and suffer poor motivation as a result of them. Thus, it seems that if these measures are to be used they must be used in conjunction with measures of the characteristics of individuals.

SELF-REPORT MEASURES

One way to take individual difference factors into account is to use subjective self-reports of satisfaction, motivation, affect, and beliefs. There are standardized, well-developed measures of these variables and they have been shown to be related to human system effectiveness (Likert, 1961). Likert and Bowers (1973) have even suggested that it is possible to put a dollar value on different levels of job attitudes as they are influenceable and have some face validity. Overall, self-report attitude measures have proven to be useful human system measures in those situations where there is no motivation for the individual to report false data.

Unfortunately, we know very little about their validity in situations where there is motivation to distort them because they are rarely used under such conditions. In some instances the use for which the data are being gathered itself creates motivation for distortion, and in these cases self-reporting would seem to be an unsatisfactory solution unless nonfakeable measures are used. At the moment there are no such measures, although some of the commonly used measures are more difficult to fake than others. For example, some of the difference measures (e.g., subtracting people's feelings of what they should receive from what they feel they do receive) are less subject to distortion than are measures that simply ask people how satisfied they are or how much opportunity they have to grow and develop on the job. In short, self-report data can be valid indicators of human system effectiveness when there is little motivation to distort them. It is **166** also important to note that there are no obvious measurement terms like dollars that can be used for attitudes and that their relationship to behavior is far from perfect. Attitudes do, however, have the distinct advantage of being an influenceable cause of behavior and, correspondingly, they can indicate the need for remedial steps to prevent the occurance of negative behavior in the future.

BEHAVIORAL OUTCOMES

One alternative to using self-report measures is to focus on the behavioral outcomes that are produced by working in an organization. Such indicators as turnover rates, absenteeism rates, mental illness rates, alcoholism rates, theft, and community service rates can be measured. This approach has the advantage of focusing on somewhat objective outcomes. It also has high face validity since most people would agree these outcomes are indicative of a poor human system. This approach has the disadvantage that it identifies bad conditions only after they have done their damage. Work situations that don't fit individuals produce dissatisfaction and a psychologically poor work environment. These, in turn, produce problems such as mental illness, alcoholism, and organizational ineffectiveness. Where possible, it is important to identify poor work environments before they produce serious negative outcomes.

This approach also suffers because negative behaviors such as these are influenced by things an organization cannot control and influence. For example, an organization may have a high absenteeism rate for reasons that have nothing to do with the kind of human system it maintains. People may come to an organization with certain characteristics that lead them to engage in these behaviors (e.g., drug abuse) and they may by caused by changes in the external environment (e.g., unemployment rates may change). Furthermore, at the moment there are no generally accepted, standardized definitions of many of these behaviors. Although most firms collect such things as absenteeism and turnover figures, the data are not comparable. This problem would need to be solved for any useful external reporting of the data.

Some interesting work has been done on developing standardized definitions and costs of such behaviors as absenteeism, turnover, and tardiness (Macy and Mirvis, 1974). This work has essentially taken a cost accounting approach and has yielded some interesting results. It requires some cost estimation but it offers the possibility of measuring these behaviors in a common way on a standard scale across organizations. The approach also yields a single summary figure and puts the measurement of behavior in face-valid terms that are taken seriously by most decision **167** makers—those of dollars. Before a generally accepted system will be realized, however, a considerable amount of work needs to be done on developing standardized definitions and costing procedures. Still, the potential appears to be large and it has some important advantages over Human Resource Accounting. Among these is the fact that behavior is costed rather than individuals and this is more acceptable to most managers and accountants, and the system.

IMPACT ON DECISION MAKING

Now that we have reviewed the kinds of human system measures that might be developed, we are in a position to consider in more detail their potential usefulness to decision makers. The major purpose of collecting financial information is to influence decision making. Consequently the usefulness of human system measurement depends on its ability to provide information that improves the decision making of some individual or group. There is a substantial cost to deriving and reporting human resource values, and only if the benefits of having this information exceed the costs can the reporting of human resource values be justified. There are three prominent classes of decision makers who use information about the financial condition of organizations and presumably would use data on the human system if it were available: investors in the securities market, managers making resource allocation decisions within the firm, and the public as represented by various governmental regulatory and legislative bodies. The crucial questions for us concern what kind of human system measurement will lead to improved decision making by any or all of these groups. At this time any systems that might provide a contribution are still in the developmental stage.

Management Decision Making

A number of writers have stressed the potential usefulness to management of measures of the effectiveness of the human system of their organizations. Usually it is argued that things like satisfaction, absenteeism, turnover, and grievances should be measured. In a classic article, Merrihue and Katzell (1955) have argued that organizations should develop an "Employee Relations Index" that would reflect the overall quality of the relationship between the employees and the organization. As far as management decision making is concerned, a case can be made for collecting data intended to measure organizational characteristics, individual characteristics, job attitudes, and job behavior. By regularly collecting systematic data on these variables, organizations

168 can do two things. First, they can determine how various organization policies and practices influence the human side of the organization and second, when called for, they can correct policies and practices that produce a psychologically negative work life before they lead to excessive and expensive problems. In short, measures of this type should in many instances enable organizations to make decisions that will alter the human system in ways that will contribute to organizational effectiveness. The measures should also make it easier for organizations to make decisions that will improve the human system in ways that don't directly lead to greater organizational effectiveness.

How important is it that measures used for management decision making be objective? Probably not as important as it is that measures used for other purposes be objective. Self-report measures of such things as satisfaction and opportunities for self-development are potentially useful to managers for decision making. The experiences of organizations that have used the measures for this purpose has been that people generally give valid self-report data if they are assured of individual anonymity. Many organizations have successfully run employee attitude measurement programs for years and they have found that people are honest in reporting their feelings about what it is like to work in their organizations. In all cases employees are guaranteed anonymity and the data are used only for management decision making. It is important, however, that attitude measures have face validity. Otherwise managers will not use them.

What kind of data then should organizations collect for their own decision making? Three kinds would seem to be of particular importance: measures of individuals' skills and abilities, self-reports, and behavior measures. Measure of individuals are needed so that correct personnel decisions can be made. It is not clear, however, whether it is important that these measures be in the form of human resource accounting. Putting it into dollar terms may well increase its saliency and face validity but there is no evidence to support this point yet. The literature does contain testimonials from corporate officers to the effect that the data have helped improve decision making, but these reports are difficult to evaluate. Some of the best examples of this are found in the Ohio State behavioral accounting studies (Burns, 1970, 1972).

It is extremely unfortunate that systematic data are not available on the effects within the Barry Corporation of Human Resource Accounting. Such data could help answer many of the questions raised about the value of Human Resource Accounting. Though the R.G. Barry Corporation and some of the early researchers deserve a great deal of credit for establishing that human resource accounting can be put into operation, it is important to note that their work does not make a convincing case for the usefulness **169** of this system. In fact, none of the experiments on Human Resource Accounting have produced any evidence that shows the effects of installing these systems. Overall, then, the work on Human Resource Accounting has been of the operational practicality variety. The literature (Flamholtz, 1974) has shown it can be done, but it hasn't shown it is worth doing. This means that a decision to put measures of individuals in Human Resource Accounting terms must be made on the basis of faith in the hope that it will improve decision making rather than on the basis of factual evidence.

Evidence is also lacking that regular collection and analysis of self-report data and behavioral data can improve decision making. Again, there are testimonials but this is not enough. A logical case can be made for self-report data since they seem to be predecessors of later crucial behaviors such as absenteeism or turnover. Similarly it seems only logical that decisions about such things as pay raises and hiring should be made on the basis of a careful analysis of absenteeism and turnover figures; yet there is little data to support the usefulness of collecting these measures. It would also seem logical that attaching dollar figures to behaviors would improve decision making but presently only a handful of organizations do this, and there is no evidence of its usefulness.

Use of Measures in Public Reporting

At the moment, companies are not required to inform stockholders about the human side of the organization. A case can be made for requiring organizations to furnish these kinds of data. As was pointed out at the beginning of this chapter, the human system influences financial success. Thus, it would seem that investors should have the right to know how the human system is functioning. Furthermore, since the human system affects such socially important issues as mental illness, alcoholism, drug abuse, and various physical illnesses, stockholders as humanitarians might want to know something about the impact their organization has on the people who work for it. Dierkes and Bauer (1973) present an important compilation of articles focusing on corporate social accounting.

Stockholders have recently demanded information from companies as to whether they discriminate against minorities and whether they pollute. Before too long they may ask for information about the kind of life their company provides for its employees. They may even demand organizational practices that will reduce profits in order to increase the quality of the life of the employees. This has already happened to a limited extent in some companies. For example, stockholders have demanded that American companies pay equal wages to blacks in South Africa, even though such payment is not required by law and could put the company at a financial disadvantage with respect to competitors.

What kind of human system data should stockholders receive? A strong case can be made that they should receive pretty much the same information as management decision makers. That is, information concerned with the attitudes and behavior of individuals, data about human resources, and data about the organization as a system. At the moment, the greatest concern in the literature seems to be with reporting HRA data, although this may not be the best approach to take and it is certainly a limited one.

If Human Resource Accounting is going to progress to the point where it can be reported to investors, our discussion so far indicates that several things must occur. First, the form for presenting human resource information must be determined. Is the traditional accounting framework the proper form or should the development of human resource information be unencumbered by the reporting requirements of the accountant and take the form of supplementary statistical information? Second, the problem of measuring human value must be solved. The R.G. Barry Corporation's approach of valuing human resources by outlay of costs for recruiting, acquiring, training, familiarizing, and developing personnel assumes an equality of cost and value. It will be several years before meaningful returns on investment variables can be calculated. The variables are elusive; and, when isolated, it is questionable as to whether human resource cost can be equated with human resource value.

Many years ago, a prominent accounting scholar stated:

> In the business enterprise, a well-organized and loyal personnel may be a more important "asset" than a stock of merchandise . . . At present there seems to be no way of measuring such factors in terms of the dollar; hence they cannot be recognized as specific economic assets (Paton, 1922, p. 486–487).

The passage of more than fifty years has brought accountants somewhat closer to measuring these factors, but only at a glacial pace and only with the most limited of useful results. Without better measurement tools, the results found by Shenkir, Sperry, and Strawser (1972) in a recent survey of major certified public accounting (CPA) firms and some 200 of the largest industrial organizations will likely continue to be valid. They found that:

1. There is little active interest in Human Resource Accounting on the part of the CPA firms.
2. Most firms report that it is "impractical" and/or "of little use" to use Human Resource Accounting costs in calculating return of investment.
3. Users of financial statements report only limited interest in many of the cost categories utilized by the R.G. Barry Corporation.
4. Human Resource Accounting for internal use was perceived to be more important than Human Resource Accounting for external use.

An alternative to HRA is to have firms present data to stockholders on employee behavior. As a first step, organizations could provide their stockholders with data on turnover, absenteeism, and grievance rates, as well as information on the rates of job-related physical and mental illness. These data could be subject to audit, just as are the financial data. They might be combined in a single "Quality of Work Life Index" that would provide some indication of the consequences of working for a particular company. If comparable data were collected from a number of companies, they could be reported in terms of the percentile standing of each company. Alternatively, as better costing methods for these outcomes become available, companies could be required to report them in financial terms.

The difficult question to answer concerning any report to stockholders is whether it should include self-report data. This is information that investors should find very helpful since they are investing in the future of the company and attitudes influence future behavior. On the other hand, if the employees are also stockholders, they might be motivated to provide invalid data. Attitude data have never been gathered for distribution to stockholders, so it is difficult to know how serious this problem would be. This is obviously an area where experimentation is needed.

Stockholders should also have measures of the quality of the interpersonal relationships in the organization, since this influences whether the members of an organization are able to work together effectively, that is, whether the sum of the individuals' competence is equal to, greater than, or less than the effectiveness of the whole organization. To some extent the character of the interpersonal relationships could be measured by self-report, but this probably would not be sufficient. People often do not realize what their impact on others is and often are completely unaware of their interpersonal relationships. Thus, direct observation by others is needed, and could be accomplished by having a skilled observer sit in on meetings to record the kind of interaction that takes place. In addition, tapes of meetings could be analyzed according to the kind of scoring systems recommended by Argyris (1971) and others. These measures could then be combined into a single measure of the overall quality of the interpersonal relations in the organization. If similar measures were taken in different organizations, they could be reported in terms of percentile standing.

The possibility of reporting to stockholders the condition of the human aspects of organizations raises the question of who would prepare these reports. Just as with financial statements, it is not a job to be trusted to management. There simply would be too much pressure on them to give invalid data, since the reputation and value of the company are at stake. This suggests that people trained in behavioral science measurement would be needed to audit the human system, just as Certified Public Accountants are necessary to audit the financial system. They would use certain standard tests and procedures, and they would directly observe management, leadership, and decision-making practices. As in financial accounting, they would have to develop over time a standardized set of procedures so that comparable data could be obtained from different firms. Presumably they, like CPAs, would have the power to certify statements. Admittedly, considerable work needs to be done before it will be practical to begin certified human system audits, but the time indeed may come. It is likely to come however, only if the federal government requires organizations to prepare such statements since, at this time, there is little incentive for organizations to prepare them.

Use of Measures by Government

In the United States, as in most countries in the West, there are a number of indices that measure what is occuring in the nation. Almost without exception, however, they focus on the economic aspects of life. These indices are valuable because they provide information about where the country is and has been, and serve as useful guides in setting national economic and social policy. However, the point has been made that they may have focused too much attention on the economic aspects of life and that, as a result, we as a nation have emphasized economic growth to the detriment of the overall quality of life. No one can argue with the importance of a nation's trying to reach an informed decision about how much, if any, economic growth it will experience. All countries certainly need to confront this question. Yet, to do so intelligently, information is also needed on how various economic and social policies affect the nonmaterial as well as the material quality of life.

Since one important component of the quality of life is the working life of employees, it too must be measured to achieve a clear picture of the whole. It should not be too difficult to develop quality-of-life measures in this area if the data are used only for the purposes of building national indicators of the quality of life and of guiding governmental decision making. Under these circumstances, it is reasonable to rely at least partially on self-report measures of employees' feelings with respect to satisfaction and opportunitites for growth, as there should be relatively little motivation on the part of the people to give invalid data. Individual responses could be kept confidential, and there would be no necessity to identify the person questioned with a particular organization. **173**

In short, individuals' responses would not be likely to affect directly either them or their organization. Thus, there would be little motivation to distort the data.

If, on the other hand, quality of work measures are to be used for regulating and influencing the behavior of the organization for which the people work, the situation will be quite different. There might well be some motivation in this case to distort self-report measures, just as there would be if the information were reported to stockholders. Yet, probably the most valuable use of indicators of the quality of work life is to influence and control those organization practices that affect employees. It may seem far-fetched to envision the government's taxing or fining an organization because it has a destructive human system, but there are reasons to suggest that these actions can and should happen.

There are already precedents for these types of actions. In the area of physical safety, for instance, there has been a long history of legislation regulating those organization practices and working conditions that can affect a person's physical health. Such things as hours of work and equipment design are specified in considerable detail. Perhaps even more pertinent to problems of the psychological quality of life, however, is the recent enactment of state and federal legislation controlling pollution.

As is well known, organizations that pollute the air, water, and soil are now subject to fines and, in some cases, shutdown of their operations. The logic underlying this legislation is as follows: It costs industry more to manufacture many products in ways that will not pollute. Consequently, any organization that tries to produce a product without polluting is at a competitive disadvantage in the market. The reason for this is that pollution control equipment is expensive and adds to the company's costs, an addition that usually forces a price increase. In a real sense, when goods are produced in a way that pollutes, their actual price tends to be too low, because their full production costs are not charged to the customer. They are borne by the society as a whole because it is the society as a whole that bears the cost of pollution, such as rivers to clean up or air that increases illness.

Using this logic, legislation that fines organizations for causing pollution is very much justified; it simply involves charging organizations in the name of the public for the cost of the pollution they are causing. It also is fair if this raises the price to the consumer. Now he or she will bear the full cost of the product rather than sharing it with people who do not buy and benefit from the product or service in question.

There is an obvious parallel between the economics of the
174 pollution situation and the economics of providing a poor quality

work life for employees. Providing people with dissatisfying, meaningless jobs is a form of pollution, and the cost at the present time is borne by the society and the individuals harmed rather than by the organizations responsible. This type of pollution leads to increased societal costs in such areas as mental illness, alcoholism, shorter life expectancy, and less involvement in the community. These are expensive outcomes and ones that are paid for by the government and private funds that support hospitals, mental health centers, and civic programs. Because these costs are absorbed by society, some goods are underpriced relative to their real costs. And, just as with environmental pollution, a case can be made for government intervention designed to correct this situation.

There are some situations in which improving the quality of working life may not in fact increase an organization's costs so as to put it at a competitive disadvantage. The research on job design, for example, suggests that job enrichment can, in some cases, reduce costs by bringing about higher quality products and lower turnover, while at the same time improving the quality of work life (Davis and Taylor, 1972). In these situations there is already pressure toward improving the quality of work life because it promises higher profit. These situations probably will correct themselves without government intervention once organizations realize it is to their economic advantage to improve the quality of work life. But the government may have to intervene to change the economics of the situation and provide stronger motivation for change when organizations realize that improvement in the quality of work life will cause increased costs. For example, despite the work that has gone into job enrichment, it is not clear how to enrich some assembly-line jobs without increasing production costs. It is clear, however, that in many of these situations enrichment would increase the quality of many people's lives. The situation needs to be changed so that organizations can act to improve these conditions without finding themselves at a competitive disadvantage. Three types of government intervention could potentially do this.

First, the government could charge organizations for the negative social outcomes they produce. For example, if a company had an unusually high rate of alcoholism, drug addiction, and mental illness among its employees, the government could increase its taxes proportionally. This is not dissimilar to present government practice in the area of unemployment insurance. The cost of this benefit to employers is based on the individual company's past history. This method has the advantage of focusing on the broad social outcomes that are to be avoided; its disadvan- **175**

tages include the difficulties of determining the cost of these negative social outcomes and of deciding whether their causes can
be directly attributed to the organization.

An alternative to focusing on behavior is to rely on self-reports
of the employees about their feelings of satisfaction and growth.
Organizations could, for example, be taxed more highly if they
had dissatisfied employees. Again, the problem with this is that
self-reports are potentially fakeable and therefore may not be trustworthy in this situation. Finally, this approach is likely to work
only if the taxes or fines charged to the company are greater
than the cost of correcting the cause of the negative outcomes.

The second approach, by way of contrast, is that most frequently used in the areas of physical safety and pollution. Here,
organizations are usually fined not for the outcomes they produce
(accidents, dead fish, sick people), but for the practices in which
they engage (air pollution, unsafe work practices). Applying this
approach to the area of the quality of work life, organizations
could be fined or taxed on the basis of their practices, policies,
and the nature of the jobs they have. For example, they might
be taxed if they produce goods on an assembly line rather than
on a team project basis. Such action could obviously eliminate
the economic advantages of producing goods on an assembly
line. The major problems with this approach are that few practices
have a negative impact on everyone's psychological life and the
practices of an organization are difficult to measure validly.

The third approach has the same strengths and weaknesses
of taxing and fining organizations according to the practices they
engage in. It involves simply forbidding organizations to engage
in certain practices that have been shown to decrease the quality
of most people's working lives, or to require them to do certain
things that are believed to improve working life. For example, the
government could simply close all factories that have highly repetitive jobs or require all companies to have a workers council
to decide on such things as hours of work. The latter approach
is presently being tried in some European and South American
countries.

Research, to date, on the effect of specific practices on the
quality of work life would indicate that we probably are not ready
for any of the three types of intervention just discussed. There
are, however, some things, in addition to sponsoring research,
that the government can do. It can, as it has done in the pollution
area, require organizations to prepare quality of work life impact
statements when they build new plants and facilities and on a
regular basis thereafter. Such action is probably a prerequisite
to widespread public reporting by organizations on the quality

of work life they provide. If nothing else, this would force organizations to think about how their way of designing and administering a plant affects their employees' lives. At the present, this is often considered only after an organization begins to have personnel problems. To start with, these impact statements would have no direct sanctions attached to them; they would, however, be made public. Such disclosure could result in bringing public pressure to bear on those organizations that engage in deleterious practices; we might even see consumers boycotting those organizations that provide a poor work life. It should also help acquaint potential employees with the kind of work situation the organization offers; there is evidence that this kind of information can help people make better job choices.

The government could also apply pressure by directing its business toward those organizations that provide a high quality of life for their employees. This pressure is already used in the area of discrimination. Organizations that are not in compliance do not get federal contracts. Similarly, quality of life in a given company could be audited and, if found deficient, government contracts could be withheld. This represents a potentially powerful intervention strategy for the government and one that could be made operational in the not-too-distant future if work on it began immediately.

SUMMARY

There seems to be no question that measures of the human systems in organizations are potentially useful. High quality measures potentially could play a major role in improving the quality of everyone's life. Unfortunately, we do not have the measures we need. Every operational measure we reviewed was lacking in one or more important ways. This was particularly true when we considered using them as a basis for government action and investor decision making. An argument can be made for doing the best we can with our present measures because going ahead will speed the development of better measures and in an area where no measures are used even poor measures can help. An argument for not doing anything until better measures are developed, can also be made. This argument rests on the dangers of a premature freezing on poor measures and on the potential disruption of the economy. We will leave it to the readers to conclude what they think is the best approach. We do want to close, however, by reaffirming the importance of our developing high quality human system measures to complement the already existing financial and internal control reporting systems in organizations.

10 DESIGNING EFFECTIVE CONTROL SYSTEMS

Now that we have looked at how the characteristics of information and control systems affect motivation, dysfunctional behavior, and decision quality, we are ready to address a final issue. What information and control system or systems are optimal from an overall effectiveness point of view? To answer this question we need to consider all the uses of information and control systems as well as all the individuals who are affected by them. Thus, we will first consider what kind of information and control system will produce a maximum amount of motivation and a minimum amount of dysfunctional behavior. Then we will consider how information and control system maintenance jobs should be designed. Finally, we will consider how systems should be designed to assure high decision quality.

MOTIVATION AND DYSFUNCTIONAL BEHAVIOR

Many of the same characteristics that produce a maximum amount of motivation produce a minimum amount of dysfunctional behavior. Thus, there is little conflict between objectives. However, there are characteristics that lead to both high motivation and a high incidence of dysfunctional behavior. This can produce conflicts in designing systems. Before we reach any conclusions about how serious the design problems are and about possible solutions, we need to review where the conflicts appear and establish their nature.

Characteristics of Sensor Measures

Intrinsic and extrinsic motivation are both highest when measures are complete, objective, and influenceable. In fact, all three of these characteristics must be present for there to be either extrinsic or intrinsic motivation. Particularly crucial are the characteristics of completeness and influenceability. As far as dysfunctional behavior is concerned the picture is not as clear. Resistance tends to be less when measures are incomplete but this is a small effect and probably should be discounted since the resistance comes from a desire not to be held accountable for performing all aspects of the job well. Further, this dysfunctional behavior can be overcome in most situations because usually not everyone will resist the new measures. Bureaucratic behavior is most likely to occur when objective, influenceable measures are used but it does not occur when measures are complete. Thus, it seems safe to conclude that regardless of the purpose for which an information system is used, it should be based on measures that are complete, objective, and influenceable. When this is not possible, then serious consideration should be given to not tying extrinsic rewards to performance, because it may lead to a high incidence of dysfunctional behavior.

Nature of Standard

There seems to be little doubt that in most cases standards should be set either by the person being measured or as the result of a mutual influence process between the person and some other knowledgeable person or persons. This seems to be optimal in terms of intrinsic motivation and the major dysfunctional behaviors. The one slight qualification necessary here concerns situations where extrinsic motivation is involved.

Usually when goals are being set for planning purposes or for intrinsic motivation purposes the employees can be counted on to give valid data. However, when goals and standards are being set for the purpose of distributing extrinsic rewards, like pay, there is strong motivation for employees to give invalid data about how well they can perform. It is to their economic advantage to get the standard or goal set as low as possible because with low-level goals they have the greatest chance of profiting financially. The research reviewed earlier on such things as piece rate incentive systems shows that this does happen and that often standards are set that are too low to be intrinsically motivating. They sometimes turn out to be accurate for planning but only because employees restrict and manage their production so that they will be accurate. This, of course, doesn't always have to happen and in organizations where superior/subordinate relations **179** are good and trust is high it often doesn't. However, in most cases it appears that goal setting for extrinsic rewards needs to be handled differently than goal setting for planning and intrinsic motivation. The employee should still be involved but the superior should take a more active role in determining the goals so as to be certain that too low standards are not set. There is a clear danger in having the superior unilaterally set goals, however. He or she may lack relevant information and as a result end up setting goals that are too difficult.

There is little question that very difficult goals produce low motivation and dysfunctional behavior. The only qualification that is necessary here concerns motivation. There is evidence to show that, *when accepted,* difficult goals produce high motivation. However, they frequently aren't accepted and as a result they cannot be counted on to produce high motivation.

It is not completely clear just what goal difficulty is optimal with respect to motivation. As far as intrinsic motivation, moderately difficult goals seem optimal. These seem to arouse achievement motivation and, of course, when accomplished produce a high level of performance and satisfaction. In terms of extrinsic motivation, it is easiest to motivate achievement of easy goals because when goals are easy $E \rightarrow P$ beliefs are high and this means that motivation will be high if rewards are tied to good performance. However, even though it is less difficult to use extrinsic rewards to motivate people to reach easy goals, it is not clear that in terms of overall organization performance or motivation it makes sense to set easy goals. First, even if low goals are achieved, performance is usually just that: low. Second, with easy goals, intrinsic motivation is minimal and, as a result, total motivation must fall considerably short of what is possible. This suggests that moderately difficult goals probably are optimal in terms of overall motivation and performance. They also seem to be acceptable as far as dysfunctional behavior, since they do not produce it to the same degree that difficult goals do.

Source of Discrimination

Except in special cases, it appears that whoever is being measured should be involved in the discrimination process. The cases where this would not be true are those in which the discrimination function is simply a matter of comparing a very objective measure (e.g., actual dollars spent) with an established objective standard (e.g., budgeted dollars to be spent). Both intrinsic and extrinsic motivation are likely to be highest when the person is involved. In the case of extrinsic motivation, the involvement is necessary as a basis for building trust and capturing information about the person's performance. It probably should take the form of a mutual process between the person and some outsider, because unless this is done the person will be tempted to distort the actual comparison. This can both lower extrinsic motivation and lead to the production of invalid data. As far as intrinsic motivation is concerned, there is no reason why the person shouldn't be the sole discriminator if he or she has the necessary skills to make the discrimination. Having it be a joint process is also acceptable as far as intrinsic motivation is concerned.

Having the person act as the sole discriminator seems optimal in terms of reducing bureaucratic behavior and resistance, although having someone else involved is also acceptable as long as the person doesn't use the result as a basis for giving rewards and punishment. Thus, in terms of most criteria, the discriminator function probably is best performed by the person doing the job except in the case of extrinsic motivation, where it makes sense to have it be a shared process between superior and subordinate.

Recipients of Communications

Intrinsic and extrinsic motivation both require that the individuals whose performance is measured receive feedback about their performance. This presents no problems with respect to causing dysfunctional behavior, so it seems safe to conclude that all information and control systems should provide the person whose performance is being measured with performance feedback. A similar situation exists with respect to information about the performance of others. Intrinsic and extrinsic motivation are often increased when information about the performance of individuals doing similar jobs is shared by everyone. This can usually be done without seriously increasing dysfunctional behavior. Thus it makes sense to make performance results available to all individuals doing similar jobs.

Extrinsic motivation requires that communications about performance be sent to individuals who can give rewards. As was noted in Chapter 6 giving performance information to individuals who have reward power is likely to produce dysfunctional behavior, particularly the production of invalid data. Thus there is an obvious conflict between what is necessary to generate extrinsic motivation and the need to minimize dysfunctional behavior. This conflict is particularly severe because it suggests that information that goes to superiors or power figures cannot be used for planning purposes because it is likely to be invalid. In fact, many superiors take this into account when they plan. They simply adjust the data given them by their subordinates to make the data more "reasonable."

Speed and Frequency of Communication

Fast communication is necessary for both intrinsic and extrinsic motivation. In both cases the reason is the same—without it, it is impossible to closely tie rewards to performance. Fast communication is a mixed blessing, however, because it can lead to some dysfunctional behavior. Still, as was noted in Chapter 6, speed of communication is probably not a major factor in influencing dysfunctional behavior. In fact, the reason it seems to have an impact is that when it is fast it opens up the possibility that the information can be used for reward and punishment purposes. Thus, the conflict between what is optimal for motivation and what is optimal for dysfunctional behavior is not a severe one.

The issues concerned with frequency of communication are similar to those concerned with speed. It must be appropriate if intrinsic and extrinsic motivation are to be present. However, having it appropriate can cause dysfunctional behavior because it creates the possibility of using the information as a basis of rewards and punishments. The one difference here is that an inappropriate frequency can in and of itself cause dysfunctional behavior, as the example of the Soviet plant managers given earlier illustrated. Thus, it seems reasonable to conclude that in terms of both motivation and dysfunctional behavior control systems should measure behavior on a schedule that approximates the time span of discretion of the job.

Type of Activity

For there to be intrinsic motivation, the activity involved must have certain characteristics. These were discussed in Chapter 5 in some detail. When combined they suggest that the activity needs to be meaningful and important to the person. It was pointed out that in the case of important activities there is a tendency toward dysfunctional behavior. As Argyris (1971) noted, the more important the activity, the harder it is to produce valid data. Thus, it appears that what is required to generate intrinsic motivation is likely to produce dysfunctional behavior. However, this conflict may be more apparent than real. The reason important activities produce invalid data is that they often influence the rewards and punishments individuals receive. This suggests that the way to reduce dysfunctional behavior is not to give everyone unimportant tasks and thereby reduce intrinsic motivation but to deal effectively with the matter of extrinsic rewards. If extrinsic rewards are not in the picture or are administered well, then giving people important meaningful tasks presents no problems in terms of dysfunctional behavior.

In Conclusion

Our review of the effects of control system characteristics suggests the following conclusions:

1. There is little conflict between the kind of information system characteristics needed to produce intrinsic motivation and the kind that lead to low levels of dysfunctional behavior. The only conflicts that appear here (e.g., recipients of communication) involve the production of dysfunctional behavior because of a third factor, the possible use of information for the giving of extrinsic rewards.
2. There is little conflict between the kind of information system characteristics that produce intrinsic motivation and the kind that produce extrinsic motivation. The exceptions that should be noted here involve the problems of who is involved in setting the standards and who acts as the discriminator. When extrinsic rewards are involved it can be hard to get the person to set the kind of challenging goals needed for high intrinsic motivation. It also can be difficult to get a valid discrimination made by the person whose behavior is being measured.
3. There is a definite difference between the kind of system characteristics that produce high extrinsic motivation and the kind that provide valid data.

CHOOSING A SYSTEM

Because of the conflict between the characteristics associated with high extrinsic motivation and the production of valid data, a number of writers have suggested that organizations use multiple information and control systems (Hofstede, 1967; Stedry, 1960). Is this a reasonable suggestion? There is no question that in most cases when important extrinsic rewards are involved employees are prone to distorting data. Thus, information systems used for extrinsic motivation often are not useful for intrinsic motivation and planning. The issue that organizations must face is when if at all multiple systems should be employed. To operate effectively the planning system would have to be designed so that it never influences rewards. This can be handled in several ways, but none of them are simple to implement. One way to handle it is to have the planning system provide information only on an aggregate basis (as suggested by Likert, 1961) so that the performance of no individual would be identifiable. Another is to only provide information to staff people who do not have reward power. The extrinsic reward system on the other hand would report data on the performance of individuals directly to the person who is in the best position to administer rewards and punishments. Every effort would, of course, be made to see that valid data were collected; otherwise, extrinsic motivation would disappear, but some slippage would be expected.

There are difficulties in implementing multiple systems. It requires an enormous educational effort and considerable attention **183** to budgeting, but it may be practical in some cases. Hopwood (1974) has reported that several British firms are experimenting with multiple budgets.

In one company, the managers are asked to formulate two budgets, one reflecting what they almost certainly expect to happen (to emphasize the inherent uncertainty of the process the wording used is "with 90 percent probability"), the other showing what they would ideally like to happen ("with 50 percent probability" is the phrase used in this case). The company operates in a high technology area and employs a well-educated work force. Another company uses a similar approach, but in this case the expectations budgets are regarded as being personal to each manager and hence relatively unthreatening yardsticks for personal review and appraisal. The monthly report received by each manager contains six columns: expectations budget, actual results, and variance, and personal aspirations budget, actual results, and variance. Columns 1, 2, 3, and 5 are completed by the accountants. Columns 4 and 6 remain empty in anticipation of the manager entering his or her own figures. Thus it seems that in some cases multiple control systems can operate.

In many cases multiple systems probably aren't necessary because a system designed to maximize intrinsic motivation and the production of valid data will get the job done. That is, the behavior will be performed adequately and the organization will be able to get the information it needs for planning and coordinating purposes. This would seem to be the approach to take when the job situation lends itself to high intrinsic motivation. The use of two systems probably makes the most sense when the tasks to be performed are simple, somewhat difficult to measure, and very important to the effectiveness of the organization.

A recent article by Cammann and Nadler (1976) has tried to specify in some detail when the decision to choose an externally or internally motivated control system should be made. Figure 10–1 lists the four questions that they say should be asked and Figure 10–2 shows how the answers to these questions should be combined to determine which kind of control system to use in a particular situation. In addition to the decision steps outlined in Figure 10–2, Cammann and Nadler state that the manager needs to consider the trade-offs between different strategies in his or her particular situation. The most obvious question is: "What are the desirable or undesirable outcomes for my particular group of subordinates." For example, if in the particular situation the opportunities for game-playing are few and the costs of game-playing are low, a tight control strategy may be more feasible than in other kinds of situations. They go on to state that in most **184** organizations, however, the potential costs of game-playing are

1. In general, what kind of managerial style do I have?

   Participative: I frequently consult my subordinates on decisions, encourage them to disagree with my opinion, share information with them, and let them make decisions whenever possible.

   Directive: I usually take most of the responsibility for and make most of the major decisions, pass on only the most necessary job-relevant information, and provide detailed and close direction for my subordinates.

2. In general, what kind of climate, structure, and reward system does my organization have?

   Participative: Employees at all levels of the organization are used to participate in decisions and influence the course of events. Managers are clearly rewarded for developing employee's skills and decision making capacity.

   Non-participative: Most important decisions are made by a few people at the top of the organization. Managers are not rewarded for developing employee competence or encouraging employees to participate in decision making.

3. How accurate and reliable are the measures of key areas of subordinate performance?

   Accurate: Measures are reliable, all major aspects of performance can be adequately measured, changes in measures accurately reflect changes in performance, measures cannot be easily sabotaged or faked by subordinates.

   Inaccurate: Not all important aspects of performance can be measured, measures often don't pick up on important changes in performance, good performance cannot be adequately defined in terms of the measures, measures can be easily sabotaged.

4. Do my subordinates desire to participate and respond well to opportunities to take responsibility for decision making and performance?

   High desire to participate: Employees are eager to participate in decisions, can make a contribution to decision making, and want to take more responsibility.

   Low desire to participate: Employees do not want to be involved in many decisions, don't want additional responsibility, and have little to contribute to decisions being made.

FIGURE 10–1
Questions a
Manager Should
ask When
Choosing a Control
Strategy

Adapted from C. Cammann and D. Nadler, "Fit Control Systems to Your Managerial Style," *Harvard Business Review*, 54(1976), p. 65–72.

high and managers should give serious consideration to an intrinsic control strategy if the basic decision-making process indicates that such a strategy is feasible.

It is possible that in some situations a single system that does include extrinsic rewards can be used. A situation that might fit this category is one where the tasks are simple and easily measured and there are known fair standards of performance. Where this is true, the opportunities for producing invalid data and bureaucratic behavior are minimized and thus a single system de- **185**

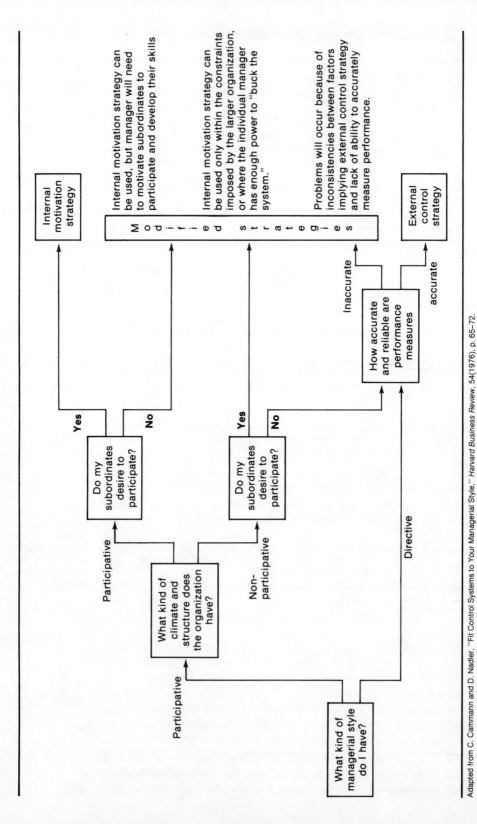

FIGURE 10-2 A Decision-Tree for Choosing a Control Strategy

Adapted from C. Cammann and D. Nadler, "Fit Control Systems to Your Managerial Style," *Harvard Business Review*, 54(1976), p. 65–72.

signed to maximize extrinsic motivation probably could be used without producing a great deal of dysfunctional behavior.

Finally, it is possible to imagine organizations where the climate is so good that only one system would be needed even though the job and organization structure is such that dysfunctional behavior might occur. Studies are now appearing on organizations that suggest that when climates are characterized by openness, trust, commitment to the organization, and mutual influence one system may be adequate (e.g., Likert, 1967; Walton, 1972). It is adequate because people don't demonstrate dysfunctional behavior even though it might possibly increase their short-term extrinsic rewards. It is beyond the scope of this book to specify how climates of this sort can be created, but it is worth noting that as a general rule they tend to occur when all employees participate in the design and operation of the organization, accept its goals, and feel they will gain when it increases its effectiveness.

EXTERNAL AUDITORS

Our review of the jobs of external auditors identified some important problems. The most serious of these concerns the pressures they are under. The pressure they are under because of their financial liability has led to their conservative behavior. The pressure they are under to maintain successful clients has led at times to the development of alternative approaches to reporting and analyzing financial data so that it is often difficult for the inexperienced individual to correctly interpret financial statements. It seems unlikely that the situation will be changed with respect to financial liability. If anything, law suits against CPA firms seem likely to become more frequent. Thus, there is little prospect that this kind of pressure will be decreased and indeed there is considerable question as to whether it should be decreased. Although it is a pressure toward conservative behavior, it is also a pressure toward high-quality audits.

The same thing cannot be said about the pressure CPA firms are under to maintain successful clients. This is not necessarily a pressure toward a high-quality audit nor is it a pressure toward producing reports that give directly comparable data for all firms. It is also a pressure that potentially can be reduced. Some tentative moves have already been made in this direction (requirements that firms disclose reasons for changing auditors), but more seem to be needed. As long as organizations select and pay their auditors this pressure will exist and it will be substantial.

Even with the pressures that CPA firms are under, it seems there are some things they can do to improve their effectiveness. Most researchers who have studied CPA firms have remarked on **187** their low commitment to good personnel administration (see, for example, Sorensen, Rhode, and Lawler, 1973). In most firms staff turnover is high, performance appraisal is poorly done, entry level jobs are boring and repetitive, and selection decisions are made based on interviews that are not valid. It is not hard to understand why these conditions exist given the history of most CPA firms and the pressures they are under. Still, there is no question that most firms can do a better job of personnel administration. The jobs of most CPA's can be improved by such things as consolidating highly segmented auditing tasks, eliminating identifiable production-line activities in auditing or tax work, permitting greater individualization in the organization of work, permitting choices of work associates, involving more lower-level personnel in the review of personnel at their level, and asking lower-level personnel for their evaluations of their immediate supervisors. These suggestions, if adopted, could go a long way toward removing the conservative image and behavior characterizing CPA firms. This would seem to be a necessary prerequisite for firms to attract and retain the high quality of individuals they obviously need if they are to perform their crucial functions well.

It is not an overstatement to say that the effective functioning of financial information and control systems both for internal organization purposes and external decision makers requires that CPA firms be well-managed organizations staffed with highly-trained, innovative professionals whose primary commitment is to producing valid, comparable, understandable data about the conditions of the firms they audit. Now this involves only financial data, but in the future it may include nonfinancial data as well. The need for comparable data is clearly illustrated with respect to the problem of functional fixation. The research shows that decision makers cannot correctly interpret data when different computation methods are used to arrive at a measure of something like profit. This means that accountants must begin to compute in the same way indicators that are called the same thing. Until this is done decision makers cannot be expected to produce high quality decisions.

INTERNAL SYSTEMS DEVELOPMENT
AND MAINTENANCE JOBS

Many of the things just said about external audit jobs can be said about internal jobs. First it is clear that for information and control systems to operate effectively, these jobs must be staffed by competent people and there must be a good line/staff relationship. The latter is necessary if the staff is going to get the kind of information it needs and if it is going to have the kind of influence it desires. The key to attracting and holding competent individuals in staff jobs and to an effective line/staff relationship would seem to be in the design of the staff jobs. They must be challenging and motivating, otherwise they will not attract and hold competent people. The job satisfaction research clearly points out that many staff jobs are not that satisfying. The reasons seem to be highly specialized job content, low power, and the negative sanction system. As was pointed out in Chapter 7, sometimes this can be corrected by simply breaking up the paper work assembly lines that have grown up in many offices. Often they are no different than the assembly lines in factories. In fact, in one respect they are worse, they are staffed with more highly educated people than most industrial assembly lines. Sometimes, however, staff jobs cannot be improved without changing the basic line/staff interface.

The question of how staff jobs can be redesigned to improve the line/staff interface is difficult to answer. Essentially the issue is power. The staff wants more of it and the line resists giving it up. However, the line badly needs the information the staff has to offer in order to make effective decisions. In many cases it also needs the counsel of the staff, since some of the data it produces are not readily interpretable. Because the line needs the staff, improved line/staff relations may be possible.

Probably the most effective solution to the problem of line/staff conflict lies in giving the staff more formal decision-making power. In effect this means reducing the amount of distinction between line and staff employees. Certain parts of this distinction seem to have outlived their usefulness. This seems to be particularly true with respect to the point that staff employees make recommendations and line employees make decisions. Gibson and Nolan (1974) recognize this in their writings on computerized information systems. In what they consider to be their most advanced situation the information system manager is part of the top executive team. The work of Pettigrew (1972) and others points out that whether or not they have formal power, staff employees influence many decisions. Thus it seems only logical to acknowledge this fact formally. It is also becoming more and more common to see divisional controllers report directly to the division general manager and be part of his or her management team. This design recognizes the inputs the controller has to make and provides a means for the controller to influence decisions and share in the success of good decisions.

Of course not all staff employees should be involved in what have been traditional line functions, but more can be. There are possibilities for this that are not utilized in most organizations. Task forces that involve both line and staff employees are but one way to break down line/staff differences and get staff employ- **189** ees involved in decision making. Getting staff employees involved in more line-like decision making should not only make them more satisfied, it should also help them design better information and control systems. As line managers often point out, staff employees tend to be unrealistic in what is expected of line managers. One reason for this may be that staff employees have little experience in line jobs.

DECISION QUALITY

The information and control system characteristics contributing to high decision quality and its predecessor utilization are not different from those leading to high motivation and a low incidence of dysfunctional behavior. Briefly stated, to contribute to good decisions information and control systems should:

1. Produce measures that are complete, objective, and influenceable by whatever is being measured.
2. Use standards set by decision makers or someone who is knowledgeable.
3. Have the decision maker or some other credible person act as the discriminator.
4. Provide information to the decision maker.
5. Provide some sort of motivation for the decision maker to use the information.
6. Provide data rapidly and at an appropriate time interval.
7. Avoid information overload.
8. Present data in an understandable form and language.

The only points that might conflict with what is optimal for motivation are points 2, 3, and 4. There might be a problem if the decision maker has substantial reward power. The guidelines for decision making suggest that the decision maker be involved in the standard setting and discrimination but when people who have reward power become involved the incidence of dysfunctional behavior goes up, particularly the reporting of invalid information. Two ways to deal with this problem are to not use extrinsic rewards to motivate or to structure the organization so that decision makers do not have this kind of power over individuals below them. Another approach is to create organizations where most decisions are made by the individuals whose behavior is being measured. Under these conditions the performer, discriminator, and decision maker are the same person. This suggests that if an organization is properly designed, situations where the decision maker is far away from the data point should rarely exist.

The relationship between decision quality and organization design raises a key issue. To evaluate the effectiveness of an information and control system, we must consider its fit to the organizational situation. Although all systems that contribute to high quality decisions have certain characteristics in common, they must fit certain aspects of their host organization. As Hop-wood (1974) has noted: "If genuine consideration is to be given to the creation of decision oriented accounting systems, accounting may well require a new vision and ideology, one based on an organizational rather than an individual view of decision making. . . . Much more attention would have to be given to the relationship between the decision centers and both the other parts of the organization and the wider organizational environment (p. 141)."

ORGANIZATIONAL FACTORS AND DECISION QUALITY

One of the characteristics of organizations that was identified in Chapter 3 and again by Hopwood warrants particular attention in the design of information systems: the external environment. For a long time organization theorists tended to pay relatively little attention to it, they tended to think in terms of universal theories of organizational effectiveness, that is, theories that assumed there was one best way to organize regardless of situational factors. Recently, however, organization theorists have been paying greater attention to the effects of the external environment. This has led to the development of a number of contingency theories of organizational effectiveness. Rather than assuming that there is one best way to organize, these theories assume that the best way to organize depends on the characteristics of the environment in which the organization operates. Overall, it is hard to disagree with the contingency theory arguments that the environments in which organizations operate require different information processing structures. Not only does it have an intuitive appeal; it is supported by a number of research studies (Burns and Stalker, 1961; Lawrence and Lorsch, 1967).

The aspect of the environment most theorists have focused on is degree of certainty. The environments organizations face clearly differ substantially in their rate of change. Some are stable and predictable while others are relatively unstable. For example, the environments of consumer-oriented firms often change rapidly while the environments of many manufacturing firms that sell to other firms often don't. Galbraith (1973) has explained why environments that differ in rate of change require different structures. He views organizations from an information processing point of view and notes that the uncertainty of the task influences the amount of information that has to be processed during the execution of the task. If the task is well understood prior to performing it, much of the activity can be preplanned. If it is not understood, then during the actual task execution knowledge is acquired which suggests changes in resource allocations, schedules, and priorities. **191**

All these changes require information processing during task performance. Therefore, the greater the *task uncertainty,* the greater the *amount of information* that must be processed to insure effective performance. From this proposition it follows that variations in organizational form are variations in the ability to process amounts of information. It follows that organizations or subparts of organizations that operate in changing environments need to process more information than organizations in stable environments. Hence they must be structured differently.

Lawrence and Lorsch (1969) have summarized one view of how organizations should be structured to deal with low and high change environments: If the environment is relatively stable, the job can be specified in a predetermined set of operating rules. The necessary messages can be handled through traditional superior-subordinate channels, which may be few and constricted but are probably less subject to error and relatively inexpensive. Fairly short time horizons are usually adequate to take account of the reactions of such an environment to the firm's actions. This makes it sensible to use a straightforward, task-oriented managerial style.

On the other hand, life in an organizational unit must become more complex to deal adequately with an uncertain and rapidly changing sector of the environment. A flatter organization must be employed so there will be more points of contact with the environment. Formal rules cannot be formulated that will be suitable for any appreciable time period, so it seems better not to rely heavily on them. More of an all-to-all communications pattern is indicated; it can keep environmental clues moving throughout the unit for interpretation at all points instead of just through superior-subordinate channels. A longer time orientation is usually needed. The growth of this necessarily more complex and sophisticated (as well as more costly) communication network is fostered by an interpersonal style that emphasizes building strong relationships rather than just accomplishing the task, per se.

Organizations facing unstable environments also need to push decisions down to the lower levels of the organization. This is necessary for two reasons: speed of response and information overload. Changing environments require quick decisions and one way to assure this is to move the decisions to the point nearest the action. This usually means moving decisions down so that the power balance is flatter than in most organizations (See Figure 10–3). Since uncertainly leads to greater amounts of information, overload can be a problem at the top of the organization if decisions are concentrated there. As we noted in Chapter 8 individuals can only handle so much information, and thus when a great deal must be processed something needs to be done to take the load off the top of the organization. The most effective thing to do

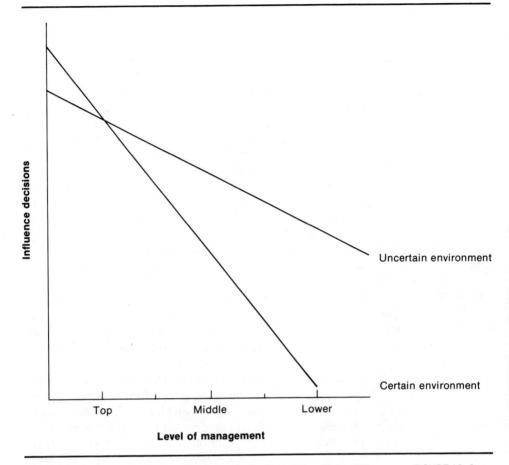

Influence decisions

Top   Middle   Lower

Level of management

Uncertain environment

Certain environment

Adapted from J. Galbraith, *Designing Complex Organizations,* Reading, Mass.: Addison-Wesley, 1973.

FIGURE 10–3
Hierarchical
Distribution of
Influence

in most situations is to have individuals close to the function process the information and make the decisions.

There are, however, other approaches that can be taken (see Galbraith, 1973). The need for information is subject to management influence since it is dependent on the desired level of performance. If senior managers are willing to accept lower standards of performance, the more traditional forms of organization may still be able to cope. Alternatively, it may be possible to reduce the degree of interdependence either by the use of inventory buffers or by creating relatively self-contained tasks (tasks that do not require cooperation).

To a substantial extent the degree of integration and communication required is a function of just what kind of relationships the different parts of an organization have to each other. Thompson (1967) identifies these different kinds of task interdependence as pooled, sequential, and reciprocal. Pooled interdependence **193** exists when each part renders a discrete contribution to the whole and each is supported by the whole (e.g., subsidiaries of a conglomerate). Sequential interdependence exists when one part of an organization must act properly before another can act. Reciprocal interdependence exists when the outputs of one part of the organization are the inputs for the other and vice versa. Pooled interdependence requires the least information while reciprocal requires the most. Thus any effort that moves organizations in the direction of pooled interdependence should lead to a reduced need for information processing. In accounting terms, for instance, attempts may be made to establish autonomous profit and investment centers. This may mean structuring organizations along product lines rather than along functional lines.

If no desirable option is available to reduce the information needs of the organization, management can improve the capacity of the organization to process information (Hopwood, 1974). In part, this can be achieved by improving existing information systems, by creating new ones, and possibly by the use of more efficient data processing methods (e.g., introduction of computers). In addition, a movement towards forms of organizational structure that facilitate direct personal contacts between managers who share a problem can do much to improve the flow of information.

Perhaps the most influential research study on contingency theory was done by Lawrence and Lorsch (1967). In their investigation of how organizations respond to their environments, they studied the structure and behavior of companies operating in three industries that experienced very different rates of change in both products and processes. Although the firms' environments could be described in general terms, in reality each firm faced a series of different environments. The environmental contexts of their production departments differed from those of their marketing departments, and both of these were very different from those of the research and development departments. Lawrence and Lorsch were therefore concerned with discovering how firms succeeded in organizing themselves to respond to the specific demands of a series of environments while at the same time maintaining the viability of the enterprise as a whole.

Companies that were successful in terms of sales, profits, and return on investment were found to have organizational structures that were consistent with the demands of their environments. Those organizations that had to respond to a number of environments had structures that were described as differentiated. That is, different parts of the organizations were structured differently in accord with the kind of environment in which they operated. The key environmental factor seemed to be degree of certainty. The results quite clearly show that the organizations that dealt

194

effectively with stable environments were organized differently than those that dealt effectively with unstable environments. Those in stable environments were more hierarchical in nature and more rigidly structured.

In addition to looking at degree of differentiation Lawrence and Lorsch looked at how organizations coordinated themselves and integrated their activities. They found that although there were differences in approach, the separate departments of the successful companies in all three industries were all highly integrated. In the container manufacturing firms they studied, where it was important to meet the demands of the customers, the activities of the production and sales departments were integrated through the management hierarchy and by the use of plans, budgets, and schedules. Overall, they found that where greater differentiation existed more integrating structures were needed.

Very much related to the issue of subunit interdependence is the issue of how technology influences organization structure. Once an organization has decided what product or service to provide, it has a limited choice of technologies to choose among. Most products can only be effectively produced in a limited number of ways. Three basic kinds of production technologies have been identified: unit, mass, and process. Unit production involves one of a kind or small batch production (e.g., locomotives), mass production involves large numbers (e.g., cars), and process production involves a continuous flow of products (e.g., chemicals). In addition to these production technologies there are a wide variety of service industry technologies for which no classification system exists. Technology has been shown to be an important determinant of both organizational structure and information needs. (See e.g., Woodward, 1958, 1965.) Technologies differ in terms of both the rate of change and the amount of interdependence they demand. Process production technologies seem to have the most difficult interdependence problems and thus require the most information. Technologies undergoing rapid changes like many of the process production technologies also require a great deal of information processing capability.

Research has also shown that the different technologies require different organization structures (Burns and Stalker, 1961). Woodward (1965), for example, found that successful firms with mass production technologies tend to have mechanistic management structures with clear cut patterns of duties and responsibilities. Higher performing firms with unit or process production technologies tend to have organic systems of management with a great deal of delegation of authority and decision making. This is not surprising, given the information demands these kinds of organizations face.

195

Several researchers have noted that the effects of technology cannot be considered separate from the effects of size (see e.g., Porter, Lawler, and Hackman, 1975). It appears that when organizations are small, technology is crucial to structure and design, but when organizations are large the importance of technology is typically confined to rank-and-file level jobs. It follows from this that technology may not be considered as extensively when information systems are designed for large organizations as when they are designed for small. Finally it is important to note that technology shouldn't be looked upon as a fixed determinant of organizational structure. While it is often difficult to change certain features of technology, it is not impossible. Action can be taken to change it in ways that make it more congruent with the needs of individuals.

In Conclusion

The research and theory we have reviewed on technology and organization structure points to one conclusion: The structure of an organization must fit the environment in which it operates and the information and control systems of an organization must fit that structure. Organizations that do not meet these conditions are likely to be ineffective because the appropriate individuals will not have the information and authority they need to make decisions. To contribute to good decision making the information and control system must get the right information, in an understandable form and amount, to the individual or individuals who need it. All too often poor decision making occurs because the information system fails to do this. It fails not because the information doesn't exist, but because the system was not designed with the characteristics of the organization and its environment in mind.

Figure 10–4 shows the three organizational factors that in particular need to be considered when information and control systems are designed. These in turn are shown as being shaped by the environment and the objectives of the organization. The degree of environmental uncertainty influences both the level at which decisions should be made and the degree of integration and differentiation. We know from our discussion so far that the greater the uncertainty the lower the levels at which decisions should be made and the more organic and flexible the management style should be. We also know that this requires an information system that emphasizes the pulling together and delivery of information at lower levels in the organization and de-emphasizes passing detailed information up the hierarchy.

The work of Lawrence and Lorsch (1967) shows the greater the variance in the certainty of the environments the organization needs to deal with the more differentiated and integrated the organization needs to be. Integration in turn can only be achieved

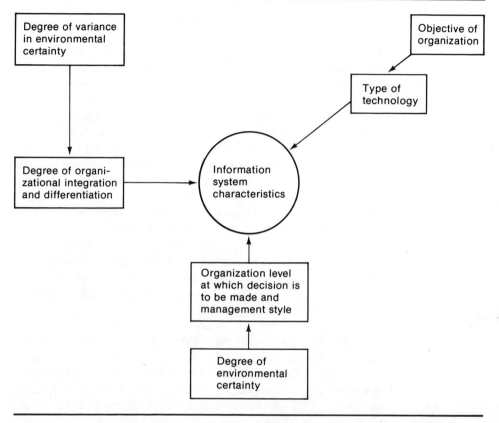

Degree of variance
in environmental
certainty

Objective of
organization

Type of
technology

Degree of organi-
zational integration
and differentiation

Information
system
characteristics

Organization level
at which decision is
to be made and
management style

Degree of
environmental
certainty

FIGURE 10–4
Factors That Should
Affect Information
System Design

when the information and control system is designed to facilitate the horizontal transmission of data and the establishment of integrating standards and reports. Figure 10–4 also shows that the technology of the organization is determined at least partially by the product it tries to produce. The technology in turn should influence the type of information systems used. Perhaps the best way to summarize this discussion of organizational characteristics is to note that anyone who wants to evaluate an information system should ask the following questions:

1. Does it provide decision makers with data relevant to the decisions they need to make?
2. Does it provide the right amount of information to decision makers throughout the organization?
3. Does it provide enough information to each part of the organization about how other related parts of the organization are functioning?
4. Does it fit the technology and structure of the organization?

If the answer to all these questions is affirmative then the data from the information system are likely to be utilized and high quality decisions made.

OVERVIEW

We began by pointing out the pervasiveness of information and control systems in organizations of all sizes and types. Because of this they have a large impact on organizational behavior. In some cases this impact contributes to organizational effectiveness and a high quality of working life while in others it doesn't. Designing an effective information and control system for an organization is clearly a complex and demanding task. It requires taking into account a number of factors: the organization's technology, its external environment, the nature of its employees, and its size. Because these factors influence the effectiveness of information and control systems no single type of control system can be effective in all situations. To be effective systems must be designed for particular situations. There are, however, some general principles that can be used in the design of information and control systems. Underlying all of these principles is the point that the characteristics of an information and control system have a significant impact on behavior.

It is crucial that behavioral considerations not be overlooked or slighted in favor of designing systems that are efficient from a data processing point of view or from a financial audit point of view. If behavioral impact is not the predominant consideration, the system that is designed is likely to have a negative impact on organizational effectiveness and on the quality of work life of both the people who are measured by the system and those who run it. The classification system presented in Chapter 3 represents one attempt to guide system design. If it is used in combination with what we know about the causes of behavior there is a good deal of evidence that it can improve the design of systems. It is the responsibility of everyone concerned with the design and operation of information and control systems to be aware of this information and to utilize it to design systems that are effective and that lead to a high quality of work life.

REFERENCES

Allport, G.W., and L. Postman, *The Psychology of Rumor.* New York: Holt, 1947.

American Institute of Certified Public Accountants, *Accounting Terminology Bulletin No. 1.* New York: Committee on Terminology, 1941.

Anthony, R.N., *Planning and Control Systems: A Framework for Analysis.* Boston: Division of Research, Graduate School of Business Administration, Harvard University, 1965.

Argyris, Chris, *The Impact of Budgets on People.* New York: Controllership Foundation, 1951.

———, *Executive Leadership,* New York: Harper, 1953.

———, *Personality and Organization.* New York: Harper, 1957.

———, *Interpersonal Competence and Organizational Effectiveness.* Homewood, Ill.: Dorsey, 1962.

———, *Integrating the Individual and the Organization.* New York: Wiley, 1964.

———, "Management Information Systems: the Challenge to Rationality and Emotionality," *Management Science,* 17(1971), 275–292.

Arps, G.F., "Work with Knowledge of Results Versus Work without Knowledge of Results," *Psychology Monographs,* 28(1920), no. 3(Whole No. 125).

Ashworth, John, "People Who Become Accountants," *The Journal of Accountancy,* (November 1968), 43–49.

———, "A Must for Effective Recruiting: Mutual Understanding Between Students and the Accounting Profession," *The Journal of Accountancy,* (February 1969), 84–86.

———, "The Pursuit of High Quality Recruits," *The Journal of Accountancy,* (February 1969), 53–58.

Atkinson, J.W., *An Introduction to Motivation.* Princeton, N.J.: Van Nostrand, 1964.

Babchuk, N., and W.J. Goode, "Work Incentives in a Self-Determined Group," *American Social Review,* 16(1951), 679–687.

Ball, Ray, and Philip Brown, "Portfolio Theory and Accounting," *Journal of Accounting Research,* 7(Autumn 1969), 300–323.

Barnes, L.B., and F.Z. White, "Power Networks in the Appraisal Process," *Harvard Business Review,* 49(1971) 101–109.

Bart, Lionel, "Who Will Buy This Wonderful Morning," *Oliver,* Lakeview Music Co. Ltd., London, England, 1960.

Beaver, William H., "The Behavior of Security Prices and Its Implication for Accounting Research (Methods)," in Robert R. Sperling (ed.), *Research Methodology in Accounting.* Lawrence, Kansas: Scholars Book Co., 1972.

Becker, Selwyn W., "The Accountant as Others See Him," *The Newsletter of the Graduate School of Business,* University of Chicago, (Spring 1969), 16–19.

Becker, Selwyn, and D. Green, "Budgeting and Employee Behavior," *The Journal of Business,* 35(1962), 392–402.

Berlew, D.E., and D.T. Hall, "The Socialization of Managers: Efforts of Expectations on Performance," *Administrative Science Quarterly,* 11(1966), 207–223.

Berliner, Joseph S., "A Problem in Soviet Business Administration," *Administrative Science Quarterly,* 1(1956), 86–101.

————, "The Situation of Plant Managers" in A. Inkeles, and K. Geiger, eds., *Soviet Society: A Book of Readings.* Boston: Houghton Mifflin, 1961.

Beyer, R., *Profitability Accounting for Planning and Control.* New York: Ronald, 1963.

Bilodeau, E.A., I.M. Bilodeau, and D.A. Schumsky, "Some Effects of Introducing and Withdrawing Knowledge of Results Early and Late in Practice," *Journal of Experimental Psychology,* 58(1959), 142–144.

Blau, P.M., *The Dynamics of Bureaucracy.* Chicago: University of Chicago Press, 1955.

Blood, M.R., and C.L. Hulin, "Alienation, Environmental Characteristics, and Worker Responses," *Journal of Applied Psychology,* 51(1967), 284–290.

Bonini, C.P., *Simulation of Information and Decision Systems of the Firm.* Englewood Cliffs, N.J.: Prentice-Hall, 1963.

Bower, J., *Managing the Resource Allocation Process.* Division of Research, Graduate School of Business Administration, Harvard University, 1970.

Briloff, A.J., *Unaccountable Accounting: Games Accountants Play.* New York: Harper & Row, 1972.

Browne, Philip J., and Robert T. Golembiewski, "The Line-Staff Concept Revisited: An Empirical Study of Organizational Images," *Academy of Management Journal,* 17(1974), 400–417.

Brummet, R.L., E.G. Flamholtz, and W.C. Pyle, "Human Resource Measurement— A Challenge for Accountants," *The Accounting Review,* 43(1968), 217–224.

————, "Human Resource Accounting: A Tool to Increase Managerial Effectiveness," *Management Accounting,* 51(1969a), 12–15.

————, *Human Resource Accounting: Development and Implementation in Industry.* Ann Arbor, Mich.: Foundation for Research on Human Behavior, 1969b.

Bruns, William J., Jr., "Inventory Valuation and Management Decisions," *The Accounting Review,* 40(April 1965), 345–357.

————, "Accounting Information and Decision-Making: Some Behavioral Hypotheses," *The Accounting Review,* 43(July 1968), 469–480.

Buckley, John W., and Marlene H. Buckley, *The Accounting Profession.* Los Angeles: Melville, 1974.

Burns, Thomas J., editor, *The Behavioral Aspects of Accounting Data for Performance Evaluation.* Columbus, Ohio: College of Administrative Science, Ohio State University, 1970.

————, *Behavioral Experiments in Accounting.* Columbus, Ohio: College of Administrative Science, Ohio State University, 1972.

Burns, Thomas J., and G.M. Stalker, *The Management of Innovation.* London: Tavistock, 1961.

Cammann, C., "Can Accounting Systems Produce Change?" Presented at the APA Convention, 1974a.

———, *The Impact of a Feedback System on Managerial Attitudes and Performance.* Unpublished Ph.D. thesis, Yale University, 1974b.

Cammann, C. and D. Nadler, "Fit Control Systems to Your Managerial Style," *Harvard Business Review,* 54(1976), 65–72.

Campbell, J.F., M.D. Dunnette, E.E. Lawler, and K.E. Weick, *Managerial Behavior, Performance and Effectiveness.* New York: McGraw-Hill, 1970.

Caplan, Edwin H., A Review of T.R. Dyckman, "Investment Analysis and General Price-Level Adjustments, Studies in Accounting Research #1," *The Accounting Review,* 45(October 1970), 810.

———, *Management Accounting and Behavioral Sciences.* Reading, Mass.: Addison-Wesley, 1971.

Caplan, Edwin H., and S. Landekich, *Human Resource Accounting: Past, Present and Future.* New York: National Association of Accountants, 1974.

Carmichael, D.R., "Behavioral Hypotheses of Internal Control," *The Accounting Review,* 45(2)(1970), 235–245.

Carroll, D.C., "Implications of On-Line, Real-Time Systems for Managerial Decision-Making," in C.A. Meyers, ed., *The Impact of Computers on Management.* Cambridge: MIT Press, 1967, 140–166.

Cartter, A.M., *Theory of Wages and Employment.* Homewood, Ill.: Irwin, 1959.

Cherrington, D.J., and J.O. Cherrington, "Participation, Performance and Appraisal," *Business Horizons,* 17(1974), 35–44.

CMA: Certificate In Management Accounting. New York: Institute of Management Accounting, National Association of Accountants, 1973.

Coch, L., and J.R.P. French, Jr., "Overcoming Resistance to Change," *Human Relations,* 1(1948), 512–532.

Cofer, C.N., and M.H. Appley, *Motivation: Theory and Research.* New York: Wiley, 1964.

Comiskey, E.E., "Market Responses to Changes in Depreciation Accounting," *The Accounting Review,* 46(April 1971), 279–285.

Committee to Prepare a Statement of Basic Accounting Theory, *A Statement of Basic Accounting Theory.* Evanston, Ill.: American Accounting Association, 1966.

Cook, D.M., "The Effect of Frequency of Feedback on Attitudes and Performance," *Empirical Research in Accounting: Selected Studies, 1968* Supplement to the *Journal of Accounting Research,* 1968, 213–224.

Cressey, D.R., *Other People's Money.* New York: Free Press, 1953.

Dale, E. and L.F. Urwick, *Staff in Organizations.* New York: McGraw-Hill, 1960.

Dalton, M., *Men Who Manage.* New York: Wiley, 1959.

Davis, K., "Management, Communication and the Grapevine," *Harvard Business Review,* 31(5)(1953), 43–49.

Davis, L.E., and J.C. Taylor, *Design of Jobs.* Baltimore: Penguin, 1972.

Dearden, J., "Problems of Decentralized Profit Responsibility," *Harvard Business Review,* 38(1960), 79–86.

———, "Problems in Decentralized Financial Control," *Harvard Business Review,* 39(1961), 72–80.

DeCoster, D.T., and J.P. Fertakis, "Budget Induced Pressure and Its Relationship to Supervisory Behavior," *Journal of Accounting Research,* 6(1968), 237–246.

DeCoster, D.T., and J.G. Rhode, "The Accountant's Stereotype: Real or Imagined, Deserved or Unwarranted," *The Accounting Review,* 43(October 1971), 651–664.

Dierkes, M., and R.A. Bauer, eds., *Corporate Social Accounting.* New York: Praeger, 1973.

Drucker, P. "Controls, Control and Management," in C.P. Bonini, R.K. Jaedicke, and H.M. Wagner, *Management Controls: New Directions in Basic Research.* New York: Wiley, 1964.

Dubin, R., "Industrial Workers' Worlds: A Study of the Central Life Interests of Industrial Workers," *Social Problems,* 3(1956), 131–142.

Dunbar, R.L.M., "Budgeting for Control," *Administrative Science Quarterly,* 16(1971), 88–96.

Dunnette, M.D., *Personnel Selection and Placement.* Belmont, Calif.: Wadsworth, 1966.

Dyckman, Thomas R., "The Effects of Alternative Accounting Techniques on Certain Management Decisions," *Journal of Accounting Research,* 2(1)(Spring 1964), 91–107.

⸺, *Investment Analysis and General Price-Level Adjustments: A Behavioral Study.* Evanston, Ill.: American Accounting Association, 1969.

Eilon, S., "Problems in Studying Management Control," *International Journal of Production Research,* 1(1962).

Elwell, J.L., and G.C. Grindley, "The Effect of Knowledge of Results on Learning and Performance I: A Coordinated Movement of the Two Hands," *British Journal of Psychology,* 29(1938), 39–53.

Festinger, L., "A Theory of Social Comparison Processes," *Human Relations,* 7(1954), 117–140.

Flamholtz, E.G., "The Development and Implementation of a Replacement Cost Model for Human Resource Valuation," *Accounting and Information Systems Research Program,* Los Angeles: University of California, Graduate School of Business Administration, 1970.

⸺, "Toward a Theory of Human Resource Value in Formal Organizations," *The Accounting Review,* 47(4)(1972), 666–678.

⸺, "Assessing the Validity of a Theory of Human Resource Accounting: A Field Study," *Journal of Accounting Research: Empirical Research in Accounting—Selected Studies, 1972., Journal of Accounting Research,* 1973.

⸺, *Human Resource Accounting.* Encino, Calif.: Dickinson, 1974.

Frank, A.G., "Goal Ambiguity and Conflicting Standards: An Approach to the Study of Organization," *Human Organization,* 17(1959), 8–13.

French, J.R.P., J. Israel, and D. As, "An Experiment on Participation in a Norwegian Factory," *Human Relations,* 13(1960), 3–19.

French, J.R.P., and B. Raven, "The Basis of Social Power," in D. Cartwright and A. Zonder, eds., *Group Dynamics,* 2nd ed. Evanston, Ill.: Row Peterson, 1959, 607–623.

Galbraith, J., *Designing Complex Organizations.* Reading, Mass.: Addison-Wesley, 1973.

Gardner, B.B., *Human Relations in Industry.* Chicago: Irwin, 1945.

Ghiselli, E.E., *The Validity of Occupational Attitude Tests.* New York: Wiley, 1966.

Gibson, C.F., and R.L. Nolan, "Managing the Four Stages of EDP Growth," *Harvard Business Review,* 74(1974), 76–88.

Gillespie, J.J., *Free Expression in Industry.* London: Pilot Press, 1948.

Goldman, Arieh, and Benzion Barlev, "The Auditor-Firm Conflict of Interests: Its Implications for Independence," *The Accounting Review,* 49(4)(October 1974), 707–718.

Gordon, M.J., B. Horwitz, and P. Meyers, *Empirical Research in Accounting: Selected Studies.* Evanston, Ill.: American Accounting Association, 1967, 164–180.

Gouldner, A.W., *Patterns of Industrial Bureaucracy*. Glencoe, Ill.: Free Press, 1954.

Greller, M.M., and D.M. Herold, "Sources of Feedback: A Preliminary Investigation," *Organizational Behavior and Human Performance,* 13(1975), 244–256.

Guion, R.M., *Personnel Testing*. New York: McGraw-Hill, 1965.

Haas, J.E., and T.E. Drabek, *Organizations: A Sociological Perspective*. Riverside, N.J.: Macmillan, 1973.

Hackman, J.R., and E.E. Lawler, "Employee Reactions to Job Characteristics," *Journal of Applied Psychology,* 55(1971), 259–286.

Haire, M., "Biological Models and Empirical Histories of Growth of Organizations" in M. Haire, ed., *Modern Organization Theory.* New York: Wiley, 1959, 272–306.

Hermanson, R.H., *Accounting for Human Assets*. East Lansing, Mich.: Bureau of Business & Economic Research, 1964.

Hofstede, G.H., *The Game of Budget Control*. Assen, Netherlands: Van Gorcum, 1967.

Hofstedt, Thomas R., "Some Behavioral Parameters of Financial Analysis," *The Accounting Review,* 47(1972), 679–692.

Hopwood, A.G., "An Emperical Study of the Role of Accounting Data in Performance Evaluation," *Emperical Research in Accounting: Selected Studies, 1972.* Supplement to Vol. 10, *Journal of Accounting Research.*

_____, *An Accounting System and Managerial Behavior*. Lexington, Mass.: Lexington Books, 1973.

_____, "Leadership Climate and the Use of Accounting Data in Performance Evaluation," *The Accounting Review,* 49(1974a), 485–95.

_____ , *Accounting and Human Behavior*. London: Haymarket Publishing, 1974b.

Hubbard, Elbert, "The Buyer," in *Selected Writings of Elbert Hubbard, Vol. VIII.* Roycrofters Press, 1922.

Hulin, C.L., and M.R. Blood, "Job Enlargement, Individual Differences, and Worker Responses," *Psychological Bulletin,* 69(1968), 41–55.

Ijiri, Y., R.K. Jaedicke, and K.E. Knight, "The Effects of Accounting Alternatives on Management Decisions," in R.K. Jaedicke, Yuji Ijiri, and Oswald Nielsen, eds., *Research in Accounting Measurement.* Evanston, Ill.: American Accounting Association, 1966.

Jaques, E., *Equitable Payment*. New York: Wiley, 1961.

Jasinski, F.J., "Use and Misuse of Efficiency Controls," *Harvard Business Review,* 34(1956), 105–12.

Jenkins, G.D., D.A. Nadler, E.E. Lawler, and C. Cammann, "Standardized Observations: An Approach to Measuring the Nature of Jobs," *Journal of Applied Psychology,* 60(1975), 171–80.

Jensen, Robert E., "An Experimental Design for Study of Effects of Accounting Variations in Decision Making," *Journal of Accounting Research,* 4(1966), 224–38.

Johnson, A.M., "The Influence of Incentive and Punishment Upon Reaction Time," *Archives of Psychology,* 8(54)(1922).

Jones, E.E., and H.B. Gerard, *Foundations of Social Psychology*. New York: Wiley, 1967.

Kaplan, R.A., and R. Roll, "Investor Evaluation of Accounting Information: Some Empirical Evidence," *Journal of Business,* 45(April 1972), 225–57.

Katz, D., and R.L. Kahn, *The Social Psychology of Organizations*. New York: Wiley, 1966.

Khemakhem, Abdellatif, "A Simulation of Management-Decision Behavior: Funds and Income," *The Accounting Review,* 43(July 1968), 522–34.

203

Koontz, H., and C. O'Donnell, *Principles of Management,* 4th ed. New York: McGraw-Hill, 1968.

Lawler, E.E., "Managers' Attitudes Toward How Their Pay Is and Should Be Determined," *Journal of Applied Psychology,* 50(1966), 273–79.

————, "The Multitrait-Multirater Approach to Measuring Managerial Job Performance," *Journal of Applied Psychology,* 51(1967), 369–81.

————, "Job Design and Employee Motivation," *Personnel Psychology,* 22(1969), 426–35.

————, *Pay and Organizational Effectiveness: A Psychological View.* New York: McGraw-Hill, 1971.

————, "Secrecy and the Need to Know" in M. Dunnette, R. House, and H. Tosi, eds., *Readings in Managerial Motivation and Compensation.* East Lansing, Mich.: Michigan State University Press, 1972.

————, *Motivation in Work Organizations.* Monterey, Calif.: Brooks/Cole, 1973.

————, *Improving the Quality of Work Life: Reward Systems.* U.S. Labor Department Monograph, Washington, D.C.: Government Printing Office, 1975.

Lawler, E.E., and D.T. Hall, "The Relationship of Job Characteristics to Job Involvement, Satisfaction and Motivation," *Journal of Applied Psychology,* 54(1970), 305–12.

Lawler, E.E., and J.L. Suttle, "A Causal Correlational Test of the Need Hierarchy Concept," *Organizational Behavior and Human Performance,* 7(1972), 265–87.

Lawrence, P.R., and J.W. Lorsch, *Organization and Environment.* Boston: Division of Research, Graduate School of Business Administration, Harvard University, 1967.

————, *Developing Organizations: Diagnosis and Action.* Reading, Mass.: Addison-Wesley, 1969.

Leavitt, H.J., "Applied Organizational Change in Industry: Structural, Technological and Humanistic Approaches," in J.G. March, ed., *Handbook of Organizations.* Chicago: Rand McNally, 1965, 1144–70.

Leavitt, H.J., and T.C. Whisler, "Management in the 1980's," *Harvard Business Review,* 36(1958), 41–48.

Lev, B., and A. Schwartz, "On the Use of the Economic Concept of Human Capital in Financial Statements," *The Accounting Review,* 46(1971), 103–118.

Lewin, K., *A Dynamic Theory of Personality.* New York: McGraw-Hill, 1935.

Likert, R., *New Patterns of Management.* New York: McGraw-Hill, 1961.

————, *The Human Organization.* New York: McGraw-Hill, 1967.

Likert, R., and D.G. Bowers, "Organizational Theory and Human Resources Accounting," *American Psychologist,* 24(1969), 585–92.

————, "Improving the Accuracy of P/L Reports by Estimating the Change in Dollar Value of the Human Organization," *Michigan Business Review,* 25(1973), 15–24.

Livingstone, J.L., "A Behavioral Study of Tax Allocation in Electric Utility Regulation," *The Accounting Review,* 42(3)(July 1967), 544–52

Livingstone, and Sathe, "A New View of the Controller's Organization," Paper presented at the Conference on Topical Research in Accountancy, New York University, May, 1975.

Locke, E.A., "Toward a Theory of Task Motivation and Incentives," *Organizational Behavior and Human Performance,* 3(1968), 157–89.

————, "The Nature and Consequences of Job Satisfaction," in M.D. Dunnete, ed., *Handbook of Industrial and Organizational Psychology.* Chicago: Rand McNally, 1976.

Locke, E.A., and J.F. Bryan, "The Directing Function of Goals in Task Performance," *Organizational Behavior and Human Performance,* 4(1969), 35–42.

Lyden, F.J., and E.G. Miller, eds., *Planning, Programming and Budgeting: A Systems Approach to Management.* Chicago: Markham, 1968.

Macy, B.A., and P.H. Mirvis, "Measuring Quality of Work and Organizational Effectiveness in Behavioral-Economic Terms." Presented at the American Psychological Association convention, New Orleans, La., August, 1974.

Mann, F.C., and L.K. Williams, "Observations on the Dynamics of a Change to Electronic Data Processing Equipment," *Administrative Science Quarterly,* 5(1960), 217–66.

Manzer, C.W., "The Effect of Knowledge of Output on Muscular Work," *Journal of Experimental Psychology,* 18(1935), 80–90.

March, J.G., and H.A. Simon, *Organizations.* New York: Wiley, 1958.

Maslow, A.H., *Motivation and Personality.* New York: Harper, 1954.

————— , *Eupsychian Management.* Homewood, Ill.: Irwin, 1961.

Massoud, M.F., "The Impact of Different Control Systems on Attitudinal Change." Presented at the American Institute for Decision Sciences, Midwest Conference, Minneapolis, Minn., May 1974.

McClelland, D.C., "Some Social Consequences of Achievement Motivation," in M.R. Jones, ed., *Nebraska Symposium on Motivation.* Lincoln: University of Nebraska Press, 1955.

————— , *The Achieving Society.* Princeton, N.J.: Van Nostrand, 1961.

McGregor, Douglas, *The Human Side of Enterprises.* New York: McGraw-Hill, 1960.

————— , *The Professional Manager.* New York: McGraw-Hill, 1967.

McKelvey, W.W., *Toward An Holistic Morphology of Organizations.* Santa Monica, Calif.: Rand Corporation, 1970.

Mellinger, G.D., "Interpersonal Trust as a Factor in Communication," *Journal of Abnormal and Social Psychology,* 52(1956), 304–09.

Merrihue, W.V., and R.A. Katzell, "ERI—Yardstick of Employee Relations," *Harvard Business Review,* 33(1955), 91–9.

Merton, R.K., "Bureaucratic Structure and Personality," *Social Forces,* 18(1940), 560–8.

Milani, K., "Budget-Setting, Performance and Attitudes," *The Accounting Review,* 50(1975), 274–84.

Miles, R.E., "Human Relations or Human Resources?" *Harvard Business Review,* 43(1965), 148–63.

Miller, B., *Gaining Acceptance for Major Methods Changes,* Research Study No. 44. New York: American Management Association, 1960.

Miller, J.G., "Information Input Overload and Psychopathology," *American Journal of Psychiatry,* 116(1960), 695–704.

Mumford, E., and O. Banks, *The Computer and the Clerk.* London: Routledge and Kegan Paul, 1967.

Murray, H.A., *Explorations in Personality.* New York: Oxford University Press, 1938.

Newgarden, Albert, "A Little Anthology of Words and Pictures About Accounting and Accountants from Antiquity to the Present Day," *The Arthur Young Journal,* Spring-Summer 1969, 47–62.

————— , "Goodbye, Mr. Hubbard," *The Journal of Accountancy,* November 1970, 96.

O'Donnell, J.L., "Relationship Between Reported Earnings and Stock Prices in the Electric Utility Industry," *The Accounting Review,* 40(1965), 135–43.

O'Dowd, D.D., and D.C. Beardslee, "College Student Images of a Selected Group of Professions and Occupations." *Cooperative Research Project No. 562.* Wesleyan University and United States Office of Education, April 1960, 38–39.

Onsi, M., "Behavioral Variables Affecting Budgetary Slack," *The Accounting Review,* 48(1973), 535–548.

205

Paton, William A., *Accounting Theory*. Unpublished Ph.D. dissertation, University of Michigan, 1922.

Pettigrew, A., *A Behavioral Analysis of an Innovative Decision*. Published Ph.D. dissertation, University of Manchester, 1970.

————, "Information Control as a Power Resource," *Sociology,* 6(1972), 187–204.

————, *The Politics of Organization Decision-Making*. London: Tavistock, 1973.

Porter, L.W., "Job Attitudes in Management: III. Perceived Deficiencies in Need Fulfillment as a Function of Line Versus Staff Type of Job," *Journal of Applied Psychology,* 47(1963), 267–75.

————, *Organizational Patterns of Managerial Job Attitudes*. New York: American Foundation for Management Research, 1964.

————, "Turning Work into Nonwork: The Rewarding Environment," in M. Dunnete, ed., *Work and Nonwork in the Year 2001*. Belmont, Calif.: Wadsworth, 1973, 115–133.

Porter, L.W., and E.E. Ghiselli, "The Self Perceptions of Top and Middle Management Personnel," *Personnel Psychology,* 10(1957), 397–406.

Porter, L.W., and M.M. Henry, "Perceptions of the Importance of Certain Personality Traits as a Function of Line Versus Staff Type of Job," *Journal of Applied Psychology,* 48(1964), 305–09.

Porter, L.W., and E.E. Lawler, "Properties of Organization Structure in Relation to Job Attitudes and Job Behavior," *Psychological Bulletin,* 64(1965), 23–51.

————, *Managerial Attitudes and Performance*. Homewood, Ill.: Irwin-Forsey, 1968.

Porter, L.W., E.E. Lawler, and J.R. Hackman, *Behavior in Organizations*. New York: McGraw-Hill, 1975.

Porter, L.W., and R.M. Steers, "Organizational, Work and Personal Factors in Employee Turnover and Absenteeism," *Psychological Bulletin,* 80(1973), 151–76.

Rackham, J., and J. Woodward, "The Measurement of Technical Variables," in J. Woodward, ed., *Industrial Organization: Behavior and Control*. London: Oxford, 1970.

Rea, Richard B., "Getting Rid of the Green Eyeshade," *The Journal of Accountancy,* 25(February 1968), 78.

Read, W. *Factors Affecting Upward Communication at Middle Management Levels in Industrial Organizations*. Unpublished doctoral dissertation, Ann Arbor: University of Michigan, 1959.

Reeves, T., and J. Woodward, "The Study of Managerial Controls," in J. Woodward, ed., *Industrial Organization: Behavior and Control*. London: Oxford, 1970.

Report of the Committee on Education and Experience Requirements for CPA's. New York: American Institute of Certified Public Accountants, March 1969.

Rhode, J.G., R. Hamlin, E.E. Lawler, and J.E. Sorensen, "Pre-Employment Expectations Versus Actual Work Experience in Public Accounting," *Accounting and Information Systems Research Program,* Los Angeles: University of California, Graduate School of Business Administration, 1973.

Rhode, J.G., and E.E. Lawler, "Human Resource Accounting: Accounting System of the Future?" in M. Dunnette, ed., *Work and Nonwork in the Year 2001*. Belmont, Calif.: Wadsworth, 1973.

Rhode, J.G., G.M. Whitsell, and Richard L. Kelsey, "An Analysis of Client-Industry Concentrations for Large Public Accounting Firms," *The Accounting Review,* 49(October 1974), 772–787.

Roethlisberger, F.J., and W.J. Dickson, *Management and the Worker*. Cambridge: Harvard University Press, 1939.

Roper, Elmer, and Associates, *The Use of Certified Public Accountants by Manufacturing Executives and Their Attitude Toward The Profession.* New York: American Institute of Certified Public Accountants, 1963.

Rosen, H., "Desirable Attributes of Work: Four Levels of Management Describe Their Job Environments," *Journal of Applied Psychology,* 45(1961a), 156–60.

———, "Managerial Role Interaction: A Study of Three Managerial Levels," *Journal of Applied Psychology,* 45(1961b), 30–34.

Rosen, H., and C.G. Weaver, "Motivation in Management, A Study of Four Management Levels," *Journal of Applied Psychology,* 44(1960), 386–392.

Rosen, L.S., and R.E. Schneck, "Some Behavioral Consequences of Accounting Measurement Systems," *Cost and Management,* 41(October 1967), 6–16.

Rosen, S., and A. Tesser, "On Reluctance to Communicate Undesirable Information: The Mum Affect," *Sociometry,* 33(1970), 253–263.

Roy, R.H., and J.H. MacNeill, *Horizons for a Profession: The Common Body of Knowledge for Certified Public Accountants.* New York: American Institute of Certified Public Accountants, 1967.

Schiff, M., "Accounting Tactics and the Theory of the Firm," *Journal of Accounting Research,* 4(August 1966), 62–67.

Schiff, M., and A.Y. Lewin, "The Impact of People on Budgets," *The Accounting Review,* 45(1970), 259–68.

Scott, William E., "The Behavioral Consequences of Repetitive Task Design: Research and Theory," in L.L. Cummings and W.E. Scott, eds., *Readings in Organizational Behavior and Human Performance.* Homewood, Ill.: Irwin, 1969.

Searfoss, D.G., *An Empirical Investigation of the Relationships Between Selected Behavioral Variables and the Motivation to Achieve Budget.* Unpublished D.B.A. dissertation, Indiana University, 1972.

Searfoss, D.G., and R.M. Monczka, "Perceived Participation in the Budget Process and Motivation to Achieve the Budget," *Academy of Management Journal,* 16(1973), 541–554.

Selznick, P. *TVA and the Grass Roots.* Berkeley: University of California Press, 1949.

Shenkir, W.G., J.B. Sperry, and R.H. Strawser, "Human Resource Accounting: A Report on the Progress To Date," Paper presented at the American Institute of Decision Sciences meeting, New Orleans, November 1972.

Simon, H.A., *Administrative Behavior.* 2nd ed. New York: Macmillan, 1957.

Simmons, J.K., and M.J. Barrett, "A Behavioral and Technical Investigation into the Utilization of Accounting Reports by Middle Managers," in T.J. Burns, ed., *Behavioral Experiments in Accounting.* Columbus, Ohio: The Ohio State University Press, 1972, 351–380.

Smode, A.F., "Learning and Performance in a Tracking Task Under Two Levels of Achievement Information Feedback," *Journal of Experimental Psychology,* 56(1958), 297–304.

Solomon, Ken, "The CPA Public Image," *Bulletin of the National Association of Hotel-Motel Accountants,* (April 1970), 3–11.

Sorensen, James E., "Professional and Bureaucratic Organization in Large Public Accounting Firms," *The Accounting Review,* 39(3)July 1967, 553–565.

———, "Professional and Organizational Profiles of the Migrating and Non-migrating Large Public Accounting Firm CPA," *Decision Sciences,* 1(3,4)(July-October 1970), 489–512.

Sorensen, James E., John Grant Rhode, and Edward E. Lawler, "The Generation Gap in Public Accounting," *The Journal of Accountancy,* 136(December 1973), 42–50.

207

Sorensen, James E., and Thomas L. Sorensen, "Comparison of 1965 and 1970 Organizational and Professional Profiles and Migration Plans of Large-Firm CPAs," in Thomas J. Burns, ed., *Behavioral Experiments in Accounting.* Columbus, Ohio: The Ohio State University Press, 1972.

Sorter, George H., and Selwyn W. Becker, "Corporate Personality as Reflected in Accounting Decisions: Some Preliminary Findings," *Journal of Accounting Research,* 2(Autumn 1964), 183–196.

"A Special Background Report on Trends in Industry and Finance—No Thanks: Stockholders Apparently Not Eager for Extra Corporate Data," *Wall Street Journal,* July 11, 1974, 1.

Sprouse, Robert T., and M. Moonitz, *A Tentative Set of Broad Accounting Principles for Business Enterprises.* New York: American Institute of Certified Public Accountants, 1962.

Stedry, A., *Budget Control and Cost Behavior.* Englewood Cliffs, N.J.: Prentice-Hall, 1960.

Stedry, A., and E. Kay, *The Effects of Goal Difficulty on Performance.* Publication BR5-19, New York: Behavioral Research Service, G.E. Brotonville, 1964.

Strauss, G., "Some Notes on Power-Equalization," in H.J. Leavitt, ed., *The Social Science of Organizations.* Englewood Cliffs, N.J.: Prentice-Hall, 1963.

Strawser, Robert H., J.M. Ivancevich, and Herbert L. Lyon, "A Note on the Job Satisfaction of Accountants in Large and Small CPA Firms," *Journal of Accounting Research,* 7(Autumn 1969), 339–45.

Swieringa, R.J., and R.H. Moncur, *Some Effects of Participative Budgeting On Managerial Behavior.* New York: National Association of Accountants, 1975.

Tannenbaum, A.S., *Control in Organizations.* New York: McGraw-Hill, 1968.

Taylor, F.W., *The Principles of Scientific Management.* New York: Harper, 1911.

"The '70's: A Decade for Decisions," in U.S. Bureau of Census *Subject Reports—Occupation by Industry,* Publication C3.223/10.970/4.2/pt7b. Washington, D.C.: Government Printing Office,

Thompson, J.D., *Organizations in Action.* New York: McGraw-Hill, 1967.

Thorndike, E.L., "The Law of Effect," *American Journal of Psychology,* 39(1927), 212–22.

Thorndike, R.L., *Personnel Selection: Test and Measurement Technique.* New York: Wiley, 1949.

Time. 99(26)(1972), 14.

Titmus, R.M., *The Gift Relationship.* New York: Pantheon, 1971.

Turner, A.N., and P.R. Lawrence, *Industrial Jobs and the Worker.* Boston: Harvard University School of Business Administration, 1965.

Viteles, M.S., *Motivation and Morale in Industry.* New York: Norton, 1953.

Vroom, V.H., *Some Personality Determinants of the Effects of Participation.* Englewood Cliffs, N.J.: Prentice-Hall, 1960.

_____, *Work and Motivation.* New York: Wiley, 1964.

Waldo, D., "Organization Theory: An Elephantine Problem," *Public Administration Review,* 21(1961), 210–25.

Wall Street Journal, 55(1975), February 18.

Walker, C.R., and R.H. Guest, *The Man on the Assembly Line.* Cambridge: Harvard University Press, 1952.

Wallace, J., "An Abilities Conception of Personality: Some Implications for Personality Measurement," *American Psychologist,* 21(1966), 132–38.

Walton, R.E., "How to Counter Alienation in the Plant," *Harvard Business Review,* 50(1972), 70–81.

Whisler, T.L., *The Impact of Computers on Organizations.* New York: Praeger, 1970a.

_____ , *Information Technology and Organizational Change.* Belmont, Calif.: Wadsworth, 1970b.

Whyte, W.F., ed., *Money and Motivation: An Analysis of Incentives in Industry.* New York: Harper, 1955.

Wilensky, H.L., *Organizational Intelligence.* New York: Basic Books, 1967.

Winther, E. "The Study of a Computer System and Work Design in a Danish Bank." Paper presented at ALTOR conference, Hindas, Sweden, 1974.

Woodward, J., *Management and Technology.* London: Her Majesty's Stationery Office, 1958.

_____ , *Industrial Organization: Theory and Practice.* London: Oxford University Press, 1965.

NAME INDEX

SUBJECT INDEX